MW00387570

BISON
BOOKS

The Price

Gerald Mohatt & Joseph Eagle Elk

The Price of a Gift

A Lakota Healer's Story

University of Nebraska Press
Lincoln and London

All photographs are courtesy of Gerald Mohatt.

Manufactured in the United States of America

∞

First paperback printing: 2002

Library of Congress
Cataloging-in-Publication Data
Mohatt, Gerald Vincent.
The price of a gift: a Lakota healer's story / by Gerald
Mohatt and Joseph Eagle Elk.
p. cm.
Includes bibliographical references and index.
ISBN 0-8032-3204-7 (cloth: alk. paper)
ISBN 0-8032-8282-6 (paper: alk. paper)
1. Eagle Elk, Joseph, 1931–1991. 2. Dakota Indians – Biography. 3. Shamans – South Dakota – Rosebud Indian Reservation – Biography. 4. Dakota Indians – Social life and customs. 5. Rosebud Indian Reservation (S.D.) – Social life and customs. I. Eagle Elk, Joseph, 1931–1991. II. Title.
E99.D1 E165 2000
978.3′62 – dc21 99-047755

To Joseph Eagle Elk (1931–91)

and

To my family, Robby, Justin, and Nate,

those I love the most and who have supported,

inspired, and challenged me. You have traveled

many miles over many years and made my

work possible.

Gerald Mohatt

In memory of Joey Eagle Elk,

who represented the Lakota ways given

to him in life.

Diane One Horn

Storytelling; to utter and to hear. . . . And the simple act of listening is crucial to the concept of language, more crucial even than reading and writing, and language is crucial to human society.

—N. Scott Momaday, *House Made of Dawn*

Contents

Illustrations

Acknowledgments

The Siċaŋġu Lakota people of the Rosebud Reservation in South Dakota welcomed me into their homes and communities beginning in 1962, taught me a new way to look at life, and made me their relative. I thank them for their patience when I failed to take my hat off at the appropriate times, mispronounced Lakota as I struggled to learn it, and tried to share what Stanley Red Bird called "my brains" without violating their culture and world view. Stanley became my mentor, friend, and a father in many ways. He guided me and gave me the greatest opportunity in my life—to help found Sinte Gleska University. I am eternally grateful to him.

The Red Bird family has always been our extended family system when we returned to the reservation. It is into this family that Tillie Black Bear brought me as a *huŋk̄a* (relative). The Bad Hand family taught me to sing and allowed me to become part of the Red Leaf singers. Willie and Rose named one of their daughters for my wife and myself, which binds us closely to this family and place. The Spotted War Bonnets and so many others were wonderful neighbors during our time living in the Sioux 400 in St. Francis. Narcisse and Martha Eagle Deer, Abel Stone, Odell Good Shield, and many other singers and helpers for the medicine men brought us into ceremonies, traveled with us, and gave our family support. Lloyd One Star helped me begin my publishing career by telling me his story of strength and the path to sobriety as embracing family. Isadore White Hat was an inspiration in both his weakness and strength. He was the great storyteller who could make you laugh. But mostly I remember the day on the back porch of the college in Rosebud when he told me how much it meant for him to sun dance after years of rejecting the old ways. He said that he had kept a promise, the promise to the spirits that he would dance. Years and years of breaking promises were over. The Menards made us feel like family, at powwows or in visiting their homes. Webster and Evelyn Two Hawk supported the college in its infancy. Webster told me in 1970, after his election as tribal president, that as a white man I had to learn to serve without overidentifying and that it never helped Lakota people for outsiders to use the editorial "we." Gerald One Feather of Oglala taught me about the seriousness of becoming involved in Lakota ceremonial life and helped me establish boundaries and limits. I learned from him what the consequences of this involvement were and how far I wanted it to go. Finally, Dorothy and Francis Crane agreed with Tillie that I would become a relative, a huŋk̄a. This brought my family a new family, for which we are most grateful.

The Jesuits brought me to Rosebud in 1962 while I was a novice and sent me back in 1968 to teach as a regent. They taught me that social justice and equity were the primary reasons for being on the reservation. Early on they turned over control of the mission school to an Indian group, worked for the Office of Economic Opportunity (OEO) and housing programs, and seemed willing to change. I thank them for the spiritual ground that I received while in training with them. I want especially to thank Fathers Joe Sheehan, Gene Merz, and Bob Leiweke for their spiritual guidance. Fr. Dick Pates married Robby and me. He was always a friend and model. Frs. Barnie Fagen and Dick Jones served the people faithfully and were friends and advisers. Although I have had disagreements with the Society and with my friends in the Society, it shaped me, brought me to Rosebud, let me blend my retreats with Lakota spirituality, and supported me in finding my own pathway.

I especially want to thank all the medicine men for their great generosity and patience in teaching me, supporting me, sharing their ceremonies, and helping me and my family. Leonard Crow Dog introduced me to the vision quest and healing rituals. He had a most influential role in guiding my early work in helping found Sinte Gleska University. Bill Schweigman helped with everything from wiring our house to telling me about the burdens the medicine men carried and the importance of thanking the spirits. Johnny Strike brought clarity to my earliest experiences with Lakota ritual. George Eagle Elk insisted always on bringing back the oldest knowledge and said that the people should always try to do things in the traditional manner. John Fire spoke of how "in the beginning was the sound and the sound was." He said that the sound preceded words and was the sacred movement of the spirits and that to pay attention to sound would lead us to meaning.

Robert Stead patiently tried to tell me numerous things, many of which I never heard very clearly and for that I am sad, but I am thankful that I had a chance to spend so much time with him. Norbert Running opened his sweat lodge to me and many friends and has always been ready to help. So, too, Earl Swift Hawk has lived long and helped many. He is the consummate joker who invites you to consider what is true and false. Gilbert Yellow Hawk often came to our home and prayed with us and for us. He was a person of incredible power and strength. Frank Picket Pen and Ben Black Bear Sr. gave me my Lakota name, Taċaŋup̄a Waste (His Pipe Is Good). I thank them for this name and their confidence in me. George Horse Looking taught me Lakota and gave me my nickname, Waṗošt̄aŋ Ota (Many Hats), for which I am grateful. Roy Stone, Richard Moves Camp, and Sam Wounded Head continue the tradition of these men and have helped my family and friends.

I thank all those I interviewed during 1993 whether their words are included here or not. Albert White Hat has been a longtime, close friend. I thank him for his friendship for the past thirty years. His knowledge of the deepest meaning of the Lakota language shaped my sense of its sacredness and brought to my attention how often it has been misinterpreted. His advice on how to present the diction in the translation was very valuable. Neva Standing Bear and Rose and Norman Wilson gave me much interesting background that, although not directly included, was very helpful for understanding Joe Eagle Elk's world and how he helped others. Bea Roderer spent a great deal of time with me and showed me how Joe opened her to new levels of growth, making me think about how to present this impact through cases. Teresa Black Bear gave me her memories of growing up with Joe. Vincent Brings the Pipe was a joy to work with. Any time I went to his apartment he was ready to share a joke and a story. Ken Stands Fast, always generous with his time, was there to advise and offered stories and songs that I have included in the book. Duane Hollow Horn Bear was a critical contributor, one who always inspired me whenever I had the chance to speak with him. The staff at the Austen Riggs Center, who read parts of the work during my seminars there, validated the relevance and importance of Joe's work for informing the process of treating those with severe mental disorders.

There are a number of anonymous contributors of cases and stories. I thank them for all their time and the careful and respectful way they helped me. Many other contributors to the final section of the book encouraged me to write and gave me feedback throughout the process. Jean-Max Gaudillière and Françoise Davoine urged me to continue when I was at the very beginning of the process. At one point they told me that they thought "I had a book," a little phrase that has meant much to me. John Muller read versions, gave interesting ideas for organization, and called my attention to its relevance to contemporary psychotherapy and psychoanalysis. Dick Katz was always there, advising how to do the prospectus, organize the summary, and structure the presentation. He kept my foot to the fire. Manfred Kazenmaier has been a great source of inspiration and help. Ute Gentner welcomed us into her home and shared stories of Joe with us. I also want to acknowledge all the students in my classes who read various versions of this book and offered their reactions. They challenged me to write more clearly and told me of the value of the story for them.

Jim and Jeanette Shelbourn have welcomed me into their home for the past sixteen years when my family and I came back home to visit. They fed me, played cards, and taught me much about generosity. Jim has managed our small cattle herd since we left, and I have never lost a night's sleep worrying about their care. Without Jim and Jeanette our connection to Rosebud and my ability to finish the book would have been enormously more difficult. Jim and his team of horses and hearse took Joe Eagle Elk to his grave in 1991. In 1997 he and Frank Sokol were there again to bring his gravestone to the burial site.

Many individuals helped with editing and advice on the writing. Sharon Boatwrite, Jeanne Anderson, and Sue Mitchell all provided editorial suggestions that shaped the book. Nancy Warren-Pitha was a gift who made it possible to complete the book. She provided the final formatting and helped shape the manuscript for the publisher. I also thank the University of Nebraska Press for publishing this book and for its continual support and encouragement.

Finally, Joe made this book possible. I thank him for his generosity in letting me into his life, the laughter and tears we shared as he told his story, and especially for choosing to accept his gift. Joe's wife, Victoria, answered specific questions and encouraged me to continue the work. Diane, Joe's daughter, advised me on a variety of aspects of the book. I thank them as well. Joe's life honors his children and grandchildren, whom he loved so very much.

Pronunciation Guide for Lakota Terms

The pronunciation guide is based on the work of Albert White Hat (1999), which derived from the work of members of the Lakota language departments of Sinte Gleska University and Oglala Lakota College beginning in 1971 and continuing to the present. There are forty letters in their recommended alphabet system: eighteen represent sounds found in English, and twenty-two indicate sounds unique to Lakota.

VOWEL SOUNDS

There are eight vowel sounds: five are basic vowels and three are nasal vowels.

Basic vowels		*Nasal vowels*	
a	as in father	an	as in calm
e	as in met	in	as in seen
i	as in me	un	as in boon or ruin
o	as in oak		
u	as in flute		

When any Lakota vowel follows the letters *m* or *n,* it becomes a nasalized sound. When *b* or *p* is preceded by the Lakota nasal vowels, this creates the sound of the letter *m;* for example, w*an*bli sounds like wa*m*bli.

CONSONANT SOUNDS

b	as in baby	t	as in tell
g	as in girl	w	as in way
h	as in help	y	as in yes
k	as in kite	z	as in zoo
l	as in light		
m	as in mink		
n	as in nice		
p	as in piece		
s	as in see		

SOUNDS THAT USE DIACRITICAL MARKS

ċ *ch* as in church

c̄ this does not have an English equivalent; the sound falls between a *g* and a *j*

c' a short explosive *ch* sound that is followed by a quick closing and opening of the throat (glottal stop) (White Hat 1999, p. 79)

ġ a guttural sound that is like clearing the throat

ḣ a guttural sound

ḣ' a combination of a guttural and a glottal stop

j this does not have an English equivalent; White Hat (1999) indicates the closest sound is the *s* in confusion

k̄ a hard sound between the *k* in sketch and skill

k̇ a guttural sound

k' the English *k* sound, as in keep, with a glottal stop

p̄ as in spell or spinster

ṗ a guttural sound

p' the English *p* sound with a glottal stop

ṡ the *sh* sound as in she

s' the *s*, as in sea, with the glottal stop

ṡ' the *sh* sound with a glottal stop

t̄ as in stay

ṫ a guttural sound

t' the *t* as in team, with the glottal stop

The Price of a Gift

Places in Joseph Eagle Elk's Life Story

Introduction

Their invaders were a long time in conquering them; and now after four centuries of Christianity, they still pray in Tanoan to the old deities of the earth and sky and make their living from the things that are and have always been within their reach; while in the discrimination of pride they acquire from their conquerors only the luxury of example. They have assumed the names and gestures of their enemies, but have held on to their own, secret soul; and in this there is a resistance and overcoming, a long outwaiting.

—N. Scott Momaday, *House Made of Dawn*

Although this is the story of one individual, his practice places him at the center of the ancient profession of Lakota healing. To better understand his life story, the teachings, and the cases that follow, we need to begin with context: the place where Joe Eagle Elk practiced and from which his power and commitment came and how our relationship came to be.

The day was November 19, 1931. A cold wind whipped the short grass so it undulated like waves on an ocean. Protected from this wind and warmed by a south-facing sun, a log home sat on Spring Creek, back in the ponderosa pine–lined canyons south of the village of Spring Creek. The midwife came that day to deliver a son for George and Adelia Eagle Elk. When he finally arrived, the midwife examined him carefully, noting a healthy young boy who entered a family of medicine people with roots among the Sićaŋġu and Yanktonais as well as the Ṡahiyela (Northern Cheyenne).

One day in 1938, seven years later, Joseph Eagle Elk fell asleep in an old Model A Ford car. He had been playing and says in retrospect, "I needed a nap." He slept deeply and awoke after a most powerful dream. The dream came back to him each night for four nights and bothered him each time. Finally, he told his grandmother, who responded by telling him not to speak of it and to forget it.

Some thirty years later, around 1965 (Eagle Elk can't quite put a date with the event), Eagle Elk followed the vision to its conclusion and became a medicine man. He had traveled many roads and seen many things but finally returned home.

In November 1967 I traveled from St. Louis to Pierre, South Dakota, to visit the mission school in St. Francis, South Dakota, where I would begin teaching in January as part of my regency experience. This was a two-year teaching experience that every Jesuit seminarian or scholastic goes through before pursuing his theological training and ordination as a priest. It was cold and windy. On the 125-mile drive, I spotted one or two trees, which my colleague told me are the national forest. This visit would be short, but it would be my third one to the reservation; I had spent two weeks there during each of the summers of 1962 and 1963. At that point in my life, I did not know that in two years I would leave the Jesuit order and that the reservation would become my home—the place where I lived from 1968 to 1983 and where my family and I have returned yearly since.

This place that became my home was to be the place of today's, yesterday's, and tomorrow's relatives. For Joe Eagle Elk, home began on the Rosebud Reservation, a little more than a million acres scattered among four counties in south-central South Dakota—but Rosebud did not truly become his home until after leaving and returning on more than one occasion and years of self-questioning. He finally decided that the reservation was his source and place.

Rosebud lies on the high plains, west of the Missouri River and about 180 miles east of the Black Hills, a sacred place for the Lakota. A few meandering rivers and creeks cut through the open spaces of tall- and short-grass prairies to create ponderosa pine- and scrub oak-lined canyons and valleys. The horizon dominates: as the sun rises and falls, shadows change the topography, constantly modifying how this open landscape presents itself. At dawn and sunset these shifting shadows create a depth that lends a mysterious quality to the land. One can imagine that the spirits have a home here. It is part of the West, beyond the hundredth meridian.[1]

A place of contrast and power greets the visitor: harsh high winds, intense cold in the winter, sudden and ferocious spring blizzards, and the intense white-hot heat of the summer, whose green and white skies bring powerful thunderstorms. Sunrises and sunsets present colors so deep and varied, so magnificent in the largeness of the sky that they leave indelible marks in one's memory. The night brings a panoply of stars dominated by the Milky Way and periodic northern lights. I fell in love with this land. The weather represented passion and challenge. It captured me with its rhythms, rhythms that seemed to mirror the struggles experienced in life, taking away and giving. The country, so seemingly physically empty, was full of relatives, alive and deceased. Small cemeteries dot the landscape. Communities of fifty to two thousand inhabitants rest in the valleys or break the horizon. It is here that Joseph Eagle Elk was raised and here that he returned from his travels throughout the cities and towns of the West. It is this place that became my home.

A Reflection on Home as Kinship

Tioṡp̄aye is a word used often to name the extended family into which one is born and nurtured. *Ti* means "to live," and *oṡp̄aye* means "the group." So it is the group or community in which one lives as a Lakota. As White Hat (1999) says, "*mit̄ak̄uye oyas'iŋ,* translated as 'all of my relatives,' is the foundation for the tioṡp̄aye. To strengthen this foundation, today we are relearning to address each other with a relative term and to bring back the honor of our names" (p. 27).

My personal experience of tioṡp̄aye has grown over the past years both gradually and at times intensely. One summer, June 1989, I became a *huŋk̄a,* a relative, during a huŋk̄a ceremony at the Crane, the Red Bird family's sun dance in 1989. I had known the family for years. Tillie was the *t̄ak̄oja,* the granddaughter (grandniece in Western relational terms), and her mother, Dorothy, was the daughter (niece in Western relational terms) of my best friend, Stanley Red Bird. Stanley was the local leader who asked me to help him start a tribal college. It was with Stanley that I worked most closely on a variety of projects over my fifteen years of living on the reservation. He was my closest friend and mentor, whom I lost to death in 1987.

The hot sun of the high plains beat down on the dancers on the day of my huŋk̄a ceremony. My wife stayed in the car because she was not used to the heat and was suffering from a slight bit of heat stroke. My two sons stood with me as we watched the dancers round after round. We moved into the circle periodically to stand behind a dancer we knew and to pray with and for him while he attempted to break loose after being pierced. I felt a deep urgency to lend energy and fortitude to him. After the dance was over and we had thanked the dancers for their sacrifice, we moved to the center ourselves to be made relatives—huŋk̄a. The family provided food and a giveaway in our honor, and everyone came up and embraced us with a depth we seldom had experienced.

But this peak experience soon turned to the need for continued responsibility and careful attention to finding a place to fit in the role of older brother or uncle or grandfather. If I were to accept being a huŋk̄a, I had to know what was the correct name to use to address another and to learn what this name demanded. To be a *tiblo,* older brother, to my new sister meant particular behaviors that were broad but specific. Every time we returned, a new challenge was placed in front of me by my aunt or father or mother. How would I help the granddaughter who was in turmoil? How would I speak to the bickering and fighting surrounding my younger siblings? How should I joke, to whom could I give advice and how? From social and psychological support to the everyday chores of helping cook or clean or celebrate a birthday or anniversary, we were part of a family with multiple roles and responsibilities.

Only as this huŋk̄a relationship grew could I begin to understand why Eagle Elk always had to come back home. What drew him was his family, his need to give back and receive. Even when he got in trouble with the law, it was often with relatives. He seemed unable to say no at times and to put a limit on himself and others. Why? Was he weak, with an unformed sense of right and wrong, or was this a kind of tenacious loyalty that came from a deep sense of commitment to relatives and a need to give back as one was given to?

Ella Deloria (1988) captured the essence of kinship to a Lakota:

> The ultimate aim of Dakota life, stripped of accessories, was quite simple: One must obey kinship rules; one must be a good relative. No Dakota who has participated in that life will dispute that. In the last analysis every other consideration was secondary, property, personal ambition, glory, good times, life itself. Without that aim and the constant struggle to attain it, the people would no longer be Dakotas in truth. They would no longer even be human. To be a good Dakota, then, was to be humanized, civilized. And to be civilized was to keep the rules imposed by kinship for achieving civility, good manners, and a sense of responsibility toward every

> individual dealt with, thus only was it possible to live communally with success; that is to say, with a minimum of friction and a maximum of good will. (p. x)

It is this sense of duty to relationship and kinship that kept Joe Eagle Elk returning and finally led him to decide to follow his vision and live in his ancestral place. Young Bear spoke of this sense of commitment to family, which underlies why one dedicates himself or herself to a particular project or life work:

> There's a Lakota saying, "*t̄ohaŋ mat'e ṡni ehaŋt̄an*" (as long as I am alive), which says that if your family history ends, if your family name ends, if the Lakota language ends, or if the blood that runs in your family ends, your family identity, your family blood almost kind of diminishes into water. In connecting this to my life as I think about "as long as I'm alive," this book will be the way for my family and myself to go on; our traditions, our way of life will never end, because now we documented it in this book. Our songs are recorded; we retained the good side of it. (Young Bear and Theisz 1994, p. xxii)

Home, then, is that place where "all my relatives" reside, where there is a deep commitment to see the family survive across generations. Elders sprinkle their public speeches with exhortations to their audiences to take the perspective of the *ṫak̄ojap̄i* (grandchildren), to think about the long-term impacts of their current decisions on future generations.

Home is a place of great humor and a place in which one can gain the support needed to weather the ups and downs of life, to withstand death, loss, the responsibilities of raising and nurturing children, and to help others find their destiny.

Frank Pommersheim (1995) spoke of the reservation as place, "a physical, human, legal, and spiritual reality that embodies the history, dreams, and aspirations of Indian people, their communities, and their tribes. The reservation constitutes an abiding place full of quotidian vitality and pressing dilemmas that continue to define modern Indian life" (p. 11).

To appreciate the position of the medicine man in today's society, we need to look back at the pressures that were placed on them and their people to renounce their ancient beliefs. The story in the next section was given to me over years but began one spring day in 1969 when I met a man at St. Francis Mission School in St. Francis, South Dakota. His name was Stanley Red Bird. He was to become my best friend and the person who with others in the community ushered me into the tiośp̄aye life, part of the evolution of my becoming a huŋk̄a. Each Friday he came to pick up his children, and he would sit in the office of my friend, Larry Leblanc, the assistant principal. Both of them loved to tease and joke, and I enjoyed sitting and listening to the repartee. Red Bird sat with his old, sweat-soaked white cowboy hat, joking about white people with a straight face. He liked to start the conversation by saying one Lakota word. The first day I met him he kept repeating to Leblanc, "*Sluśluťa.*" Leblanc would try to translate and kept missing it. Finally, Red Bird pointed with his chin to the window. We could see it was raining and sleeting, and the snow was turning to ice.

Leblanc said, "Slick, icy, slippery!"

Red Bird replied, "Slippery, just like a Frenchman."

We all broke into laughter, Red Bird leading the way.

He savored the victory of his joke. With a wide, smug grin he exposed a missing front tooth in which he held a smoking Salem. I had never seen someone laugh with a Salem stuck between two teeth.

After a few months I thought to myself that this man was somebody to ask about medicine men. I was afraid to ask him, because he was a pretty impressive fellow, but one Friday I ventured into this territory. I went from being a listener to a questioner.

"Say, Stanley, did you ever hear of these medicine men?" I asked.

"Never did hear of them," he said. "Have you seen a ghost? I thought Leblanc told me you were the ghost detective."

We laughed, and Leblanc made a joke about psychologists not knowing a ghost if they met one in the graveyard.

"Yeah, I have heard there used to be medicine men, but you white guys killed them all. That's what I heard," Stanley said. This was going as I feared it might. So I thought I would bring out my big story. I told him that I had seen somebody who I thought needed a long time in counseling before she would show much improvement. She was taken by her grandpa to see a medicine man named Joe Eagle Elk who lived in Grass Mountain. She saw him four times and became much better. "Quite a deal!" I said. "So I have been asking the Jesuits what they think. In fact, I asked that Iroquois Jesuit what he thought, and he said that medicine men are devils, that it is all witchcraft, and that I should not even mention the name 'medicine man.' Some of the other Jesuits tell me that the medicine men seduce women with their power. So, here I have somebody who I know got better, and some of my superiors tell me not even to mention the name 'medicine man.' "

Stanley looked right at me for a long time. He rarely looked at me directly, but this time he locked right onto me. He said, "I'm going to tell you a story."

A young girl's story

Each day I would walk to the creek and throw pebbles into it to see if they would sink. I was ten years old and not yet a full woman who had gone to the *iṡna tip̄i,*[2] so I had more time to do little chores and dream a little. I would skip these rocks upstream against the flow to see how I could join with the spirit of the rock and resist the current. Other times I would pick up a piece of grass or a clump of weeds, put them into the current, and wonder where they would go. Each time I did this I would talk to the spirits of these rocks, grass, and weeds, like my grandpa and grandma had instructed me. I would apologize for moving the rock and taking the grass out of the earth. I didn't quite know about the weeds because they were pretty ugly, but to be on the safe side I would talk to them once in a while. I liked to be alone because the tents became crowded by brothers and sisters, aunts and uncles, and the never-ending stream of visitors. The family had one large tip̄i that my grandparents occupied, where I loved to visit to hear Grandpa tell the *ehanni* (ancient) stories. Even if some of them scared me, I loved them. I pretended that I was sitting at the edge of the water like Ikt̄omi in order to entice the ducks to come to shore and dance with their eyes closed.[3] I sure liked to eat duck.

I threw a few more rocks and then went home past the long row of cottonwoods on the bank that divided the meadow from the creek. As I reached the bank, I glanced to the north and saw a wisp of dust pass over the horizon. I looked again and saw more clouds briefly melt into the blue of the sky and knew someone was coming to our place. I ran home, hollering to my mother that someone was coming. Grandmother and Mother were already standing looking to the south but quickly returned to cutting meat for the soup. I helped build a stronger fire but continued to watch, wondering who the visitors would be.

After the dust became thicker and did not blow away so fast, we could hear a rumbling that said this was a team and wagon and some riders. Maybe my cousins from Two Strike or Grass Mountain would come and we would play with the old wagon wheels and try to balance them in teams of two as we raced to the line in the sand.

I looked as the team came over the last hill before they turned into our place and knew it was agency people and Indian police. The black of the suits contrasted with the reddish white faces. The sun seemed to bounce off the hair on their faces and the golden brown skin of the Indian police in their blue and yellow coats. I had seen these policemen in Rosebud as well as on the trail to Cody or Valentine. They always joked with my father and grandfather but with little ease and with the sharpness that came from some sense of superiority. Grandpa would simply say *ao zi,* which meant yellow armpits.[4] I could not understand this since everything looked blue.

When they arrived, it was the agency superintendent, a priest, and four Indian policemen. One of the Indian police was a mixed-blood with a long white name from the *ikc̄e wiċaṡa makoce* (France) that I could not pronounce because of all the strange sounds. They asked where Grandpa was, and Mother said he was sleeping in the tip̄i. "Go get him up!" said the superintendent. "We need to speak with him about important issues." Grandma walked slowly to the tip̄i and emerged from it quickly. "He will be out soon," she said. The Indian police moved their horses so they could see all sides of the tip̄i and stood saying nothing. In a few minutes Grandpa came out and walked over to us, but only after going to each of the Indian policemen and shaking their hands. He then shook hands with the priest and superintendent.

"Well, what can I do for you?" he asked.

"The priest needs to talk to you, Jesse. It is about your medicine." The priest stayed on the seat where he was and talked for a long time about somebody named Jesus and how he had come to offer a new life. He said that the old ways must be put away and the new would bring something called eternal life. He said he knew that Grandpa had done ceremonies and had a medicine bundle and he was asking him to give it to him so that he could bless it with his holy water. He said he would take it away so that Grandpa and his family could come into something called a bosom. The priest spoke Lakota and used the word *aṡk̄aŋ* for breast. He kept asking for Grandpa's bundle, which I had seen many times under his cot in the tip̄i.

Grandpa just stood and said nothing. Finally, he said to the priest, "I have my ways and you have yours. We worship one God who is good. I was given this bundle by the spirits, my friends, and it is mine. I cannot give it to you."

The superintendent then spoke and told Grandpa that those ways were finished and that the great Grandfather had said that the Sioux people must embrace the new world. The wars were over, and no one should hold to the past. Grandpa said that this was not the past. His vision was for the people, not himself, and he could not give it up. The superintendent said, "You must give it up. It is the Grandfathers' law." Grandpa said nothing. This superintendent kept mixing up *T̄uŋk̄aṡila* with *Ṫuŋkaṡilapi* and seemed to talk about the grandfather, Ṫuŋk̄aṡila, that we prayed to and a bunch of other grandfathers, Ṫuŋkaṡilapi. Grandma told me later that this Ṫuŋkaṡilapi was the U.S. government. Well, finally this superintendent got down from his wagon and told the interpreter to tell the police to go into the tip̄i and look for the bundle. They all got off and could barely wait to see which one would go into the little doorway first. I heard them make the sound of coup and saw them come out holding the bundle in the air. The police brought it to the superintendent.

The priest got off the wagon and pulled a little black leather case from his dress. They always wore a dress of black, and I wondered what was under this dark thing. He pulled out a bottle of yellowish water from it and sprinkled it on the bundle, saying something in some language I could not understand. Then he took a metal cross out with a man hanging on it and kept laying it on top of the bundle and saying more of these strange words. We just watched, and no one moved or spoke. Finally, the priest said to Grandpa, "We will take this and never will you have it returned. You should come to me for baptism and to learn of our ways so you can teach your people. You know that some of the medicine men have found Christ and now study with us to become catechists. They will translate for us, help with the Mass, and do weekly services for the people. You can still pray for the people each week." Grandpa just looked and said nothing. He then went to the bundle and put his hand on it and turned to the four directions and looked to the sky and touched the earth and went into his tip̄i.

The superintendent looked at us and said: "Remember today. Remember to put away these ways. They are not allowed anymore. Today you have a new way. The great Grandfather has given you to the Black Robes to become part of the Black Robe church. They will build schools so you can learn to read and write and have the power to live in this new world. I will only tell you today that the medicine bundle and its ceremonies are not allowed anymore, and if we find you doing them they will put you into the white man's jail."

He stopped, and the interpreter told us what he said. He did not talk about any bosoms or milk and honey. His words were neither funny nor friendly. Well, I know today why these people are ao zi. Who could take orders from such hairy creatures?

After they left, our life just went back to normal. No one really talked about what happened. Everyone joked about the priest's interest in bosoms. They made bets on whether he was half man and what the other half was under the dress. The problem was how would they find out, and no one volunteered to pull up his dress. No one said anything about the medicine bundle except to talk about how the white men and police were going to all the homes to take away their pipes and the medicine bundles of the *wapiya wiċaṡa* (medicine men). Did they not know that there was much pipe stone? They must not have known about the black stone by Black Pipe that was so soft that one had to be especially careful when molding the bowl. I guessed they did not know much. But they kept going from tioṡp̄aye to tioṡp̄aye. First they took the medicine bundles and then the people's personal pipes. They just did not tire of looking.

Meanwhile, some of the medicine men did become catechists, but not Grandpa. He was quite close to these men, and they would often visit. They would sit in the shade and talk for hours about the big questions of who was this great mystery, what was good and evil, and how did one find his *siċuŋ* (his gift). I could hear them talking and laughing as they smoked. They examined every black mark in this book called the Bible and loved to listen to and discuss the stories of Jesus. Then, as the evening faded and the sun went down, they gathered in the tip̄i and one of them would place his *owaŋk̄a* (altar) in the center in order for someone in our family to be doctored or for us to celebrate a birthday or to do a thanksgiving for the good health and good fortune of our family.

I continued to go to the creek to throw my stones and float my grass. I wondered who the current was and who the rocks and grass were. The world might not have a place for our ways. Sometimes Mother would tell us that if we were not good the white man would be looking for us. Well, he seemed to have found us. Was he the current or the rock or the grass? I didn't ask anyone about this but just kept thinking and wondering.

Then one day I was walking home, up the bank near the cottonwoods. I tripped on a root that was just at the edge of the bank and fell right down by a tree and bumped my head on the trunk, just a little. I brushed my hair and noticed that the trunk was a little warped and cock-eyed. I pushed on the tree and it moved. It looked like a piece of trunk came out. I wondered what it was, so I pushed some more and pulled until it came out. Then I looked in very carefully. My aunt had taught me that the rattlesnakes loved cool places and would feel the warm arm reaching into a cool place and strike. I had seen the results of this and did not want to have a swollen arm and vomit for days. So I looked. I did not reach. I looked again. Grandpa's medicine bundle was right there. I looked again, and sure enough it was the same bundle the police had taken. How did he get it back? I asked myself. I had seen him put an altar up, but only with a few of those articles he used to use. It then became clear what I had seen. It was a new bundle they had taken. He had found this place for his real bundle and hid it here. I closed the place up and walked home. Not a bad joke, I thought. If they were collecting medicine bundles all over the place with no power, then they could never become the current in the stream.

Stanley stopped and smiled with that Salem still lit. He got up and left.

Stanley Red Bird became my friend, colleague, and teacher for twenty years. The stories he told me were echoed by many other Lakota people. They told me of the many other medicine men who had continued to practice, how they held tightly to their visions and ceremonies and did not let them disappear. The man who spent a full six months weekly teaching me the Lakota language, George Horse Looking, told me how the medicine men went underground by practicing in remote areas and early in the morning after the priests had returned home from scouting for suspicious signs of ceremonies, like too many cars and wagons at a home. In the face of such opposition, the healers became stronger in their conviction to keep their ways and more clever in avoiding scrutiny. They became catechists while remaining medicine men, because they knew there was only one great power.

A tenacious holding on to what was central to their spiritual life, loyalty to their visions, and ingenuity in fooling the authorities ensured the survival and development of their practice. But it was possible only because the community as a whole continued to support traditional spirituality. Its members shared the same convictions as the medicine men. They did not betray the medicine men or their beliefs but gritted their teeth and literally maintained their sacred center. Stanley, the medicine men, and many others taught me more and more about this persistence and strength of belief, what Stanley spoke of as *wowaċiŋ t̄aŋk̄a,* translated loosely as a great and strong mind and persistence. He and they were strong in holding to their land and serving the people. I saw Stanley's daughter die, his wife leave him and be murdered, his grandchildren die tragic deaths, and his sons have trouble with the law. But in spite of his hardships, Stanley never quit believing that he could make his world better and that it was worth his effort.

So what held him to this place? What held the healers to their visions and to integrity in following them? My sense of the center is simply kinship, that nexus of relationships so clearly and complexly elaborated in the Lakota language and by the two words used as the basic prayer for all Lakota rituals—*mit̄ak̄uye oyas'iŋ* (all my relatives).

In the early part of the 1960s, Joe Eagle Elk lived on a farm and ranch in western Nebraska near Scottsbluff. During this first part of the decade, he lost his close friend, employer, and supporter, Henry Griswold. Moving to Alliance, Nebraska, he worked for another non-Indian rancher named Ed Sokol. Slowly, he moved closer to the reservation. More rapidly, he faced uncanny experiences that "scared" him, put him in fear of his sanity and the safety of his family. His vision returned and unsettled him with its vividness and intensity. He sought help from family, returned to the reservation in Rosebud, went to medicine men in the neighboring Oglala reservation, Pine Ridge, but still he had no peace. Then he decided he would fast on a hill and ask the spirits what was his destiny. He would not avoid it any longer. It was now maybe about 1964, he recalled.

A red brick building stood in the center of the Rosebud Agency. It was the original agency office building for the Bureau of Indian Affairs, later housed the Rosebud Sioux Tribal offices, later still was made into some apartments, and finally was condemned. But in 1970 the tribe gave it to the board of the new Sinte Gleska University, which took the old wreck and turned it into a vital center. Students came in and out. Community members came in, took a cup of coffee, and walked into our offices to visit. Small talk is an art on the reservation and highly valued. I shared an office with another faculty member, Frank Pommersheim. We were the human services department at the time, and our office was the hub for the medicine men, who came to sit and drink coffee and ruminate on any number of abstract philosophical issues or simply tell stories and tease one another. The room was ten by twelve feet with wood paneling, two desks and chairs, and other chairs for our visitors.

On one day a small group of the medicine men and their associates were gathered at one end of the office while Frank and I went on with our daily work at the other end. We met monthly with these men, who gathered to discuss issues of importance to them, everything from how to reduce alcohol abuse and the number of teenage school dropouts to how to create positive relationships with the white doctors and hospital.[5] The entire group was to meet the next day, and the first agenda item was to design a card for the medicine men and another for the associates who were their helpers. Some were singers; others were supporters who attended most ceremonies. The card would identify each one as a medicine man or an associate wherever he went. Therefore, they needed an identifying name. On this day in our office there were four medicine men and two of their helpers. They went around and around about this key issue: how should they refer to themselves? What was their name—medicine men? At first they said maybe it should be *pejuta wiċaśa,* or herbal medicine man. No, they said, that was too limiting. There were herbalists who could be called *pejuta wiċaśa* or *wiŋyaŋ,* but those typically known as medicine men had functions beyond administering medicine. Ben Black Bear Sr. spoke of his work with herbs that he had learned from his parents and others. He gave the herbs to people, but he was not a medicine man.

"What about *wiċaśa wak̇aŋ,* or holy man?" Some people already called them that.

"*Hiya!* (No!)" they all agreed.

"We are not holy or sacred. We are men, common men, with a gift but not holy," said Robert Stead, strongly rejecting this term. The others agreed.

"How about *iyesk̄a,* or interpreter?" offered Bill Schweigman. This led to much discussion because it was a term they used, and they all understood that they were interpreters for the spirits. But they felt it was a single function, primarily done during their *inik̄aġa* (purification) or *lowaŋp̄i* (evening songs or ceremonies). It was not a generic name, although it was used generically at times. They also led sun dances, took people on the hill for vision quests, and performed other rituals. So they agreed this should not be on the card. But they discussed the fact that each of them had specific powers that came from their visions. Such powers allowed them to do certain ceremonies. There were some with *waŋbli,* or eagle power, some with *wanaġi,* or ancestral spirit powers of former medicine men, who could do *wanaġi lowaŋp̄i.* Many had *ikt̄omi* power, or that of the little people, and they could do *ikt̄omi lowaŋp̄i.* Some had *heyok̇a* power, that of the contrary and the *wak̄iŋyaŋ* (thunder beings). Some had *yuwípi* power and could do *yuwípi* rituals, during which they were bound or tied up (*yuwípi*). They agreed that each one's specific powers should be listed someplace on the card. But still they needed a generic name, which eluded them.

Finally, one of the medicine men or associates brought up *wapiya wiċaśa.* They talked animatedly about this term. Everyone seemed not only to agree but to find the term quite humorous. "That's it!" said Joe, Gilbert Yellow Hawk, and Bill Schweigman. "We're fixer-uppers." Another said, "We fix the people, so let's use *wapiya wiċaśa.* It means the man who fixes. Our ceremonies fix up people and 'the people.'" One of the helpers said, "Well, then, why don't you just fix up my car? It never does run really good."

The next day at the Rosebud Medicine Men and Associates meeting they offered this to the entire group, and everyone thought it was a good idea. Finally, someone made the motion, which was seconded, and the group adopted *wapiya wiċaśa* as the generic title for those whom the people called medicine men. They did not change the English title of medicine man, even though they thought it was not precise. A more precise translation would have been "healer," but they thought the English was a bit arrogant and that it implied that they did the healing rather than the spirits. They wanted it to be clear that they were good tools in the process of healing.

Frameworks for Understanding Lakota Healing

Among those who have written recently about Lakota healing, the concept of the medicine man as iyeśka (interpreter or intermediary) is well accepted. The overarching identification of the medicine man as one of the *wapiyapi,* derived from *piya,* "to cure," is identified by William Powers (1977, 1986) and James Walker (1980) as the subcategory of the more general category of wiċaśa wak̇aŋ, or sacred men. My experience both that day at the college in Rosebud and throughout my time with Rosebud medicine men was that they consistently rejected use of the word *wiċaśa wak̇aŋ* with regard to their role. Powers's references to the distinction between power and rituals are quite consistent with my experience. It is clear to me that the levels or types of healing match the type of vision and the power communicated in this vision. Most authors who have written about this seem to agree about the types of medicine men even if the interpretations of certain words vary. For example, White Hat (1999) would interpret *wak̇aŋ* not as sacred but as full of power or energy.

The person at the center of this book, Joe Eagle Elk, stands at the heart of the ancient tradition of medicine men among the Lakota. Robert Stead, a highly respected medicine man who is now deceased, would ask other medicine men who were from Pine Ridge and spoke at the healing conferences we held at Sinte Gleska University in the 1970s and 1980s, "*T̄ak̄u wowak̇aŋ luha huwo*? (What power do you have? or, What is the power that comes from your vision, or *woihaŋble?*)" The answer would situate the person for him and the other members of the audience. Joe Eagle Elk possessed multiple visions and multiple powers, which allowed him, as Powers (1977, 1986), Lewis (1990), Walker (1980), and White Hat (1999) have described, to perform particular rituals of a curing nature. Eagle Elk and other healers with whom I worked did not use the precise taxonomic structure identified by Powers (1986), however. The accompanying figure situates Eagle Elk within a structure that is consistent with his presentation and that of other medicine men with whom I worked between 1970 and the present.

FIGURE 1
Lakota Structure of Visions and Sacred Powers

woihaŋble
(vision)
❑
wowak̇aŋ
(power based on a vision), which leads to
❑
wapiyapi
(types of doctoring or evening song—*lowaŋp̄i*)
❑
itt̄omi, wanaġi, yuwípi, wak̄iŋyaŋ (heyok̇a),
waŋbli, ċekp̄a nup̄ap̄i

I have used *waŋbli* as one example to designate those visions that involve animal spirits (e.g., eagle, weasel, bear). The structure in the figure varies a bit from that of Powers since I do not make the distinction of the *wak̇an k̄aġa,* those who do performances but do not do individual doctoring. I agree with Powers that such a role exists separate from individual doctoring. In my experience the role of wak̇an k̄aġa is that of healer of the community at a symbolic level. Eagle Elk was both wapiya and wak̇an k̄aġa, as he did the *heyok̇a woze,* was a sun dance leader, and led people on vision quests. Others could do the latter and not be considered medicine men (Powers 1977, 1986). Eagle Elk's primary role was that of wapiya wiċaṡa, which involves both individual and tioṡp̄aye (community) healing.

These rituals, according to Eagle Elk and other medicine men with whom I worked, are learned through the process described by Powers (1977) as one of vision, apprenticeship, and renewal. Eagle Elk certainly followed aspects of this process, but he and some other healers moved immediately from the vision quest into a particular type of practice delineated in their visions and confirmed as authentic by the medicine man who "put them on the hill," that is, who guided them on their vision quests. This process of the *hanbleċiye* (crying for a vision) is well described by a variety of authors: Brown (1953), Neihardt (1979), Lame Deer and Erdoes (1972), Lewis (1990), Powers (1977, 1986), Walker (1980, 1983), and White Hat (1999). The sequence as stated by Powers (1977) appears to me to differ from healer to healer: some have a vision early in life, immerse themselves for years in ceremonies, and begin to practice in early adulthood, whereas others wait until middle age or later. As both Lewis (1990) and Powers (1977) indicate, some medicine men receive the medicine power or powers of another medicine man rather than have a set of powers specific to their own visions. In my experience, however, this type of medicine man had a dream that directed him toward the profession of wapiya wiċaśa. He then became connected to an older medicine man and in a sense became his apprentice in order to take over his practice as he began to discontinue his work. Eagle Elk is not of this genre of medicine man because he had an early vision from which he tried to escape and which he finally followed.

Joe Eagle Elk followed the process stated by Powers (1977): "The initial mystical experience was normally not acted upon immediately, but often obsessed the person throughout this early life" (p. 61). Lewis (1990) also describes most medicine men as achieving this status in middle to later life.

Eagle Elk is best situated as one of the wapiyapi (Powers 1977) or wapiya wiċaśa (Walker 1980). He came from a family of medicine men with a long tradition of immersion in this practice. Although his family tenaciously held on to the traditions and defended them against both church and state, his relatives were ambivalent about his vision and actively encouraged him not to speak of it or remember it, nor did they support him in trying to make meaning of it. It is important for us to understand the intense persecution of medicine men and the difficulty of their lives as good reasons families would try to protect the young from this role.

The role of the medicine man is rigorous and demanding. His life is neither his own nor his family's. Taking such a role is both his choice and not his choice. Often fatigued by the sheer amount of work, the healer suffers from what in contemporary psychological literature is called "compassion fatigue." But it is beyond this concept. A type of reciprocity from the patients and the community is necessary for healing, but when families are in crisis, that is too often not achieved.

Without this reciprocity, life can become quite difficult for the Lakota healer.

My wife and two children and I remained on Rosebud until 1983. Then we moved to Alaska, where I had accepted the position of dean of the College of Human and Rural Development at the University of Alaska Fairbanks. In Fairbanks I continued practicing psychotherapy on a private basis, and I worked with individuals diagnosed as psychotic at a local day treatment center for the chronically mentally ill. Joe and I continued to consult by phone, by letter, and through his periodic visits to Alaska to teach in courses at the university.

In 1987 Stanley Red Bird died after a prolonged illness caused by a rare autoimmune blood disorder. His death was a great shock to me. My own father had died when I was fifteen, and Stanley had been my personal adviser for years. I felt an intense loss. He was also one of Joe's best friends. When Joe needed advice or help, he would turn to Stanley. When Stanley needed doctoring, he turned to Joe. The funeral was in August 1987. The day afterward, I drove back to Rapid City to catch a plane for Fairbanks. I stopped to see Joe and his wife, Victoria, on my way to the airport, and they gave me a star quilt to remember Stanley and our bond. It was made up of the Lakota colors for the four directions: red, yellow, white, and black. This was a most special gift, reminding me not only of Stanley but of the tasks that he, Joe, and I had accomplished together and the relationship we had. When Joe and I embraced that day, we said we would see each other soon.

Over the next few years Joe and I maintained a close relationship. I visited him whenever we returned to Rosebud. He came to Alaska twice after Stanley's death. I asked Joe to do ceremonies for our family, for thanksgiving and to renew strength. We talked of cases I was working on in counseling. He shared knowledge about his own cases to help me understand how to treat people; our relationship was that of friends and colleagues.

For me, the community of Rosebud was and is home. It is a place of many memories, some tragic and marked by loss but others full of humor, friendship, loyalty, and courage. It was the site of some of my best and worst moments, of great accomplishments and big failures. It is a living community that perplexes and confuses me, one that feels close—yet at times inexplicably distant and untouchable. These feelings made it difficult to write about my experiences. I did not want to talk about this world that is part of me in a way that makes it other, makes it an object, and robs it of its subjectivity. Nor did I want our experience to become part of a "new age" tradition. If this occurred, I feared that the complexity of healing would be oversimplified or romanticized, patronizing and belittling both the healer and the tradition. So it was with some hesitation that I asked Joe if I could write a book about his life. It was with the same hesitation that I shared what I have of my experience.

I told Joe I thought his story would teach others about the life of an authentic Lakota healer, in all its complexity. I told him that both those in the healing professions and his own people would learn much about healing. I thought it would inspire readers. After all my agonizing, our discussion of the book was short. He said he thought it was a good idea.

"When do you want to begin?" he asked.

I procrastinated. I put my work as a dean ahead of this book. He would ask me when I was going to call, but I seldom had time to do so. When I was back in Rosebud, we would talk, or when he was in Alaska, we would talk, and I would make notes.

Then in 1990 our house was destroyed by fire, and I had to think again of loss and about what was most important to leave as a legacy. The quilt Joe gave me after Stanley's death was gone. I asked myself what really constituted an enduring symbol of the past. What could symbolize memory in a more permanent manner? Is any symbolization more permanent, less subject to loss? I thought that a book might partially resist this inevitable undoing by keeping his life and memory alive among many people. I decided I must do the book and made arrangements to interview Joe during the summer of 1990. I completed the interviews and planned to do more in the fall but did not. Then we suffered another tragic loss. Joe died in March 1991. He and I talked a number of times during the weeks he spent in the hospital before he died. After he was gone, I knew that I had to complete the biography without him.

In the spring of 1992 the board of regents of our university reorganized our college, the third such reorganization in the nine years of my tenure. I resigned as dean and moved to a faculty position. I received a sabbatical for the spring of 1993. My family and I returned to Rosebud in January to complete the work for this book.

In constructing this narrative I had to rely on many people other than Eagle Elk because of his death. As I reflected on how to proceed, my thinking went back to the first article I ever wrote. It was a chapter for a book by David McClelland and colleagues (1972) on drinking that reflected his theory that there existed a strong positive correlation between power motivation and cultures and individuals with higher rates of alcohol abuse. My chapter presented a number of brief life histories that seemed to point to this theory as justifiable in helping explain both alcohol abuse and the recovery process. McClelland sent me a note saying that the first draft needed to be more clearly embedded in the words of the people and the data needed to drive the inferences. As psychologists, we needed to make clinical interpretations and reflections on the experiences of those we interviewed, avoiding "putting words into their mouths"; that is, our inferences were important only if they could clearly be justified by the words of the people we wrote about. As I read David's letter, I recalled how my literature teacher in the Jesuits, Fr. Lenny Waters, made us interpret with ample evidence from the text. We must bond ourselves to the text if our interpretation was to make sense.

As I listened to the tapes, trying to figure out if I understood the words and sentences, marking those I was unsure of, laughing at Joe's inflections as he related his experiences, I found myself amazed at how little I knew of his life, and I felt deep commitment and excitement in the chance to relate his life as he told it. Bind yourself to his stories, I reflected. At the same time, however, I was struck by a certain incompleteness that came out of such a limited formal time with Joe and the tape recorder. I noted that I must interview some of those he mentioned in the tapes, and I made a list of names.

I continued to poke at the computer with some of these reflections, listing names of those to interview. I sat and asked myself who had influenced how I interviewed Joe and how I wanted to approach the work of constructing his life. I knew my methodology of gathering the data had been shaped by the work of Robert White, George Goethals, Erik Erikson, Harry Stack Sullivan, and Robert Coles. All were psychologists or psychiatrists for whom the study of lives and human development had become a lifelong work. I thought of my first abnormal psychology text by White and how each chapter was introduced by a life history. Goethals taught some of same type of courses as White at Harvard and used a book that he and Dennis Klos had written on adolescent life histories in order to present a study of clinical method and personality. My interviewing, my interest in what shaped Joe's life, was clearly derived from exposure to this tradition of the study of lives.

Erikson added a more clear attention to context when he stressed that one could not understand a life unless one focused on the context and culture of the individual. The goal of raising a child in Cambridge to become an attorney shaped childrearing practices, and raising a child in Alaska or on the plains to become a hunter led to radically different practices. The goals of the culture and demands of the context differed. I knew that to reveal Joe's life I must present his context and times with their inherent ambiguities as he experienced them.

This tradition shaped by psychoanalytic theory and informed by interdisciplinary contact among anthropology, psychology, and sociology seemed to have a significant blind spot, however. I recalled sitting in Goethals's undergraduate class while I was one of his teaching assistants and listening to his lecture on Erikson's research on the Sioux. He was recounting how the sun dance was an example of a ritual designed out of the unresolved oral hostility derived from a long childrearing period followed by a sudden weaning. I was amazed by this interpretation, and Goethals noticed my frown and fidgeting during the lecture and asked what I thought of it. I told him that his interpretation seemed to assume that the explanatory structure of the Sioux was useless or secondary to a universal interpretive conceptualization based on psychoanalysis. Wasn't this a form of cultural hegemony? I didn't see why Erikson's view was not simply a culturally based set of concepts with nothing to add to understanding the sun dance and perhaps something that distracted from its meaning and what we could learn from it. I said I liked the Sioux explanation that the sun dance was for the purpose, as the Sioux said in their language, "that the people may live." Perhaps we could learn something about how an individual's actions can affect the whole in a salutary manner.

This blind spot came out even more clearly when I read some of the interpretations of shamanism by George Devereaux, Bryce Boyer, Jerome Frank, and Claude Lévi-Strauss. It appeared to me they missed the inimitable in seeking a more universal theory of healing. At this time in my intellectual development, I had learned in my sociolinguistic courses about the distinction between etic and emic and related it to Goethals's lecture on the sun dance. Our blind spot in psychology was to assume universality for our etic interpretations, losing an interest in and close attention to the emic. Although my early training in clinical method had stressed an understanding of the "emic" of my patients, it appeared that an interpretive perspective could really miss this point of departure by ignoring the reality of the culture and its goals. The emic-etic distinction has fallen into some disuse, and some scholars are concerned as to whether it is even a useful idea (see Jahoda 1995), but I continue to consider it critical for my work.

Reflecting more on the interviews with Eagle Elk, I was struck by how Joe told his stories. Following Robert Coles, I had stimulated him with a prompt of "tell me of your life" (see Coles 1970, 1975, 1989, 1990). In response, Joe talked of his life from age to age and place to place, at times in great detail. I tried to follow Coles's prompt with his advice to pay attention to making interviews free flowing and unstructured by a priori assumptions. I wanted my writing to come as close as possible to how Joe wanted himself to be seen. The tapes brought me immediately back to the days in which we sat together. I heard him telling me how he felt, what he did, why he did it, what was in his control and out of his control, what he loved and what he disliked, his regrets and joys, and his love for his children and the center of his life in both his work and his family. His cultural context and his struggle whether or not to become a medicine man was pivotal in shaping his life. But how central it was and the intensity of the struggle was amplified and formed by the attitudes of his family, their desires for him, and the ambiguities and conflictual context surrounding the question whether the tradition and practice of Lakota medicine and spirituality should survive. This conflict was both within his own culture and in the larger context of the institutions of our society that affected his tribe. So the more I listened, the more I realized that much of what Joe was saying was molded by his context.

Nevertheless, much of it resonated with me as a human being and a psychologist. In its treatment of questions of destiny, place in the world, vocation, family, love and intimacy, loss and death, and what leads to the temporary and permanent removal of symptoms, Joe's narrative revealed much about our common humanity. Joe's story also told a great deal about the diversity of cultures and the diversity of human experience.

But still a nagging question remained for me: How would I deal with the interpretive task? I knew that the life history would be based on Joe's life and interviews with others who were close to him, but how would I interpret or would I interpret? I made one important decision after these reflections. I would relate his life in four stages, because he himself related it in this way. Since he had died I could not ask him, so I presented the idea to various Lakota friends to see what they thought. They liked the idea but made it clear in their responses that the decision for the book's structure was mine and that they would not interfere with it.

Listening to the tapes over and over and talking to those who knew him well, I was able to see more clearly one of the patterns of Joe's life after he became a medicine man. His life was his work. I was struck by how central this was, so I decided to include a case within each of the sections of his life as an ending illustrating how Joe doctored. It seemed to me that each section of his life had a theme, and from what I knew of those he doctored or helped, I believed I could find a case that would correspond to this theme. During our interviews he had shared with me some of the cases he found most interesting and, at times, most perplexing. My interest in Joe's life had been shaped by my interest in the process of helping and curing. Training in cases and the study of lives had informed my method, so including cases would sharpen the focus of the book on cross-cultural clinical methods.

But something was still missing. Joe's narrative included his thoughts on certain questions I asked him about or on which he reflected. During one section of the interviews he talked about the relationship of medicine to the body and vice versa as well as medicine to disease. In another part I asked him about his notion of the importance of *ṫawaċiŋ waŋjila* (singleness of desire and thought among the people attending a ceremony) and how it was connected with why the doctoring worked sometimes and at other times didn't. Thinking about these sections of the interviews made it clear to me that the narrative of his life should include his reflections.

I spent the next two months at our home south of Rosebud. I interviewed individuals who knew Joe, relatives, and six people he had treated. I transcribed and translated and had Lakota friends translate sections with me. Tillie Black Bear spent long days listening to the tapes, translating, reading my translations, and correcting or confirming them. Albert White Hat translated the more esoteric terms Joe used. Joe's widow, Vickie, filled in questions but didn't want her recollections to take the place of Joe's. She chose not to participate in the construction of his life. I determined early on that some things others remembered were at variance with Joe's account and ultimately used only his recollections. For example, some people thought he had been a veteran of the armed forces, but he said that one of his disappointments in life was that he could not get into the service. When those that I interviewed amplified or helped clarify certain things Joe said, I included their accounts as part of his narrative. In this way I added two paragraphs on his childhood that were not his words. Some individuals gave me stories that were Joe's teachings, which I included in the sections on teachings. The source of each is indicated.

For the next four months, I transcribed interviews I had done in Rosebud. I would send questions on language to Tillie, and by the time I returned in July 1993, I had shared the transcriptions with those I interviewed. During that same month, I completed the first section and shared it with some of those I had interviewed. They uniformly liked the translations and how I had been able to keep Joe's English diction in the narrative as well as how the chapters fit together.

It was nearly a year after I had completed the first draft of the book that I decided how to deal with interpretation. Clearly, my clinical experience as a psychologist and my anthropological background made me want to stick with the emic and have the focus of the book on understanding healing. I reflected over and over on my interactions with Joe and other medicine men about cases I had treated. They never commented directly on my cases by saying, "This is what I think this means." The way they offered opinions on my work was to tell me about their own cases. I also remember an occasion when Joe presented a case to a group of psychologists and psychoanalysts and asked us what we thought caused one of his clients to be so resistant. He wanted us to share our views of this case. But when Joe made interpretations about our cases, he shared his cases. I thought this made sense for a final interpretive chapter. I had interviewed a number of people who were clinicians about Joe's effect on them and then decided to construct a conversation that said, "This is what we think about our work because of our contact with Joe; this is our framework influenced by Joe Eagle Elk." This conversation became the epilogue for the book and is a form of interpretation, to me a form of active and prudent interpretation. It is active in that it is a framework that shapes our practices, whether those of ritual leaders or of clinicians; interpretive in that the application is our construction; and prudent in the sense of ensuring that our interpretations establish the boundary between our work and Eagle Elk's. We don't comment on what we think Joe's work meant to him or for Lakota society. Perhaps others will read this and do so.

In a Lakota framework everyone is a meaning maker, everyone must make sense of his or her experience. *Woableza* has been translated as "realization." It has always seemed to me that this word acknowledges that each person has a capacity to make meaning; that understanding is very personal, is timed by him or her, and is not predictable; and that for woableza to exist, a change in the person should take place. Stanley Looking Horse, the father of the current keeper of the sacred pipe, articulated that Lakota philosophy implies that we should not persuade others to act in one way or another.[6] We should remain as neutral as possible. We should take a position that allows the maximum opportunity for every person to choose, make meaning, and apply knowledge to himself or herself.

As I was deciding how to construct this book, I recalled Stanley Looking Horse's admonition and associated it with a talk by an architect who designed contemporary churches. He showed slides of recently designed churches and explained why he disliked so many of them. They cluttered the space with shapes, colors, signs, and figures that distracted rather than engaged. He wanted to create what he called "anonymous spaces," in which each person was free to worship and experience. In such spaces participants could struggle to achieve meaning and make sense of what they experienced. I decided to try to present Eagle Elk's life and teachings in a way that creates for the reader such an anonymous space. My desire was to allow the readers freedom to find meaning and to learn. The last chapter then provides a context for how a group of clinicians, some from Western cultures and others Lakota ritual leaders (wakȟaŋ ḱaǧa) steeped in their tradition, have made sense of their contact with Joe in their lives and practice.

Thus my method for this book has been a journey that began with my early training as a clinician and researcher in psychology, continued with a strong influence of psychoanalytic practitioners and scholars and the work of anthropologists and social psychologists, and was further shaped by experiences with Joe and other Lakota medicine men. My goal is to elucidate how a healer, Joseph Eagle Elk, is formed and what constitutes his work of helping others relieve themselves of significant spiritual, psychological, physical, and social suffering. The book is limited by the untimely death of Joe Eagle Elk and, therefore, the lack of an iterative process between the two of us to construct the final narrative, teachings, and cases. In place of this process, I have depended on the advice and memories of those who knew him well to elaborate his teachings and cases. The framework and structure for the book are mine and reflect my training, background, and world view, which I have presented in some detail in this introduction.

1 Place and Destiny

That was July 20, 1890, at the great bend of the Washita. My grandmother was there. Without bitterness, and for as long as she lived, she bore a vision of deicide. . . .

The old people have a fine sense of pageantry and wonderful notion of decorum. The aged visitors who came to my grandmother's house when I was a child were men of immense character, full of wisdom and disdain. They dealt in the infallible quiet and gave but one face away; it was enough. They were made of lean and leather, and they bore themselves upright. They wore great black hats and bright ample shirts that shook in the wind. They rubbed fat upon their hair and wound their braids with strips of colored cloth. Some of them painted their faces and carried scars of old and cherished enmities. They were an old council of war lords, come to remind and be reminded of who they were.

—N. Scott Momaday, *House Made of Dawn*

1 Joeiela

I was born November 19, 1931. My Indian name is the same as my last name, Ḣeḣaka Waŋbli, Eagle Elk. My mom and dad had me only; then they broke up and each had other children, so I have a half-brother, Eugene, and a sister. I lived with my grandpa, *k̄ak̄a,* and grandma, *uŋc̄i,* after my dad broke up with the woman he was with after my mother left. K̄ak̄a's name was Jesse, but I just can't seem to remember my grandma's name. They were Eagle Elks. I had two uncles, Ernest and Silas. You knew them. We all lived a few miles west of Spring Creek on the Harrington road in a log house and tents. We moved quite a bit so my dad could work in Nebraska on ranches, but we had our home base right there. You remember that place in the canyons west of Spring Creek?

My dad was George Eagle Elk and he was a Siċaŋġu and a medicine man. My mom was named Adelia Coleman. She was a full-blood and her father's original name was Chief, *Nac̄a* in Lakota. He went to Carlisle in Pennsylvania to school like Stanley's dad and a lot of other people in those days, so when he got there, they gave him a white name and he was called Coleman. He continued to call himself by that name. K̄ak̄a Eagle Elk was also a medicine man. He was both Dakota from the Yanktonais reservation and Ṡahiyela, Northern Cheyenne. Uŋc̄i was Siċaŋġu, but I still can't remember her name. Her mother was Siċaŋġu, but I didn't know her. We all lived down in that canyon west of Spring Creek. That is where I had my home. Uncle Ernest lived further down on the Little White River in Grass Mountain. You know, where we used to have the ceremonies and the sweat?

I was taken when I was really young and raised by my aunt, who then was with my dad, George. My dad and mom broke up real early. I understand that they broke up about seven months after I was born. My dad was at that time with my auntie. I was there until I was nearly seven. She did not have any children and never did have any. I was very important to her and everybody thought she just spoiled me. She gave me my own room and really kept it neat. She cooked a lot of good food and baked a lot, so I always had the best food. I remember that

I had this wonderful star quilt on my bed, and she would often put other ones, that she made, on it. She was quite the beader, so she made me beautiful moccasins and caps and other things. The one thing I remember most and really liked was the beaded bridle and saddle for my horse. It was my favorite.

She always called me Joeiela (Joey). You know it is in our language a term of affection. So my relatives, like Teresa Black Bear, always knew me as Joeiela, the really quiet and friendly little guy. I wasn't very big, but I liked everybody and I tried to be nice to everybody and get along. Who I truly loved was the animals. My auntie had lots of animals and really loved to have cows, horses, pigs, chickens, geese, and everything around her place. I guess that is why I ended up being the same way. You know how it is around my place with all of my animals. I remember many good times as a kid when my cousins were there and we ran around and played and played.

But the first thing I remember was this one day. I don't know where we went, but we were in a wagon and we went over to this man's house. He lived alone. He came out and my dad got down from the wagon and they shook hands, shared a cigarette, and then talked for a while. Just like when we talk sometimes, and you say, "Have a seat and throw out your words like the webbed feet of the ducks."[1] Well, they did the same thing and would begin to talk. After a while he got up and went over to his corral and caught a horse and led the horse back. It was a young one and a little wild. The man came over, and my dad and my mom were there with me, and he gave it to me. Mom and Dad said that he wanted to give me this horse. I was around five then, and I was still with my dad and mom. Well, he just gave me this horse, and no one even told me this man's name.

So about this time my dad and mom split. All at once he left her. I don't know why. I don't remember any fighting or arguing, but they split, and I went to live with Ḱaḱa. And this man had given me this horse. Ḱaḱa and someone else trained it, but then my Uncle Silas came over and went and sold it. Well, Ḱaḱa came home and found out about this. He was really unhappy. So he went and bought me a horse, so I sometimes rode it with my friends. We all had horses, and about that time I must have been about six years old. It was great fun.

My friends in those days were Thomas and Lloyd Walking Eagle and Joe Kills Enemy's boy. I would play with them. We would make a wire man and a cow and a horse. The wire man would have chaps, a jacket, a hat, and we would make all of these out of wire and play with them. We would have our own rodeos and our own races and break our horses. We also took the wheels from wagons and would push them with a little hook on them and have races. This was when I was about four or five, as I remember it.

I didn't go to ceremonies in those days because my grandma told me not to go. But you know, I did see K̄ak̄a doctor people and help people. I remember that he had four powers: *heyoka, wanaği, yuwípi,* and *taȟčā.*[2] I saw K̄ak̄a use the *wayağopa* power, or the sucking power, in the sweat lodge. He would find the spot on the person and take it out of him, the sickness. He would suck out the sickness.

The other power he had was *taȟčā,* the deer. He was used for finding lost things. One time a grandfather came over and told him that he had lost his granddaughter. They knew she had drowned in the river, but no one could find her. For a ceremony like this, you must give a very large gift, *woȟyak̄a.* They brought a team, a wagon, and a saddle and a horse for the woȟyak̄a. Grandpa had the ceremony, and he told the man that he should take a walk in a certain place. When he was walking, a deer would come from the bank of the river, and they should go down to where the deer had come from and they would find the girl. They did as he said and the deer came up. They went down and found the girl under a branch.

I don't remember why I did not go to the ceremony, but they just told me not to go. Grandma told me not to go. They went quite a bit because K̄ak̄a was a medicine man so he was also a busy person. I remember they attended the Native American Church, the peyote religion. They would go for the weekend ceremonies to these *unčela* (peyote) people's ceremonies, but always left me home. However, K̄ak̄a would talk to me about things. He told me things I have not heard others say. For instance, he told about an old man who came to a medicine man, and before the old man gave the pipe to the medicine man, as he was packing the pipe, he talked to the pipe. He didn't just talk to the pipe, but he also talked to the tobacco. He talked to it like a relative. He encouraged it as it gave itself to us to smoke. He also explained the origins of the tobacco. He would always say that the tobacco is alive and one must speak to the spirits of the tobacco. One must understand the meaning of every aspect of the ceremony, even when it is this little part. I think today too often people are doing things and they don't know why they are doing it and what each part of the ceremony means or even what the whole ceremony means. So in the old days they even spoke to the tobacco and encouraged it and spoke to the spirits of the tobacco.

Well, this is how it was. We had lots of fun playing and I had lots of time with Ǩaǩa and Grandma. I still saw my dad but did not live with him.

Then one day Ǩaǩa said, "Joe, it is time for you to go to school." So I went to school in Spring Creek. There was this day school there, and we were all Lakotas. I was seven years old and I spoke only Lakota, not a word of English. None of the other kids spoke English either. There were twenty of us together from the first grade to the sixth. We were all different ages and none of us spoke English.

We could get along pretty good, because there was this breed in the school who was about twenty years old and spoke English. He worked there and his name was Jimmy Quigley. The Quigley family was called the *iyesǩa tiośp̄aye.* You know the interpreters were called *iyesǩa* (to speak white), because they spoke English, and so we just called that place the *iyesǩa tiośp̄aye.* It was right around Spring Creek, and they lived like Indians. He would work with the teacher and translate whatever the teacher said and whatever we said. Like, for instance, if we wanted to go to the toilet, he would translate for us. The problem was that it was hard to get the teacher's attention or get him to understand sometimes. The worst was when Jimmy was not there and we had to go.

We went to school every morning on the bus. Well, not really what we know today as a bus, but it was a team and wagon that picked us all up and took us to Spring Creek. After a few months the school got a car and used it as a bus to pick us up and take us home. We learned a lot in school. We would draw, learn to write our names, and we learned to use the pencil. Some were colored pencils, and we made pictures and drew things. We even began to learn to read. I really enjoyed school and started to use these tools. Ǩaǩa always told me that we should learn to use the white man's language.

Then one day things changed. The school people told me that the priests had told them that I was a peyote eater and also attended lowaŋp̄i or other ceremonies. I could not understand what this person said, so Jimmy had to translate and seemed really uneasy with what he was saying. I think he knew that my grandparents would never let me go to ceremonies. Anyway, the man told me that they were suspending me from school. That meant I could not come back until our family stopped going to ceremonies. My grandma had to stop going, he told me, if I wanted to come back to school.

Well, I went home and told my grandparents. This was when I was seven years old. Ǩaǩa was very unhappy and told me that this was not right. It was wrong. He had always wanted me to go to school and acquire the white men's tools. He was unhappy. He said, "Joe, do not go to school anymore!" Grandma did not say anything. This was the end of my school days.

Then, about the same time, a very strange thing happened. One day a priest and catechist came. The priest was Father Buechel. He spoke Indian really good, but he had his translator and catechist with him, Joe White Hat. Joe is the dad of Albert and Isadore.

Father Buechel said, "Well, Joe, you are the right age to take Holy Communion, so we need to teach you and then you can make your first communion."

So they instructed me for a while. Don't remember exactly how long, but they came or just Joe came.

Finally Father Buechel said, "Joe, you are ready to take Holy Communion, and you can do it at mass next Sunday."

So Sunday came around and we went to the church, and I made my first communion. I was very happy that day to receive the Holy Communion. But I kept thinking about my situation. I really wondered why it was that they did not want me in school where I could get an education, but here they were giving me instructions so I could make my first communion. Why is it this way that I could not learn to read and write at school, but I could learn to go to communion.

So here I was *iyoǩogna,* right in between. I went to the church and took the communion happily, but I never did attend ceremonies. Ǩaǩa was teaching me something and spending time with me, but no ceremonies. So I was about seven or eight and right in between.

Then one day I was playing outside. Like I said, we spent all of our time in the summers outside. When we finished playing, I needed a nap, so I went over to an old Model A or some kind of car body and crawled into it, laid down, and went to sleep. I really slept. While I was sleeping, I had this strong, strong dream. It was really something. I cannot say what was all in it, but there were three things that were in it that I can tell you. My grandma, a bow and arrow, and two gourds were in it. When I woke up, I thought only of this dream, all of the time, nothing else! I could not get my mind off this dream.

Well, I was now living with Amy He Dog and Dad. Dad was remarried, and I was with them. So I went to them and told them about the dream.

They said, do not talk about this dream, it is bad. "It is dangerous."

So I went to Ḳaḳa and Uŋc̄i and told them, and Grandma told me, "*Wiċoh'aŋ ḳi he sic̄e*" (This event is bad). Ḳaḳa did not say anything. Papa again told me twice that doing this was bad and that I should forget it and ignore it.

I was about eight, I think. So I had come straight to this point of having this dream find me. It offered itself to me. It came and went. So I was in sort of a bad way. I felt really in between, and I was unhappy in between. Here I was: not in the vision and the ceremonies nor the church and school, but a little bit in both. I knew for sure that I had this dream that stayed with me. In fact, that first time it stayed with me for about two weeks, recurring almost every night. It finally lightened up, and I felt a lot better.

About that time I moved in with my dad and Amy He Dog. He lived with her, and I made my home there. I stayed with them for the next five or six years. The dream came back every so often, but then it went away. It did not stay like that first time, but maybe only for a night. I would tell them about it, but they would not talk about it and told me it was dangerous.[3]

Ḳaḳa had died and my grandma was alone, so I could no longer be with them, so I was with my dad and his woman. I was over there, and I had to do a lot of things. I cut wood and carried water. Every morning she would have me get the wood and water. I really had to work a lot. Dad moved quite a bit, and we went into Nebraska to work, especially around Cody. We went to various ranches and worked, and sometimes we lived in tents near the town of Cody. I was about nine then and remember going to all of these different places. I learned for the first time about a calendar then. It was the first time I knew this. Of course, I had only spent about two months in school, so I could not read. I have always wanted to know how to read, but just didn't learn how to do it except some real simple stuff. Victoria would always read the letters I received, but a lot of people would send me tapes.

Well, anyway, it was about 1940 and I learned the calendar. Then we just pretty much did the same things for the next few years, 1941 and 1942, travel, work on the ranches, nothing big. But then in 1944 my grandma died. Before this my dad was going to get called up again for the Second War. Well, they told him if he worked for somebody, then they wouldn't take him. So he went over to Tom Arnold's and got a job, and they gave him a paper that excused him from the war. He was in the First World War, but he would have gone to World War II if it was not for that paper. Dad was born in early 1900, so he was in his teens when he went to war for the first time. It would have been tough if he had gone, especially after losing Grandma.

Around 1945, I was thirteen and was still with my parents. Dad was a medicine man and he did ceremonies, but I didn't know what they really were. He would ask me to help him sometimes. I remember Willie Crow Good Voice asked him one time to help, and they went in the sweat bath and I watched the door. Now there was a man in there by the name of Perry One Shield, and he asked me one time if I would help him set up a sweat. I said okay, and he said, "There are only going to be two of us in the sweat, so why don't you join us?"

So I went in, and this was my very first time. I didn't even know what they were doing, but I wanted to see. I was real curious. I had seen Grandpa do it, but it was quite a ways away and I never did see it up close. So I went in, and here he had a bucket, and he sat over there near it and the other guy over there across from him and me back in the back of the sweat. They filled the pipe, set it outside, and brought the bucket in and then put this cold water on the rocks. Then they started to sing, and I didn't know the songs and what or why they were singing. I just didn't know what the hell they were doing. Pretty soon they opened up the door and the first man gave him some water and said *mitakuye oyas'iŋ* (all my relatives), and then they gave me some and I drank it and he said, "Say *mitakuye oyas'iŋ*."[4] So I said it. Then they closed the door and poured some more water on the rocks and sang more songs. After that they opened the door and brought in the pipe, and after they smoked it, they said *mitakuye oyas'iŋ* again, and then gave it to me and told me to smoke it and say *mitakuye oyas'iŋ*. So I did it, and then we went out. That was my first sweat. I was still with my dad and his woman.

Dad worked for Tom Arnold for three dollars a week, and I was about to begin to work myself and leave home, because I just could not get along with the woman that my dad was with. That was definite. I just could not get along with her. I was sort of crazy, and she would keep getting after me so I was pretty unhappy. She told me to do a lot of things: get the wood, get the water, keep the house clean, work all the time. So I couldn't take it anymore and I took off.

I went over to Lloyd Brown's place, and there was a lot of snow. It was deep, like we no longer see. It was so deep that you could not go anywhere. So Lloyd told me to help the chore man, and he said, "After the winter I will take you back." I still only had a little English, so he took me over there and I worked with this man, who is still alive today, Willie Points at Him. He is the last man from those days who I knew who is still alive. He must have been a tough one, because he is still kicking. So I helped him.

Well, one day the winter was over and Lloyd said, "Well, Joe, do you want to go back?" I said, "I think I will stay." So he gave me three dollars a week, and he took me to Valentine and bought me clothes. I got some really good clothes, and I ate so good that I hated to leave, so he asked me if I wanted to stay there to help the people, and I stayed. I stayed one whole year. They would tell me to do some things like herd the sheep or cows, but I would go out and play around someplace. I would just go around the river and play and sleep a little and fool around and then in the evening come home.

When I was working for Lloyd, I had a really bad bloody nose one day, so I decided to go back home. I felt like with this bleeding nose, I should take a rest, so they took me over to my place and I stayed with them for a while, right at first. That is when it happened again real strong. I was resting there and was asleep, and the same dream, the very same dream, came to me really strong. It lasted again for maybe eight or ten days, maybe nearly two weeks. Again I asked about it and received the same answer from Dad. You know, the dream would come every so often but not strong like the first time. This was the first time it came to me a second time, exactly like the first. I could not think of anything else and probably was pretty quiet. I stayed with the Kills Enemy family after that, because I just could not get along with the woman that Dad was with. So after the dream lightened up and the nosebleeds stopped, I went back to Lloyd Brown's to sack corn.

Emerson Fish was there, and we worked together doing this. I stayed the winter, and when it came to feeding the cattle, Willie Points did the pitching hay, because I was small and pretty weak. I drove the team and hay sled. I was about fifteen at this time, or about a year or so after the second dream.

So I did a lot of this type of work in the Cody area. They always treated me real good, but I decided to move one day and went to work for Niles Dunbar. I remember this real well, because he asked all of us if anyone knew how to drive a tractor. I said I didn't but I had seen one over at Lloyd Brown's when I worked for him. I never did drive one.

"Well," he said, "why don't you try to drive it?"

So I did. It was a Farmall A with the mowing machine on it, and I put it in first gear and practiced with it. This was pretty much the end of my days of playing. I had friends, like Vincent Horse Looking, but I didn't see them much unless I met them by chance. Most of them were in school. I enjoyed being around the guys a lot but did not have many opportunities to date girls. You know, they were all in school, and the ones my age went out with the guys they knew from school. We would go to town, but I didn't drink much. I grew up with the White Hats and all the Spring Creek guys. We all knew each other.[5]

When I was about eighteen or nineteen and the Korean War was starting, I was drafted and went to Sioux Falls for the tests. My health was excellent and I passed the physical. So I went home and then I got a letter saying that I had been rejected for service. The reason was that I could not read or write. I wanted to go and even tried a second time. That time I went again to Sioux Falls and passed the physical and was able to read and write on some of the tests. I even was able to get quite a few right answers, but not enough. I was real close to going. I always say, "close but no cigar." So I went back to working on ranches.

I did return home at times to see my dad, but I couldn't get along with Amy He Dog so I didn't stay too long. Then one day Amy took sick. It was pretty fast, and all of sudden she died. They came to me and told me, and I left right away for the funeral. There she was, dead. Memories started to flood in on me. I had ate all of her cooking for quite a few years, and she did a lot of other things for me, and then all of sudden she died. They had the funeral and wake and I was there for all of it. All around me at the wake were all of her things. She had made a really nice home for us. She had one of those really big, nice wood cooking stoves. You know, the kind with the warmers and shelves with cast iron and silver. She had tables and chairs and all of these nice things. The beds were all made so nice, and we had quilts, beautiful ones. So we were always in great shape. It was a home. So after the funeral I went back there and saw all of these things and was sad. I really didn't understand why. So I left and went back to the ranch where I was working.

But at work I was sad. Why I was sad I didn't really know, but it was really bad. I didn't feel like working, so I headed home. I was coming home and got there to the place and no one was there, but I knew somebody had to be there because my dad and Eugene stayed there. So I thought they must have just gone someplace. So I opened the door and went into the house and all of the furniture was gone. They had given it away. In the corner was a mattress, a couple of blankets, and pillows and some old pots, coffeepots and little pots, just two dishes and two cups, one bigger one and one smaller one. That is all I found. My dad and my brother, who must have been about six then, were staying there alone. So I really became sad.

Dad returned and I stayed with them for about a week, and then I just could not stand it, so I left and went back to the ranch. I worked for Jack Stotts for about a week and then decided to leave. I took the train to Chadron and then a bus to Crawford and then a train to Cody, Wyoming. I was hopping trains and hitchhiking. Well, I had no idea where I was going. I had this one small suitcase, and I thought I would look for a job over there somewhere.

I was resting one day and met this man. He was hitchhiking also and coming the other way. He stopped across the road from me, so we stopped and talked. I told him I was going somewhere to find a job. He asked me where I was from and I told him.

He said, "That is where I am going. The way I read it in the paper, there are a lot of jobs over there. But why are you going over this way, because there are no jobs here? That is why I am going over there. It is haying time, and there is plenty of work over there."

So we were sitting there talking, and he was kind of an older guy. I decided I would tell him why, so I told him the whole story of what I had run into and that our home was all gone. I explained to him about Amy and Dad and the home she had made for me and how it was all gone now.

So I said, "I am going someplace so maybe I will find my home someplace."

Well, he was sitting there real quiet, thinking, and he reached into his pocket and pulled some graham crackers out. He shared them with me, and we sat there and ate graham crackers, and he said: "Joe, if I was you, I would go back and work over there. You work over there and you help your dad, and if you help your dad, you will make a home again. If you do it this way and you look for your home over here, you will never find it."

We finished the graham crackers and said so long, and I left and kept going.

2 Destiny and Life's Purpose

At the most one could say that his chi *or personal god was good. But the Ibo people have a proverb that when a man says yes his* chi *says yes also. Okonkwo said yes very strongly; so his* chi *agreed. And not only his* chi *but his clan too.*
—Chinua Achebe, *Things Fall Apart*

As a medicine man I use the pipe in my ceremonies, but I would not have to do so. My vision did not have the pipe in it, so I did not have to use it. They told me what altar to put up but never did tell me to use the pipe. However, I use it because the people expect it to be so, and it does no harm. In fact, when I give the pipe to Victoria, it is for her to use her power to help me in praying for the persons who requested the ceremony. Other medicine men use the pipe because it is in their vision. It is the vision that is most important. It tells you what your work is to be, how to do the work, what songs to sing, how to set up the altar, and how to bring your spirits into the ceremony. So the vision is most important for the medicine man.

We renew this vision whenever and however we are told to do so by our spirit friends, who are our helpers. They tell us when to make the vision quest. It is done when we are told to do so, not simply because we have decided to do so. For others, they do it for a promise or based on their own decision. I did this at one time, but it is different now that I am a medicine man.

The vision, though, is not simply something that we receive in the vision quest. For me, I had the dream and vision when I was seven. The vision was a gift, and it was for me and for the people. The vision would tell me what to do if I could understand it and follow it. Although I didn't know how to follow it when I was young, I learned later that I would have to perform the vision quest to learn what I was to do. Otherwise, I was alone with the dreams, and they were very frightening.

Those dreams kept after me and after me and would not let me go. I would try to escape, but it was persistent. Probably they were real kind to me, because I would have forgotten it, but it kept reminding me that it was there and was going to keep coming.

Other people have their own *ṫawaċiŋ,* or purpose, which they will find in their visions. I have found in my travels that many young people from various tribes, and even white people, have these visions. I even have been told about young people adopted out who have always lived with white people but who have these heavy dreams. Just the other day in the class a young Indian or Eskimo lady asked the same question of me. She wondered whether it was possible that people could be haunted by their dreams and not understand that the dreams were really visions. She wondered if the problem was that they no longer had a place or a person to go to in order to learn about these dreams. As you know, I told her that she was right. Their problems are that a person's ṫawaċiŋ is often communicated in this type of dream, which are hard to understand without help and are very scary if one is alone. The dreams don't let one go. Because they keep coming, these young people, like I did, go to others to ask about them and don't get good advice. They become lost. Some are even told they are insane and given medicine.

What they need to do is find someone with some wisdom who is able to do the sweat. They should learn to make this sweat and learn to pray sincerely with others. Then they can get some help and begin to find their own ceremonies. The other young person I met here, who talked to us the other day in your office, might have such a possibility, but he needs to learn to pay more attention to the reasons for going into the sweat than how the sweat is done. It seems to me these days we are stuck in two poles. On one hand people become rigid that this must be done this way, with this movement, these songs in this order, this person and only this person, this kind of bucket, and so on and so on. He had a bit of this, but it was mixed with the sincerity. The sincerity and the respect are the most important aspects. You should build that sweat, follow the main directions, like for example no woman in their moon being in the sweat. Bring these young people who are lost into the sweat and pray with them. This will help them. It will give them *woableza,* realization, and *wobliheċa,* courage. You must be humble and sincere when you do this ceremony.

But then there is another pole or side to this situation, like I said. Nowadays there are people who are trying to do too much. They believe they have more power than they actually have, and are doing ceremonies they should not perform. They are without the vision. There is no "instant coffee" in this business.[1] So one must realize that the vision and its interpretation are most important.

So there are a lot of visions today that go unanswered and even unknown, because people do not have the rituals I had when I decided to do something about the dreams. This is a very big problem. It is not just the big and powerful dreams we think of as those for the medicine man, but it is for the ordinary person. We are all given gifts. Stanley always said that every human being had a gift, and that was why the college was there, to help them find that gift and make it come alive. I agreed with this. This is why I agreed to help Stanley when he asked. Each person needs to seek their purpose in their dreams, through their education, through the rituals. Parents, relatives, schools, and the college, as well as your college here, need to support these young people so they can find their purpose. The people must treat them with great respect and help them.

So it is your ṫawaċiŋ. It is your way, your purpose, your reasons for living. That is most important. One is born with this ṫawaċiŋ. The old people say that a person is not born just by chance into this family or that. Instead they say that the spirits choose the parents for a child. We in a sense choose our parents with the spirits. This is quite a bit different than maybe what you have heard, but the women were taught to speak to the child in the womb and welcome it to the family and thank it and the spirits for choosing them to bear this child. We were to talk to the child in the womb about this family it was entering and the tioṡp̄aye and explain who we were—sort of introduce ourselves. We were then to welcome this gift to us, this child who chose us, and work with the children to help them find their ṫawaċiŋ. We were to teach the child how to find himself. Uncles, aunts, parents—all had ways to do this.

The medicine man was not the only expert. Everyone has a purpose. Everyone is born to a family and community for a reason. Like I explained about the tobacco, or the tree, or the animals. We are all alive, all have a purpose, and we all help each other. So each of us must learn to pay close attention to what we hear from our dreams, what the animals tell us, and what nature says.

3 A Family's Destiny

I think in the end what happened to me was about remembering, to remember myself, to relink myself, to re-member myself, to put myself back together through my spirituality and remember who I am and where I came from, to bring my members back together.

—Duane Hollow Horn Bear

A Story told by Duane Hollow Horn Bear

I would like to tell you about how I changed and the influence of Joe on me and my family. It is our own story. It is not just me as an individual but my family and our larger extended family of relatives, the Hollow Horn Bear family and tiośp̄aye. We are part of this tiośp̄aye which had been led by my great-grandfather, Mat̄o Ḣeḣlogeca, Hollow Horn Bear. He lived during the period of 1850 to 1913. This man who I never knew has had such a great impact on my life that I would like to tell a little about it.

You know that a tiośp̄aye is made up of a group of families who followed this leader. He was one who they gathered around and who was leader as long as he had their respect. The tiośp̄aye had a name, and ours is Aśk̄e, the people of the Hollow Horn Bear tiośp̄aye. Many of our tiośp̄aye memories were sort of distant for many years. We knew who we were related to, but we did not function as a tiośp̄aye like in the olden days.

A good example of this distance was an experience I had while I was living a different life. I was living a life which was full of laughter, and many friendships, with a companion at my side. I was happy. It was a life where everything was in order and had its place. People would come and go, bringing what they had to numb my mind and spirit. Everyone knew me, and I was content. I was happy. I had no responsibilities to fulfill. I was able to go where I wanted, when I wanted, just about do anything I saw fit to do. It was in those days that a stranger happened to be passing through our country, and it just so happened that our paths crossed. And so I invited him to my home, being the nice guy that I am.

It turned out that he was very interesting. His work was with stone: carvings of small animals, figures of people and pipes. He talked of his travels and his work, which took him to many places across the country. He talked about Native people and pipe-stone [the stone used to make the sacred pipes of the Lakota]. He showed me some of his work that he could do with stone. I was very impressed. He talked of many people unfamiliar to me and places that I had never been to and things I could only dream about. Then he spoke of one person in particular who really got my attention. He began talking of my great-grandfather, Chief Hollow Horn Bear, and a pipe that had belonged to him. He said that he had seen this pipe and told me where it was. He said that he felt I should look into this since I was a descendant, and perhaps there was a way to get it back. This all was very interesting, but I asked myself, "What would I do with such a pipe? These ways did not apply to me. I was happy with my friends and my companion. Why should I want to confuse all that with a pipe? Everything was in its place, and I was happy, wasn't I?"

I had left the reservation and lived away. But even though I lived away from the reservation, I always felt that I had to come back. I always wanted to be back here for some reason which I didn't understand. I tried living in Dallas, Texas, tried to make it there. I tried in Denver. I would have been able to make it with the education and training I had. Financially there was no problem. I had good jobs, and we had enough money to live comfortably. But for my own personal reasons, I kept wanting to return to this place. I did not know why, was not able to see what was in line for me, or what was being guided into my life. Something was going to get into our paths.

So in 1983 there was a tragedy in our lives, Celeste and mine. I had to make a choice. Suddenly one day we found ourselves not laughing; we couldn't. The tragedy that found its way into our circle very viciously brought us back to reality. The eldest of our children had been stricken with a sickness that even modern technology and men of expertise could not help. Nothing could be done for our child. Laughter was replaced by tears as my companion and I would argue and blame each other for our shortcomings, our lack of knowledge about what needed to be done. All we could do was watch and cry, watch and utter prayers the best way we knew, watch and wonder, "What can we do?"

One day we visited my mother-in-law. We were looking for some consolation. She talked to us at length and then she literally scolded us. She told us that we were Lakota and that there was a way, but that it would take the two of us to make it work. She said, "Pick up the pipe. Pray! That is where the answers are." I was unsure and scared because I knew very little about the ways of the pipe, but we both knew that we had to do something. And so we did. We opened our lives to a whole new way of life. We opened our hearts and our minds and prayed in our Lakota way. We went to a medicine man, Joe Eagle Elk.

I didn't know Joe that well. I had met him in passing, had maybe shook hands with him, but didn't really know him as the person he was or even as a medicine man until we needed his help. I talked to him, and he said he could help me. We had ceremonies for four long days and nights of purification rites and sacred healing ceremonies. He helped us with his gift of interpretation. Things happened to us after these ceremonies. Our child was healed. Her sickness was taken away forever. In the ceremony they told us that there was a better life to live. So we asked for continued help and we knew we must give proper thanks. So now the question was before us, "Who will stand behind this child?" My companion spoke in a soft and trembling voice, "I will. I will change my life and my ways and give you proper thanks." With these few words and knowing that this was the right thing to do, she changed her way of life. She gave up her friends, the drinking and laughter that we shared with them. I sat there and wondered, "Why? Weren't we happy?" And then somewhere in the darkness of that room on the fourth night of the ceremony, I heard myself saying, "I, too, I will stand behind my child."

So we stood there, and we vowed to do our vision quests and sun dances. So in the spring of the next year we were ready to fulfill these promises. My wife first completed her vows to spend time on a lonely hilltop praying and giving thanks for the healing of our child and new way of life. When the summer of that year came, she went to the sacred circle of the sun dance, prayed, sacrificed, and gave thanks. Now it was time for me to fulfill my vows.

The following spring, I was out on the hill praying, sacrificing, and giving thanks. I asked for help because I was weak and my friends never let me forget it. You know, when you change your life, many times your old friends, drinking buddies, do not stop bothering you and reminding you of your weaknesses. They said they wanted to share their laughter with me. Now they were laughing at me. I prayed. I remembered.

Suddenly I remembered this stranger who had passed through here some time ago. I remembered what we had talked about and a certain pipe in particular, the pipe of my grandfather, Hollow Horn Bear. This came to me so strong that I began to pray about it, begging for guidance. I talked to my creator, Wak̇aŋ Ṫaŋk̄a, if it was his will, to show me a way to regain this pipe. I prayed to my great-grandfather, Hollow Horn Bear, who was my beginning, "What must I do?" Memories flooded me. Many hurtful memories from my childhood flashed through my mind. Memories of people I had used for my personal gain came vividly before me. Things I wanted to forget were remembered. Things I had long since forgotten came back to me. My life had been opened like a book before me. My eyes were opened to see what I was becoming. I didn't like what I saw. I cried and told Wak̇aŋ Ṫaŋk̄a how sorry I was. I asked for forgiveness because I was weak and blinded. I humbled myself on the hill and took my place in reality, where I belonged. I was an equal with the rest of my relatives, the two-leggeds, four-leggeds, the winged ones, all of plant life, even the smallest of insects who persisted in being with me on the hill. I acknowledged that we were all relatives.

During this time, Joe was a mentor to me. He put me on the hill. He doctored my child. He had a lot to do with me, my spirituality, and my destiny. He was of it, and it was of him. He must have sensed the positive in me that was weak and needed rekindling. That is exactly what he did for me: he rekindled me, brought me back to life. He rekindled in me the desire for something good, something more meaningful for me than what I was doing. For myself, Joe had a gift, this man, that he used to its fullest extent in a very wise way. He took a stand for all that we as Lakota Oyat̄e (the people) put our beliefs in. At times I could not comprehend his teaching. But through this he taught me patience, acceptance, and understanding. He did this both in his ceremonies but also as a relative. When he met me, he called me by a relational name and explained how we were related.

What Joe did for me began that day we went to him in '83. So I continued after I saw what this pipe and the ceremonies could do. Previously I had never got involved. I had gone to sun dances and observed, but I never had the yearning to get out there. I would think, "I should be saying my prayers," but I was with alcohol so I did not pay much attention until we needed Joe's help. Then, of course, he was there. After our daughter got better, Celeste and I discussed what we could do to thank the spirits. We had fulfilled our vows, but we felt this was not enough. Celeste and I talked about it, and we decided that there was not anything material that we could give them that would give adequate thanks for what we had received.

So we asked Joe to teach us and let us help him. He agreed, and Joe and Vickie came to rely on us, and we felt that continued obligation. We traveled with them to ceremonies, became their helpers. I sang for Joe's ceremonies. What the work with Joe did for me had to do with remembering. I could remember myself, relink myself, re-member myself, and put myself back together through my spirituality, through remembering who I am and where I came from. I helped Joe during these years. We could go to the center, to the altar of his ceremonies, and pray and sing the songs from our hearts. That is where I found that the answers lie.

Although many questions persisted, the one that kept my attention was about my great-grandfather's pipe. Four winters came and went with no insight into what I should do, yet we continued on this road with Joe. Many sacrifices were made, many long nights of prayer. We were learning. Slowly the laughter died away in the silence and the ways of the sacred. My friends, well, they found new friends, but most importantly we had found ourselves.

Then in the spring of the following year, four years from my hanbleċiye, we were preparing and looking forward to another great summer. One day word came that our tribal president wanted to have a meeting with the Hollow Horn Bear family. This meant my dad and mom, my brother, and my sisters. "Sure," we said, "why not? But what is going on?"

"Just come to my house this afternoon," was the only reply I was given. So we went and we were all there waiting for the tribal president to show up. Nephews, nieces, Mom, Dad, my brother and four sisters, as well as many other relatives—the tiośp̄aye. We were talking and sharing stories, teasing and joking. I found myself sitting there and enjoying a new kind of laughter with my relatives.

Anticipation filled the air when word came that the tribal president would soon arrive. We kept guessing what would happen today. Finally he arrived. We were greeted and welcomed in the proper way with him shaking each of our hands. We were asked to sit, and he began to talk to us. He talked about what he knew about us, good things, things for which we were to be proud. He talked of Chief Hollow Horn Bear and what he had stood for—honesty and justice—and what he had fought—greed and corruption. He said we were to be proud to come from such a man, to have the kind of blood that he had, a Lakota blood. We should be proud of where we had come from and never forget it. He also spoke of his travels and all the struggles he had to endure to do what was right for the people. He talked of his recent trip, during which he had met a man who was quite interested in where he came from. The man asked him if he would like to see something in which he might be interested. He said he was, and the man showed him a pipe, a very old pipe, but in very good condition. It had writing on the stem saying who it had belonged to. Our tribal president said he would like to take it with him, but the man said he couldn't because it didn't belong to him.

But the man said, "On the other hand, it does not belong to me either." He then asked, "Are there any descendants from this chief?"

Our tribal president replied, "Yes, there are, and I know exactly who they are." "I don't know why I said this at this time," the tribal president told us, "but I did."

The man then replied to him, "Then take this pipe back to them. It belongs to them."

At this point I looked around at my family. I saw what looked like tears in their eyes. I also noticed that things were getting kind of blurry for me too. Then the pipe was brought out. It was handled very carefully, like a baby. We smudged it with the sacred sage, and prayers were made as a drum group sang the sacred songs and the tribal president walked toward us with the sacred pipe. Mom and the girls were crying softly. I had a big lump in my throat, who knows how big it was, but it was beginning to bounce up and down and my breathing was getting a little difficult. I had to be pinched, kicked, elbowed, and finally shoved before I realized that Dad was trying to get my attention. When I finally made it over to him, stumbling, on my two left feet, it seemed like I had traveled a hundred miles.

He spoke to me in a sincere but shaky tone: "Son, you and I both know that the ways of the pipe are sacred. And that the ways of the pipe and alcohol do not go together, and that I still have a problem with alcohol, and so I cannot accept Grandfather's pipe. You have changed your life, and this was your prayer. It is into your hands that this pipe should go."

I stood there trembling as my hand slowly came up from my side, as our tribal president said, "Accept this sacred pipe on behalf of your father and your relatives." My prayer was in my hands, the prayer of my relatives, of my tiośp̄aye. I cried softly as I looked down into my hands. My heart was beating with the drum. My mind was reeling. At this moment my mind instantly went back to the day that I was praying for this on the hill.

That day that we received our grandfather, great-grandfather, great-great-grandfather's pipe burns forever strong in my mind. I cannot nor will I ever forget. From that day our tiośp̄aye was rekindled. We have over time begun to regroup, rebound through the sun dance. My relative Albert and I talked, and we decided to create a Hollow Horn Bear sun dance. We went to Joe and asked for his advice and help, and he was there to help us. So for the past five years we have been doing this sun dance, and it seems each year more of the relatives participate and the dance becomes stronger.

Joe is there. My relatives are all there. The people are there. They are all waiting for me to say mit̄ak̄uye oyas'iŋ from my heart and mean it. To know how good it feels to know that I am not alone anymore, not alone. I am not afraid. I am not afraid to die. So over the next years I came to realize that this man knew something about me that I didn't know about myself. He saw some good in me. During those earlier years it was only a few old people who called me by a relational name, by some kinship term. And here was Joe and he knew immediately how we were related, so he used the relative term with me every time we met. He called me *taȟaŋśi,* cousin, all the time. We addressed each other as cousins, and our friendship grew, so sometimes we would take him and Victoria with us when he went to doctor or help someone. Other times he and I would go alone. I still think the most important part of his influence on me was his role as a relative to me. He fulfilled that for me by being older and wiser. He looked out for me, the younger one. It is for the older brother to give guidance to the younger in our Lakota way, not just in terms of spirituality but in terms of family life. He would talk to me about family life that pleased him and the things that he had done that pleased his family and made them happy. He also told us honestly what he had done that made them unhappy. He told me what were the things in your life that make you unhappy. He would say that someday your children are going to make you cry. So he taught me during our travels. He didn't talk a lot, but when he did I listened and learned.

So my contact with him changed my life and our lives. We now live here in Grass Mountain. We have built a post-and-beam house next to our trailer and have plans to expand it. We have brought our grandfather's pipe, the Hollow Horn Bear pipe, back from the east to our tiośp̄aye. We have our annual Hollow Horn Bear sun dance that brings the relatives together as a tiośp̄aye. We follow many of Joe's instructions for the sun dance. He helped us begin it. We remember him. We remember that he taught us to welcome everyone who has a sincere heart. He taught us that we are all related. He taught us to do our ceremonies with care and respect for all that is alive. Things can become difficult, but I have the strength of my remembering. This was the gift he gave me.

Because of this great capacity of his, he was open to people like myself. He became generous to people like myself. Often we do not realize that a person like Joe suffers, sheds tears, is so human that he grows and ages just like the rest of us and has feelings similar to ours. He too must travel on and leave us. His loss has left a hole for me, but knowing where he has gone eases the pain. I still hunger to satisfy my own spirituality. This lingers on. I know that I have been pointed in the right direction through all of the sacrifices that Joe made for me.

2 Traveling and Searching

There are ordinary men who have lived very well. They are good at everything, but if the power does not want to go to them, it will never come. Even if this person cries for it, it will never come to him. On the other hand, there is a man who is very poor and pitiful. He doesn't have anything and is very pitiful. If there is ever a time when the power is to come, the power can freely do this for such a man. This may seem strange, but it is true. Today, if one were to look back carefully, there are a lot of young men who want to handle this power. They are very expectant, but this cannot be. They look and seek but are not chosen. There are other young men who do not concern themselves with this power. They are just living ordinary lives. These, or some of these, may have had a vision or dream, and a promise is attached to them. They may have an obligation. These obligations, even one, are a very hard undertaking. Eventually, they will have to confront their obligation.

—Stanley Looking Horse

4 Steps and Missteps

A physician must be a cosmographer and a geographer.

—Paracelsus

So I kept going and went so far and got a job in Wyoming. I worked on ranches, sheep ranches. I made money and then I would take it to town. I would think of my stepmother and get real sad. So I would buy anybody a drink, anybody, not just friends. I started to drink really heavy. We could not go into the bars at that time so it was a little hard, but not too hard. We just would stay in the back outside, and we would buy it and then go to someplace else and drink over there. This was in Gillette, Wyoming, and I was nineteen years old. I was there for quite a while, maybe about two or three months. So I kept this up, and then one day I started to think about what this man said to me about my dad and my home—where I could find a home. I thought to myself, Joe, here you are spending all of this money. Every time you have money, you lose all of it. You drink it up and come home broke. Well, maybe your dad and brother don't have anything. Maybe they are suffering someplace, maybe or maybe not. So I thought, if I go back there and work close to home I could make money and maybe I could give my dad some. Maybe they could buy something. Instead of me spending all my money on other people, I could help them out. So finally, after thinking about this a lot, I went back.

When I arrived at my dad's place, there was nobody there. No one was in the house. In fact, he had moved out. There was nothing in it, just the shell. So I went inside, but couldn't stay, too many memories. I walked outside and went over to our neighbors, Plenty Horses—Joe Plenty Horses—and stayed overnight there. The next day his boy, Guy, took me over to Cody and I found a job at Krueger's. My dad found out I was back and where I worked, so he came over to see me. Walter Krueger said to me, "Well, Joe, you are going to visit your dad for a while, so why don't you take the day off and visit with him." So he wrote me a check for sixty dollars, and my dad and me went to

Cody. I gave him ten and told him to buy some dishes, some chairs, and a table. He said okay and also bought some groceries. He then went back. I told him to come back again, which he did. Each time he came back, I would tell him to buy some things, like beds. But he told me he had beds and mattresses, so I told him to go and buy some groceries and some horses. He said, "I already have two." So then I said, "Buy two more," since horses at that time were pretty cheap, like twenty-five to thirty dollars. So he went and got another one, and I bought two for myself. I then went home to visit, and it looked a whole lot better with the table and chairs. But I was still really sad in the house.

I missed her, really bad. She had taught me a lot of things, to cook, to wash, to wash my own clothes. She forced me to do these things. After she died, I realized how much she had given me. Yet I knew that I had never told her that I appreciated her. She had died. Lots of times I wished that I had told her, but I didn't.

I never spent too much time at home. I did go home, and every time I felt the same. One time I was invited into another sweat lodge. I didn't want to go into it because my grandma had always told me to stay away from them. Like I said, I didn't know what the hell was going on the first time I went in, but the second time I knew a little more. When I went in that second time at Black Mountain Sheep's, they told me a lot of things. He said that your grandpa and grandma did ceremonies so you should do them. I told him that yeah, that is true, but she told me not to do that, told me not to do it, and that is the reason I don't come over. He said, "Well, Joe, whenever you get a chance, come over and we will do this." So whenever I was home and had a chance, I went over there and took part. Sometimes everything was prepared. Other times we needed to prepare things, so I would help him and then take part in the sweat. I kept this up for quite a while that year until I decided it was time to visit my relatives in Denver. I quit my job and went to Denver.

When I got to Denver, I found a job loading fruit crates onto trucks. I met a girl there who I really liked. She was a *hašapa* girl.[1] We were really close and spent every day together. She was very well educated although she had left school. She could read and had a very good job. I stayed with her for quite a while. Her parents were really nice and liked me a lot. I liked them too. While I was with her, my dream came back to me but not too strong. The main problem was that I didn't have anybody to talk with about it. I couldn't talk to her. She wouldn't understand. I didn't think that the friends I hung out with would understand, so I kept silent. But the dream was not too strong, so it didn't bother me much. The girl and I stayed together. In fact, we almost got married, were really close to doing it, but it didn't work. She didn't like my friends. They would come over, and we would sit around and talk in Lakota. She didn't like it. All of sudden our relationship changed and it was not right between us. She became really possessive, stingy, and ill-tempered, so we did not fit when my friends were around. When we were alone it was good, but then my friends came over to visit lots of times.

One day some friends of mine and I were sitting in a café drinking coffee and in walked three Indian girls. We started to talk to them, and they told one of the guys that they were going to a movie, a Gene Autry western. So this one guy said he would pay for this one girl and then the other guy said that he would pay for the other girl, so I said I would pay for this other one. It just seemed easy. They were all Crows. I got along good with them. After the movie they said, "Why don't we go to Montana?" It seemed like a pretty good idea, so off we went. We headed up to Crow Agency, and I lived with this woman.

I lived with her and worked for white ranchers in the area. We would be together, and then I would be at the bunkhouse on a ranch. Well, she got pregnant and had a boy. We named him Joe, Joe Jr. Her name was Virginia. I was really happy with this boy. I thought about him all of the time and wanted to be with them. But her father didn't like Sioux. He would get drunk and come over and we would argue. Every time he got drunk, this would happen. So I tried to take her away with me to where I worked, but he would come over and get her and the boy. So then I would be left alone. While I was at one of these ranches, my dream came again. But this time it was different. It was really heavy. Dreaming every night, every night you dream the same dream. I wanted to tell someone, but I was afraid and nervous to tell anyone. Even when my friends or the guys I worked with talked, it seemed like I didn't hear them. All I could think about was the dream. I tried to be happy. I went to parties. I was with her and my son, but I couldn't say anything.

When I was in the bunkhouse, it seemed like somebody was going to say something to me, like somebody was right next to me. I would get ready to say something and the words were not there. It seemed like somebody wanted to talk to me. At night I could hardly sleep. It looked like somebody was going to do something to my spirit or mind. I just was not clear. I really noticed it when the dream went away. Then I was clear and happy and could enjoy other people and have good times. I guess I felt like I couldn't get away from it. If I was ready to go to bed, I would fear that it would come again. It was really powerful. But then, while I was there, it went away. It came back there once in a while but not so strong while I was there.

I kept trying to live with Virginia and my son, but her dad would not let us alone. Finally I was broke, had no job, and decided I should go home, but it was really cold. I was walking around outside and saw this man who worked at the agency. He told me it was too cold to be outside, so I should stay in the agency building overnight. I stayed in the boiler room on a mattress he had there. That night I decided I should take Virginia and the boy and go back to Rosebud. The next day Virginia and her mother came over and talked to me. Her mother said that if it was her, she would never kick me out, but it was her husband. She said that if I took her daughter and my son to Rosebud that her father would go and get her again. She said that he would make a lot of trouble. She said that Virginia and I had to talk this over between each other and decide. It was our decision. So she left and we talked for quite a while. We decided that I should leave and she would keep the boy and stay at Crow Agency. I didn't have any money to go home, but the vice-chairman of the tribe gave me a job as a janitor to make enough money for the trip. I spent three more weeks there and left. Virginia brought the boy to me every couple of days. Then I went home. I was twenty-two.

When I got home, my dad talked to me and told me not to go any place out of the way and get married someplace away from home. He told me that was no good to go there and have kids and stay there, so I never did that again. But I dreamt that someday I would have the chance to take my boy back here, that I would make enough money that some way she and the boy could take off and we could be somewhere where her dad could not find us. But I couldn't get enough money to do it, and finally I gave up.

I spent time at ceremonies back home, again at Black Mountain Sheep's. He would teach me songs, but I couldn't become a singer. He taught me other things, especially to trust myself. But then I was still pretty young and didn't listen. I wanted to leave, so I dropped the ceremonies and left. I began to travel again, place to place, farm to farm, state to state with the combiners.

I did this for a while, but I still didn't make much money. I never had much as a kid. My dad didn't have any income at all, so I wanted to have things. Other people had a nice big income, so when I was a kid, an adolescent, I saw that they had a lot of nice things and I had nothing. I wanted to work so I could make money. I went to Douglas, Wyoming, and herded sheep and made quite a bit. I was there for six months and had about six hundred dollars. I made between eighty and one hundred twenty-five dollars a month. So I decided to go home. I lucked out, because the man who I worked for liked me and he paid my ticket back to Cody, Nebraska. He was a really good white man. So I arrived back in Cody with six hundred dollars in my pocket.

Right off I bought a car for five hundred dollars. That left me with the one hundred dollars, so I bought some beer and wine and really drank. I drank heavily in those days. But when I decided to go see my dad, I quit. I stopped and went home. But my dad wasn't there, but my friends were, and I had a car and we drove around. One time I met a woman, and we started to live together. We stayed together for quite a long time while we traveled all over. During our time together we had two girls. I worked for ranchers, farmers, doing all kinds of things. We went to Fort Collins, Colorado, and lived there for quite a while. Then we were in Douglas, Wyoming, then Casper. Finally we decided this is too far from home, so we went home, but no one was there. I wanted to stay closer to home, so I found work in Bridgeport, Nebraska, about one hundred fifty miles or so from home. I herded cattle, which is pretty lonely work, but I liked it and they liked me. My friend, we weren't married, decided she wanted to go home, so she left me there alone and went back to Rosebud. She stayed for a while and somewhere over there by Martin they got drunk, her and some friends. They were coming home and near the town of Vetal they rolled the car and wrecked. The youngest child we had was hurt real bad. They called, so I went back and saw them and it didn't seem so bad. For that reason, I went back to Bridgeport to work. The next day or so I was coming in from herding and they told me that they had taken my daughter to the hospital. She had made a turn for the worse. I called and they reported that she was better and it was looking good, so I stayed and worked steadily. Then they called and said she is dead. I went home right away and attended the wakes and funeral. After them

I decided to return home. My dad said he would go with me and help me. No one believed that this had happened, but it had. I went back alone and worked hard, really hard. The woman wanted to come back, but I didn't want her anymore. I said, "No, this is what has happened, and I don't want you." I was very sad.

I lived there, but from that time forward I left Bridgeport and that job and for the next year and half or more, I traveled and worked all over. I went to Scottsbluff. You know all those towns are down in western Nebraska on the edge of the sandhills and have a lot of irrigated farmland and sugar beets. I worked for a guy named A. C. Smith, learning to build roads and move dirt. I did this for that year and half. Then when I was twenty-three I went to work in the sugar beet factory. I traveled a lot with Mexicans during those years. They harvested sugar beets just like us. About this time I met another woman. She was from the Norris area and was named Minerva. I liked her quite a bit, and we had two girls. She stayed with me and traveled all over with me. I stayed at the sugar beet factory for quite a while and liked it a lot. One day something happened that really surprised me. It was November 9, 1956. They called me into the office. I didn't know why, maybe I was a little afraid. Well, they gave me a cake, and this man, the field boss, honored me on my birthday. I did not know anything about such things, birthday parties and cakes, but he taught me about them. It touched me. I really felt like nothing bad could happen after that. I had my twenty-fifth birthday at the sugar beet factory in Scottsbluff, Nebraska.

I kept up that work throughout the spring and into the fall. Minerva was with me. We had a girl while we were there. Our life was very happy; we were very happy. Then the boss who I got along so well with, he retired. The next boss was a woman, and we got along real good too, but she sometimes wanted it one way then another time a different way. I just decided I didn't like it. I missed my old boss. I quit and found a job with another rancher. Finally one day Minerva and I started to fight. We had another girl. Things had been really good. I liked the work. She liked the place and we were really happy. Then one day nothing was good. We argued. We fought. I was not nice. She was not nice. We really argued. I was twenty-eight at the time. We finally couldn't be together. She was pretty jealous. I was getting letters from other women who I had been with early in my life. I couldn't read, so she would read the letters and get mad. We couldn't get along together, so she went home. She wanted to be at home with her mother, she said. At times we got together, but it did not work. I stayed in Scottsbluff, where I met another rancher named Henry Griswold. He asked me to work for him, telling me that he would give me a good job. I joined up and worked at his ranch six miles south of the river near Scottsbluff.

I did all types of ranch work. He liked my work. I spent a lot of time watching the cattle. He traveled a little, so he would let me alone with the cattle and I would take care of them. I stayed there for quite a while but really wanted to go home and see my dad. I told Henry I wanted to go home. He asked me how I was going to get there because I didn't have a car. I said I didn't know. He told me that his son was working in California and had left his car there. Henry said I could take it and if I liked it that I could buy it later. He didn't want to hire anybody else, he said, so that evening when I came home I looked at the car. It was a good one, really good. I thought, "This will cost a lot and I will have to give a lot of days of work to get it." Henry told me not to worry, that I did really good work, and that I could have the car and pay him off gradually. He said he would give me back my job whenever I came back so I should go and see my dad and come back when I was finished. I left with the car and went home. I saw my dad and friends, like Ben Swift Hawk, Seymour Kills in Water, and Willie Redbird. Willie was really crazy, and I liked to travel with him sometimes. Seymour died, but I kept traveling with other friends. We drank a lot, really heavy. But then I would go back to Henry's and work. There I didn't drink. I also visited in Denver with my mother and my aunt and my grandmother, Josephine Douville. When I was there I might stay for two weeks. There was no drinking there, none! Nothing bad happened when I visited my relatives in Denver. So I want back and forth from Henry's.

One time I decided I wanted to spend more time at home. I told Henry that I wanted to spend a month there. He said okay, so I went home. I had a good car and found Romeo Kills Enemy. We started to drink. We drank and drank and got drunk. When we were broke, he said to us, Ben and me, let's sell some iron. We can take the iron over to this white man, Paul Gregg's father, and he will buy it. Romeo knew where it was, so we went there in my car and found this really old mower and drill, one they used to drill grain. We got out the wrenches and took them apart, stacked them up, and then took them to Parmalee, to Paul Gregg's father. He gave us money, maybe about twenty-eight dollars. So again we started to drink and drank pretty heavy, but all of a sudden they caught us, the police. They caught us right there in Parmalee and took us to jail. We were charged with stealing property.

They took us to jail, and Romeo got really scared. He cried and cried, because he was really young. He said he was afraid to go to jail and asked what will he do because he could not stand to go to jail. Romeo told the police that I did it. My dad came and I told him that I didn't do it, but it was my car. I didn't know the property was someone else's. The Kills Enemy family came, and Romeo really cried. He was terrified. He said, "Do it this way. Tell them you did it." I felt sorry for him, because he was so young and he really cried. An FBI woman came in and questioned me. I told her it was me and me alone. I used my car and had stolen all of the iron to get money to drink. They left the room and came back and asked me more questions. I told them the other two guys were not involved at all. So they let them go.

I sat all alone in the Rosebud jail, the old jail, way in the back. It was bad. Some of my relatives got thrown in, Abel and Harvey Walking Eagle. It felt good to have someone to talk to, especially because I could talk to my uncle. We were visiting when I heard my name called. A man stood by the door talking about a statement he had that I should sign. It was what I had said, he told me. Well, I couldn't read, but I signed the statement they made. Right after that he told me to get my stuff because a U.S. marshal was going to take me to Sioux Falls. I didn't have much, only a shirt and a few things. I picked them up but was trembling. I knew the bond was set at five thousand dollars. They told me that as we walked to an office. I just kept trembling, shaking all over. That day they took me to the county jail for an overnight before we headed to Sioux Falls. The jail was crowded with white and Indian guys, all pushed together in this dirty little place. I laid down and slept a bit, woke, washed with the cold water, and went to eat. An inmate cooked some pancakes, which they gave us with no syrup—only coffee, sugar, and a pancake—bad, real bad. The marshal came to get me about the same time, Tom Slattery. He said, "I am here for my prisoner to take him to breakfast." The jailer told him no, he has had his breakfast. But Tom said, "This is my prisoner. I will feed him breakfast." So he took me handcuffed out of the jail, then took them off and turned me loose to eat. We had a real good breakfast.

When we finished, he handcuffed me, but as soon as we were away from town he took them off. Well, we went to Sioux Falls, and he put me in the federal tank. I was there for about two months, until March. It was an awful place with the worst food I had ever eaten, really awful food. There is a bowl like this with a little bit of oatmeal, a butter sandwich, and coffee. You could buy more coffee if you had money, but I didn't have any money. The white guys bought me extra coffee and even some candy, because we were all friends. One day they brought me a letter from my dad with five dollars in it. I was happy to have money to buy coffee and candy for my friends. In the letter there was another letter from Henry Griswold. Henry said he had gotten me a lawyer. I shouldn't worry, because he would get me out and there was money waiting for me in the Mission bank, back on the reservation, to travel to his place. I didn't know what to think, could this be possible. I said to myself, "If I could only come out!"

Then a few days later a man came and called me into another room. He asked me where I was from and where I had worked. I told him for Henry Griswold, who is a real good man. He told me Henry had sent him over to help me. He was going to talk to the probation officer and the judge, and even if I went to the big house he would get me out. He would see me in a couple of weeks with the decision. To top it off, there I sat for two more weeks. Then about March 19, no March 15, I went to court and this lawyer is there. The judge asked me my name, asked me a lot of questions, where I worked and who I worked for and how long I worked there. I answered all the questions. Finally he said: "I'll tell you. I am going to give you a break, an easy break. You go back and work for that guy who you worked for, because he likes you. He did all of this for you. So I am going to give you an easy break if you go back and work for him. I will put you on probation for one year while you work for Henry Griswold and don't drink or get into any trouble. If you go back to the county jail, now they will get you a bus ticket and everything so you can go home." I was really happy. In fact, it is hard to describe how happy I was.

I stayed one more night in jail. The next morning a different marshal came around, gave me a bus ticket, then opened a drawer and pulled out forty-six dollars cash for the trip. It was winter, cold and snowy, so he told me that they might have problems on the bus ride so you better have some money. I remember him saying, "Good luck, Joe, and don't come back!" I waited for the bus but kept thinking this isn't real. Maybe they will come and get me, put me in the big house. Then the bus came. I jumped on, and boy, did that make me feel good.

The trip was long, Mitchell, Lake Andes, and finally Winner. I asked the police in Winner if they knew anybody going to Mission or Rosebud, so they asked why. I told them everything, which made them have some pity on me. They said, "Just wait and we will look around." About that time some Indians came by who were going to Okreek. I didn't know them but asked them if they would take me to Mission if I paid them a little extra for the trip. They said, "Well, get in, because we are going that way anyway, so come along. We are going to Okreek, and Mission isn't much further, but get some beer for the trip." I went into the liquor store and got a few six-packs of beer. Back in the saddle again!

When I got back to Mission, there were a lot of people there because it was St. Patrick's Day. There were two bars there, Irish's and Arlo's. I stood outside of Arlo's. I kind of held myself back, but somehow I went inside, and boy, that is where we had it again. I was off and running. But by some luck I didn't get thrown in. I was kind of careful. About that time Ben and Aloysius Eagleman, with another guy, Lavern Stuart, who had a car, stopped to talk to me. Abel Stone's wife, Theresa, was also with them. They said, "We will take you home to Spring Creek." I really wanted to go home and not stay around there because I knew I was on probation. So I got in and he said, "Hey, I got some drinks, but I don't have enough, so what do you think?"

I said, "Well, I'll get a gallon of wine."

I just couldn't keep away from it. You know, these are my relatives. So I went into the Checker Board Café and bought two gallons of wine and they took me to my dad's. I didn't drink much, but just a little. I just paid them for the trip with the wine.

When I got there, no one was home. I went next door to Albert Points at Him's tent, and he told me they were in He Dog and they would come home tomorrow, but that I should just go in and stay there. I did and the next day went to my Uncle Ernest and talked to him. They were all happy to see me. He told me that my boss had come over and took the car back to Scottsbluff, but told him that he wanted me back there. I went over to the school and called Henry. He told me to go get the money at the bank in Mission and come back. But I hung around home for a week, saw Ben Swift Hawk, who was with me when we got the iron. He said he was sorry about what happened. I said there was no problem; it was over. My dad talked to me about what I was going to do. He told me I was lucky to have a boss like that and a job. My car was over there and a good job. So I got the money and Uncle Ernest took me back. Henry lectured me. He told me he never thought I would do something like that. That I was a good guy, a real good worker. So he told me not to do that again because that's not a good place for you. I remember he said, "You need to enjoy this world and be happy!" I said okay and went back to work.

Things were real good. I felt better and was very happy. Every month I had to report to the probation officer about how I was doing. Me, I got along with everybody. I would still go to the beer joints and drink a little beer at Hogi's Smokehouse, but then go home and go back to work. But I don't know why, but one time, I came out of the beer joint and here were these two guys fighting, white guys. This one guy was a good friend of mine. I knew him pretty good, so I stepped in and stopped the fight. About the time I was doing this the police came and took all three of us into jail. Oh boy, here I was back in jail. They said the next day the judge would come and see us. I told the cop that I worked for Henry and asked him to call him. He said he would and that Henry would be over the next day. Well, the next day here comes Henry and another guy, the probation officer. The probation officer asked me if I was drinking. I said no. I didn't tell him I had only two beers, but just said no, I wasn't drunk. I tried to stop the fight and got thrown in. The problem was that one of the guys had a really bad cut, really bad, right up here on the head near the eye. The probation officer said, "It all depends on what the policeman says. If he says you were drunk and fighting, then you are cooked. If not, then we'll see." The time came. The judge was there. We were there. The judge asked us what happened, and I told him my story. He then asked the policeman, and he said I wasn't drunk but just tried to stop the fight. So the judge freed me. Boy! I just made it! The probation officer said, "You just better stay at Henry's and not come over here. If you get in more trouble, you will see Tom Slattery and Sioux Falls jail again."

So I stayed at Henry's and never went to town for two months. Then one day the probation officer came over and said someone has filed a complaint on you that says you have been in the street, in beer joints. He says, "You better stay away because you have only six months left on your probation." I said okay and for the next two months I again stayed away from the bars. I would go to town, but not the bars. Then the marshal came around and said that he had received a complaint that I was drinking again. I told him I wasn't. He couldn't say who complained but that he would investigate who was making these accusations. He said to keep working, which I did. Finally he came around with a paper, which was the results of his investigation. He asked me if I wanted to read it or he would. I said go ahead and read it. The paper said it was Minerva's mother who was trying to get me into trouble. I told him I never did do those things but that is what she is saying and trying to get me into trouble. They believed me, and I kept going until the final months were over and I was done with probation. The probation officer congratulated me and told me, "Don't you ever do that again." I was now twenty-nine years old.

After these six months I really wanted to go home. I told my boss that I would like to go back to the reservation and visit my dad. I had my car again. He said I could and gave me my pay so I could go visit home. I visited around for about a week and ran out of money. I called to Henry for some money to go back to Scottsbluff. He told me that he would send some to the bank. About that time my cousin Ed came over and wanted a ride back to Alliance, where he was working. I told him that I was broke and had to wait for the money. He said, "Don't worry about it. Why don't you take me to Cody, Nebraska, and on the way I know where there are some spools of barb wire that I can get. We'll sell them and have enough money for the trip." We took a cut across, stopped to get the wire, but nothing was there. Somebody took them. We went on a ways, and there were some new wells being drilled near Tom Arnold's. Ed said to stop the car. He went over there and found two big boxes of socket wrenches. We looked at them, and Ed said, "Let's go to Cody and sell them." So we went to Cody, and he disappeared for a while. I don't know what he did, but he came back with some money and beer. He got the beer and we went to Martin, South Dakota. In Martin he sold those wrenches. We got money, bought some beer, and headed back to Rosebud. There is this small town, Vetal, near the area we call Tuthill. We were driving back that way drinking our beer when we had a flat tire. All of sudden we lost control of the car and went into this deep ditch. We were all right, but after we changed the tire we still couldn't get out of the ditch because it was so deep. I saw two tractors over in a field and went and started the one and pulled the car back on the highway. As I was doing this, a car came by and slowed down and then speeded up. We sat there for a while because we couldn't get the car started. I had returned the tractor to the field, and as I was coming back I could see red lights coming from the west, from Martin. We ran and the police came up and spot-lighted around and found Reuban and Ed. They didn't find me. I waited until they left and went over and started that tractor and went across country toward Harrington and Spring Creek. The tractor didn't have much gas, so it ran out and I had to walk. I knew the country because it was north of Lloyd Brown's, where I had worked when I was a teenager. I walked and walked and saw this car coming. It was Red Tibbitts, the sheriff. He said, "Well, Joe, I guess I am going to have to take you to the county line and the Martin sheriff will come and pick you up." So we got there and the sheriff came and they talked for a long time about something, I don't know what. Finally he told me that I had to go with the Martin sheriff.

He took me to jail there. Ed and Reuban were there, as well as my relative Herman Arapahoe. Herman and another guy had killed a cow and got caught, so they were headed to Sioux Falls. The court time came, and I got thirty days and had to pay back the wrenches. I didn't know it, but they had a lot more on Ed and Reuban. They had stole a lot of things in that area, including gas, bedrolls, wrenches, wire, lots of things. The police came in and showed me a statement from them that said I was with them all of the time. I was only with them a short time, but now I was part of the whole thing. I was there when who shows up but the marshal, Tom Slattery. He asked me, "Well, what happened, Joe?" I said, "I don't know, but here I am!" He told me he never had wanted to see me in jail again but now I must go to Rapid City to jail and then to another jail in Deadwood for Federal Court. We sat in the Deadwood jail for thirty days. It was a lot better than the Rapid City jail.

My dad and Uncle Ernest came over. Ed is my uncle's boy. They asked me what happened and I told them. Everyone was really worried because they thought this was it. I was headed for the big house. Uncle Ernest said my boss had called and asked where I was. They had told him, and he was pretty mad. The probation officer told us the same thing, saying that this time he just might not back me up and I would go for quite a while. I had only been off of probation for maybe two months, so it didn't look good. The probation officer and my dad asked me about the statement that Ed and Reuban had given. I told them it wasn't the truth. I didn't have anything to do with those other times that things were stolen. They asked me if I was going to tell the truth and I said yes, I will. The probation officer told me that I should tell the truth if I wanted to have any chance of getting off. They left me there in Deadwood in the jail. We stayed there for the next two months.

Jail was not so bad during that time. I even got a job to make some money. We needed money to buy little things. There was this woman whose husband was over three hundred pounds. He was so big he couldn't even walk, which made it impossible for him to go up and down stairs. He stayed only on the second floor. They hired me and some other guys, including Ed and Reuban, to carry him up and down with the wheelchair. Every time we did this that gave us a dollar apiece, so we made money off of this guy so we could buy candy bars and other stuff like meat and rolls, instant coffee and sugar. We went there three times a week, Monday, Wednesday, and Friday. So things were pretty good there.

Finally the time came for court. One day a lawyer came to see me. He was an old guy. First he asked me if I knew anybody named Henry Griswold. I said yeah. Did I work for him, he asked. I said, yeah. Tell me the street number and the address and house number, he asked, so I said East 20th, house number 109. How long did you work for him, he asked, and I told him for quite a while, for five years now. He wondered if I liked working for Henry and I told him, yeah, I did. He then asked about whether I owed him any money, and I told him about the car and how I still owed him for the car. At last he told me that Henry wanted me to come back and stay there for three or four years. Henry said that every time you go home to the reservation you get into trouble, so you should stay over there and work and not go back. The lawyer told me that if I let you go on your own, you are going to get six years, six years in the big house. But if you agree, I will work for you, but don't tell anybody that I am a good friend of the judge and I will talk to him. I agreed and asked him about these other two guys, what about them? He told me not to worry about those guys, just yourself. I said all right.

Sure enough, about a week later they called us to court, and there was the same judge who I was in front of the last time. I thought I was really a goner. He stood up and said: "Joe, do you remember what I told you? I said I don't want to see you again and here you are." Yes, I said. He then asked me: "If I turn you loose, what are you going to do? Are you going to get along like you have been or will it be different?" I said I didn't know what to say. What he said to me just stuck me right there, I was stumped. He looked at me real closely and said: "If I send you out, will you do good or bad? I don't know. Tell me if you will do better." I said, yeah, I can do better. He then said he would give me a break, but do not go back to the reservation. He then told us that he would put me on three years' probation, during which time I should avoid the reservation. After the three years he said he would like to see me tack on another two years of not going back. I said okay, all right, and here I was again with a lawyer who helped me, talked for me. I got off.

The probation officer was waiting for me, and he scolded me some more and said that three years is a long time to stay straight. "If you mess up," he said, "this next time there will be no one to stand up for you, to help you, and you are going to prison for sure. Two years was tough the last time, but this time there is not room for messing up." He then gave me a bus ticket to Scottsbluff, but no money this time. I got on the bus in Deadwood and went straight to Scottsbluff through Chadron, Nebraska. Henry was there waiting for me. He shook my hand and said: "Oh, oh, Joe, don't you go back to the reservation. You stay away from there. If you want to see your dad, you invite him here. I will call him, and he can come and visit you over here. I will even pay for it." Henry was really, really nice to me. He told me he liked my work but that I really made him mad at times and he even thought about firing me, but still he liked my work and decided to keep me. But I had to stay there for three years. This was the late '50s. My dream came to me sometimes, but just a little. It was like it would come close but not quite come in. I could forget it easily.

5 All of My Relatives

The physician comes from nature, from nature he is born; only he who receives his experience from nature is a physician, and not he who writes, speaks, and acts with his head. . . . The physician is only the servant of nature, not her master.

—Paracelsus

A WILD TURKEY

A story told by Ken Stands Fast

Joe loved animals. He respected them. At one point he had cows, horses, geese, chickens, and that one wild turkey. He also had the big pig. He was so big that one day I was over there talking to Joe. We were sitting in the car chatting, and all of a sudden the car started to roll and shake, roll and shake. We looked around, and here is this huge pig scratching himself against the bumper of the car. We really laughed. But the one I remember the most was this one turkey. Joe had two turkeys, but the one, the female, was killed by the coyotes, and so the other one was left alone and turned out to be aggressive and kind of mean. One day Joe asked me to come up for some reason. I drove up to his place and got out of my car to go to the house when all of a sudden around the side of the house comes this turkey. He was coming really fast and kind of scared me, so I got back in the car. He had his wings all spread out and his chest puffed way out. He looked scary because he didn't have many feathers left from fighting all of the other animals. He fought them all, even the hogs, who would bite on him and pull out his feathers. Joe saw what was happening, so he told one of his kids to get a stick and chase the turkey back around the house. So he did it, and I got out and was talking to Joe. Well, here comes that turkey again. I was standing there, and he has his wings up and his chest out and begins to push on me. Joe and I are standing together, but he is pushing on me. Joe was drinking a cup of coffee and took the cup and dinged the turkey on the head to shoo him off. But then the turkey started to peck on me and use his feet and his chest, so Joe says to me that maybe he is just too ornery and we had better get rid of him. He said he lost his mate, his friend, and can't get along with nobody anymore. So Joe said, "Why don't you come over tomorrow and we'll do something about the turkey."

I went home and the next morning I came over. As soon as I got out of the car, here comes the turkey. I stood there, and he kept pushing on me while Joe came out with a coat, a really big one like you see in the army. The turkey backed away a bit, and Joe told me to edge around behind the turkey and throw the coat over him. We just kept talking sort of nonchalantly trying to be real smooth and sneaky while we shifted around by the turkey. Then when it was the opportune time I threw the coat over the turkey. He was squirming and fighting, but I held him real tight, maybe extra tight. Joe hollered at Vincent Brings the Pipe, who stayed with him, to bring over a rope, which he did. I tied up the turkey real tight, real tight, to get back at him.

We wrapped him up and put him in the back of the pickup and went down to the Spring Creek junction. We went past Quick Bear's place and went maybe another five or six miles and turned into an old wagon road that went back into the canyons by the White River. When we got to the river, we stopped and got out and took the turkey out of the pickup. "This is the place," Joe said, "for us to turn the turkey loose." So he unwrapped him very carefully and turned him loose. You could see that Joe felt bad about letting this turkey go. So he talked to the turkey. He apologized a little and told him that he had to do this because he was getting too mean to be around kids and people. He said: "We have to do this. You can't stay around people anymore, so I am letting you out here. You be careful and take care of yourself. You will meet someone out here, so don't worry." The turkey just stood there and listened. So he let him loose and we left. Today we have lots of wild turkeys, which we never had before that crazy old turkey got started. I often wonder if he is not the progenitor of all of these turkeys. He talked to this turkey like a human being and told him to take care of himself.[1] He really liked his farm animals. He respected them. He knew that this turkey had to find his home, his place, and his people.

THE BLACK MAN

As told by an anonymous person

I want to tell you a story about our trip to Kansas City. We were there to participate in a protest against nuclear power and missiles at one of the silos. We had gone there and spent a few days in preparation for the action, which was to take place early one morning. Joe was to be one of those who prayed prior to the political protest of some of the members of the group. We prepared at a convent in a retreat-like setting. After the police had come and arrested some of us and let others of us go, Joe and I left to return home. In fact, those that they took got a year sentence out of this. We started back home and were on the interstate near Kansas City when Joe said to me that he wanted to go back there and see the black man. I asked him where, and he told me at the convent. I was sure that there was no African-American or black man at the convent, but I wanted to be respectful to Joe and didn't question him. We turned off the interstate and went back to the convent.

When we arrived, the place was open but no one was there. This was odd because it was in a fairly rough part of town and I thought they would keep the doors locked. But they were unlocked, so we went in and Joe said, "Wait here for me," so I did. He walked into the next room, and there was the nuns' dog, Bart, black Bart, a black Labrador retriever who stayed there. Joe sat down in front of the dog and started a conversation with the dog. He told him that he knew when we were there before that Bart was lonely. He knew he was not around other dogs and missed them. He told him he knew he was there in the city all cooped up and only able to get out for a walk every day and that this made him depressed. He told Bart about all the important things he was doing to help the nuns and all the good things that were in his life. He should be thankful, he said, and focus on the good things that he has right there in his hands. When he finished, he came in to where I was and says: "Well, we can go now." I knew from our conversation afterwards that his talking to Bart was every bit as important to Joe as what he did when he prayed at the missile site. To Joe, animals were persons. The black dog was a man.

6 A Life Changed

I am grateful that I was born a Lakota, because if I had not been, I would not be alive today. It was my traditions that saved my life. When I was ready to kill myself, when nothing could help me, my grandpa found Joe, and I am alive today.
—The narrator of the following life story

A STORY OF BEING HEALED
As told by an anonymous person

The sixties were turbulent for everyone, but for me I felt like I had been dropped into Mars, right back on the reservation from the middle of San Jose. In the early sixties I had married a man from another reservation who I had met in San Jose. Our life seemed like what marriage was supposed to be. I always thought that marriage was supposed to be a special relationship that lasted as long as both partners lived. We had a child, a boy. I had found a job in San Jose at the telephone company and sat all day taking calls. I guess sitting in classes at the Mission school had prepared me for long hours of tedious work. Outside of work we lived an urban kind of life.

My world became pretty predictable and stable; however, what was on the surface was only skin deep. My husband was abusive. He became progressively worse. I couldn't understand why it was happening or what I should do. Nothing I did pleased him. I felt increasingly tense with the focus being in my neck and around my shoulders. It was very tight in those areas, but I disregarded how I felt because I thought it originated from sitting all day as a telephone operator. But it was not that; it was tension. I called home frequently to ask for advice and support from my mother. As he became more abusive, I became more tense. I tried to juggle my work with being a mother and dealing with the abuse. Mom told me to leave and come home for my own sake and that of my son. But I was torn. As I said, I really believed what the church taught about the sanctity of marriage. But it did not get better. He scared me more and more. I worried more and more about what he would do to us. When my husband became physically abusive toward my son, I decided to leave him immediately! We left the city for the reservation to live with my mother, where I knew we would be safe. I then filed for divorce.

He did not let me go, but tried over and over to persuade me to return to him. He played the pitiful and helpless man, trying to get my sympathy, trying to get me to take him back. But I refused. I would not go back to that life. One day I was sleeping late, and he came into the house. Everyone had gone to work when I heard the door open. As I was laying there I heard footsteps come toward my room, and it was him. He talked on and on, very rapidly and disoriented. He told me that he had locked the doors of the house so I couldn't leave. He had come in order to kill himself in front of me. He told me that he wanted me to watch him die and to know that this was my fault. I was scared, very frightened. He held me as his prisoner all day. During this whole day he slit his wrists. He would cut a little and bleed while ranting and raving. Then he would cut some more. He walked all over the house spilling his blood everywhere. I was terrified because I didn't know from moment to moment if he was going to die or kill me. Periodically he seemed to pass out; I even thought that maybe he had died, so I would sneak over to the phone to call for help. As I stood with the phone, a bloody hand would reach out and grab the receiver and hang it up. He would tell me not to try that again, that he was watching my every move. I was all alone, nobody knew about it, nobody knew what was happening.

Then my brother came home from school, maybe in mid-afternoon. He looked through the window and saw what was happening and immediately ran to get help and let people know. They called the police, who came with an ambulance and took my former husband away. My ordeal was not over; the trauma remained. In fact, I think this was the straw that broke the camel's back. I had been stressed before, tense and down, but now I had a bigger set of problems to face. In those days there was no counseling, no sense of what trauma involves. No one had invented post-traumatic stress syndrome, so I was left with only myself, my family, and my new husband. But no one actually seemed to know what it was that was my problem. My new husband was sympathetic and cared, but that is not counseling. I know now how vulnerable I was, but then I just wanted to survive and to make it through each day. But I worried that he would return to kill me. I ruminated about the whole affair and wondered what he would do next to me or to those I loved. I tried to live a normal life, to get back to feeling secure and safe. Then about this same time my former husband came to see our son. He took him for a ride and kidnapped our son. Now I felt like I lost my life. My life was here and then all of a sudden it was gone. I didn't know how he was or what was happening with him. I tried to get him back, but there was nothing one could do in those days. He lived in a different state and different reservation, so nothing could be done. I went to many people, agencies, the police, but nothing could be done. I thought about my son all of the time and became more and more depressed and afraid.

One day after this I was going to Valentine, Nebraska, to the dentist. I had borrowed my mom's car. I drove first up to Mission to do some shopping. I then headed south toward Valentine on Highway 83. The day had been uneventful, and I really did not notice that I felt any different than any other day. Everything seemed fine until I was a few miles out of town. I began to feel like I couldn't drive anymore. I felt like Chicken Little says, the sky is falling, like everything started to crash in on me. I felt dizzy as if I would faint. I sat there in the car immobilized for a while. I lost track of the time but just sat and couldn't drive. I would try but I couldn't. I tried again and was able to turn the car around and go home. I didn't know what to think or what to do. I really didn't talk to anybody about it but waited to see if it would happen again.

Although that did not happen again, my state of mind got worse rapidly. Over the next month I got progressively worse. For example, I remember sitting at the table with my family. The meal was beautiful. Everybody sat around laughing and talking but I felt like crying. I would try to sit and eat but I had no appetite. I simply couldn't eat, so I would leave the table and go to my room. It was awful because I couldn't eat. This was not a periodic thing, but it was always this way, day in and day out. I am not a big person and have always been thin, so as I ate less and less, I became thinner and thinner until I started to look very gaunt. If the not eating was not bad enough, I started not to be able to sleep. I would go to bed and even go to sleep, but then wake up and not be able to go back to sleep. It was a horrible time!

I talked to my mother, who suggested that I go to the Indian Health Service hospital. She had worked at the hospital for several years previously. So I did as she suggested, and my journey through the reservation and Western medical system began. They gave me sleeping pills. The pills did help me sleep, but I would wake up every morning not feeling rested. The pills didn't work for long because I had built up a tolerance for them. As a result, I couldn't sleep anymore. Not eating and not sleeping made me weaker and weaker and more and more distant from other people. I stayed close to the house and did not want to leave. I couldn't drive because I was afraid of being paralyzed again somewhere in the middle of the boondocks. Because it was winter, cold, I would have been putting myself into a life-threatening situation. Some people say that not eating and not sleeping must have been awful. Certainly that is true, but I think the worst part was during the day when I couldn't concentrate. I couldn't think straight anymore. My thoughts became jumbled. I remember specifically this one time that I was trying to go to sleep when I saw a bundle of sticks in front of me, a bunch of twigs and sticks, all mixed together. This really scared me. I thought I was completely losing it and was going to start hallucinating. As we both know, little or no food or sleep can do that in and of itself.

I kept going to the hospital and getting new and promising pills, but the promises were always broken; the effects were either temporary or nonexistent. Often the pills seemed to make me feel worse. I was on what I learned later in school was called the polypharmacy, a little of this and a little of that, one medication to help with sleep, another for anxiety, another for depression, and then others to offset the side effects. The biggest problem was that none of it helped me get better.

Things kept getting worse. I didn't know what to do. I was truly at my wits' end. I thought I had better give the hospital another try, so I went to see Mom and the doctors. They gave me more pills. Now they were giving me antidepressants. The sleeping pills were not affecting me even though I still took them. Now I was on other pills. I remember going to the hospital this one night. They gave me a prescription of something which I took, but it didn't affect me. I decided to return to the doctor, and he said that I should go to the state hospital in Yankton. He threatened that if I didn't get better, he would soon have to send me to Yankton. I didn't want to go to Yankton. I had all of these pills, and nothing seemed to work. Then I started to have other problems. I smelled death when I woke up, or what I thought was death. It would have been in my dream, and when I woke up I could smell what I thought was death. My new husband said he would go and get a doctor to treat me who was his friend. He got the doctors from Eagle Butte to come, and they took me down back to the hospital to the morgue in order to smell all of the chemicals and what death smelled like. I said, "No! What I smelled was nothing like that, but it was death." I never did go back to see those doctors.

It looked like everything was hopeless. My family was worried, so my mother said, "Let's go see a doctor." She worked with him at the hospital and they were old friends, so we took off. He was a general practitioner there. Mom had called him to see if he could see me. It was the late afternoon, so by time we would travel the ninety-five miles, it was going to be after hours. He said he would wait for us at his office. I decided that I should take all of my pills with me in order to show all of what I was taking. We arrived after 5 P.M. and he was waiting. I showed him all of the pills, told him I couldn't eat or sleep, that I had headaches and couldn't concentrate. I spoke to him about how I was totally, like they say these days, "out of it." It was the most horrible and helpless feeling, like being caught between realities. You don't know what is going to happen to you and what is happening to you. It is completely like an unknown that you are living. He looked at the pills and commented that they must be trying to make a zombie out of me. Then he went to his cabinet, a little cabinet, and opened it. He said, "When you can't sleep, I want you to just mix one of these." He pulled out a bottle of blackberry brandy and bottle of soda. He had a little ice chest there and mixed Mom and me a blackberry brandy and soda. We were all sitting there having this drink, and he was sort of joking or making light of my problem. He told me that if I was anxious or couldn't sleep that I should fix a drink. Just relax and have a drink, he said. This seemed absolutely crazy to me. But when we left, we bought a pint of brandy and went home. The first night it sort of helped. I could sleep a little, but then it didn't help after the first night. So here I was, right back where I started.

Grandpa took notice of all of my troubles. One day he came into my room where I was laying and crying, really crying. He said: "Get ready, we are going to look for a medicine man. We are going to try to find someone to help you." He told me to get ready and drive. I don't know how I did it, but I drove. We went to Pine Ridge and visited all kinds of medicine men, all the medicine men down there that Grandpa knew, because he was originally from there. My grandma, who was Grandpa's sister, was there. She had been married to a medicine man named George who had healed me of an eye problem when I was a child, but unfortunately he was dead. We looked and looked for a medicine man all day long, even though it was winter and had been stormy and cold, but nobody really clicked that day, so we didn't present the pipe to anybody. At the end of the day we came back home.

The next day Grandpa came and said he had another idea. I didn't know where we were going, but just followed Grandpa's directions and drove and talked. We went to Joe's. We sat around and chitchatted for a while and had some coffee. I didn't know what to do or what was going on, but Grandpa told me what to do. I presented Joe the pipe like I was told, and he smoked it. He finished and then told us what to do and shortly after that we began to have ceremonies. The men had an *inipi* [the purification rite, or sweat lodge] before the ceremony, and then that night we had a ceremony for me. During that first ceremony they had to tell me what to do. I didn't know what was happening and how to act.

During the ceremony he told me that his friends had told him that they could help me and that he would give me medicine that would help. After the ceremony he gave me a long, grassy-looking rope, not sweet grass, which he had me inhale. He showed me how to light it up so it made a smoke and put a blanket over my head and inhale it. He said to take it this way and it would help me sleep. It helped me. I would inhale it, and it would spread throughout my head and I could sleep. I didn't sleep perfectly, but I could sleep without any pills. Joe told me his spirits said that I was not to take any more of the pills. He said that if the medicine was to work, I was not to take them. I decided that day to follow Joe's advice, and to this day I still do not take pills, perhaps an aspirin once in a while but never any other pills. Joe said he had medicine to give me but it had to be prepared each day and should be stored in the refrigerator. The spirits showed him which plant to pick and prepare for me.

He would bring the medicine to me daily. He did this every day, whether stormy or not, and it was often stormy; he would come and give me this medicine to drink.

He came for a whole month, not just four days. It was really quite nice. He would come and sometimes he would be my only visitor. He and Grandpa would visit. We would simply sit around, visit, and drink coffee. Following that first ceremony, we had more ceremonies for three or four days in a row, and after these four nights of ceremonies we had more ceremonies over the next four months whenever I felt like I needed to attend one. Joe had told me that I would gradually get better, but not immediately. He said that by April I would feel a whole lot better. He said that I might not feel great every day but that I was steadily getting better. Joe told me that someday he would take me out and show me where the medicine grew, but we never got to that point.

I was full of questions. You know me. So I would ask him all of these questions. He answered directly, telling me that during the ceremonies that the spirits, who were his friends, told him where to find the medicine, and he went there to get it. They would tell him exactly how to prepare it. My husband and I spent a lot of time with Joe. Even after he stopped giving me medicine, he would stop by to visit and we went to see him. Victoria and Joe would welcome us into their home and talk with us. He would spend as much time with us as we wanted. It was up to us to leave, and we never felt rushed. Sometimes we drove around with Joe in our car, and he would tell us all kinds of things about his work and answer the many questions I had. I had been treated once before when I was a child by another medicine man who cured my eyes. The mission had put drops in them in order to dilate my pupils. We all got these drops, but my eyes never went back to normal. I had to drop out of school because I could not see. The doctors did not have any idea what to do with me, so we went to the medicine man and he cured me. So I had a lot of questions, and Joe would answer them.

Then one time I had a relapse. I got real bad, so my husband drove me right down to Joe's. Joe told us to go up to one of his singers' homes where we had ceremonies in the past and that we would have the ceremony there. There were only four of us in that ceremony: Joe, the singer, my husband, and me and also my son. My husband was still skeptical, but that night made a believer out of him. There were old bedsprings in the house, and they just seemed to move all over during the ceremony. But that little ceremony got me over the crisis. I just got better and better over those four months so that by April I was really coming out of it.

I was able to eat and sleep and began to be able to concentrate, but I still had problems. When I felt that I needed help, I went to see Joe. Whenever I was anxious, I would go there and talk to Joe. He always found time for me. He was very patient. I never asked him about the nature of my illness but more about the ceremonies and his work. He always answered simply and directly. He let me tell him all of my troubles and always listened closely. He would tell me what to do, so even though I didn't understand everything, I followed his directions. This was probably the first time in my life that I followed anyone's advice or instructions!

He told me one time that I would reach the day where I could walk past my ex-husband and not feel fear and that I would get back my son. Soon after this conversation, my ex-husband called my mother and said, "If your family wants the boy back, you have to come and get him." Nobody else had been able to help me get back my son, but now I was getting him back.

While I was in the process of getting better, I did have one other relapse when I started to have headaches. So I went to Joe, and he told me that they would do a *k̇aŋak̇p̄a,* a bloodletting; *k̇aŋ* is the blood vein. Joe told me to come to a special area of Grass Mountain. I arrived, and the men were having an inipi in preparation for the ceremony. When the men finished the sweat, they came out and went into this little clearing. Joe had been sitting there sharpening a dime. He slowly sharpened it until it was really sharp. Everything was now prepared. All of the men sat in a circle and had me kneel in the center. I was looking toward the west, toward the hills and the river. It was really beautiful. I knelt in the middle on this bed of prairie sage and I was scared, but not really very scared. I kept thinking, this is a beautiful setting for a movie. They put something around my head. It was very tight. Joe took the sharpened dime and popped it on each of the sides of my head. The men were all singing sacred songs during the ceremony. Although I was scared, I went through it, and it helped me with the headaches. I was impressed by how supportive all of the people were. Everyone helped me. I went back to Joe and Victoria many times, and they always had time for me. I sort of felt like a pest, because whenever I was down or anxious I would go to their place. But now he is gone and I have to get along on my own.

He taught me a lot. Maybe I became overly dependent at times. I thought that in a ceremony they could take away my craving for cigarettes. This was my last resort, but now he is gone and I have to do it on my own. I quit a year ago! I have learned to cope. I don't take pills. I have a phobia of elevators with which I have learned to cope. So all in all I am doing well.

I stayed in contact with Joe for many years while I worked and went to school. I enrolled at the tribal college and then went to the city and finished my associate and bachelor degrees. Then I worked for a while and went back to school to get my master's. So now I have been working back in the city for a while and maybe ready to change professions again. All this was possible because I came out of that sickness because of Joe.

I remember Joe. I remember that his friends, the other medicine men, asked me to come once and help them in a ceremony after he lost his power temporarily. I went to that ceremony to pray and to help him. We did a *wopila* later in order to remember the gift we were given. So I remember and am grateful. I am alive today because of my traditions and the wisdom of Grandpa in taking me to Joe.

Comments of Joe Eagle Elk on the Doctoring

When I first saw this young lady, I didn't know what to think. I had been doctoring people for only a few years and still felt *wiš̄teča*—bashful. I did not know if I should take the pipe. She looked really bad, really bad. But I took the pipe and we had the ceremony. I wondered what they would say. Maybe they would say she was going to die or maybe there was no hope. So we had the ceremony and the spirits came in real strong. They examined her and told me what to do. They said that she had a bug on her brain. Not exactly on her brain, but there are three linings between the skull and the brain and there was a living being there which did not belong. It should not have been there and was causing her problems. What had to be done was to remove this bug. I don't know how white doctors would call it, but my friends called it a bug. So they told me what to do. I went and prepared the medicine and gave it to her. It was going to be a long doctoring, so I had to give her the medicine in just the right way. I did it that way and she got better. The medicine I gave her for sleep was just for sleep. I have used it a lot of other times. But the other medicine was specially for her problem and only hers. It had to be able to speak to that bug to get rid of it. She came a lot of other times to talk. We talked, but the first part was done when the medicine was able to work.

Talking is like the medicine; it has to be the right words, the right way of talking that goes along with the person, fits the person just right.

3 Vision and Choice

"What is my unique gift, my authentic talent?" As the great Carlyle saw, this is the main problem of a life, the only genuine problem, the one that should bother and preoccupy us all through the early years of our struggle for identity. . . . The question of what one's talent is must always be related to how he works it on the world.

—Ernest Becker, *The Birth and Death of Meaning*

7 Marriage, Family, and Vision

Well, here I was, a lucky guy to have met Henry Griswold. I decided I better stay there, so I did. My dad wrote me. He wanted to see me, but I couldn't go, so I sent him some money, maybe twenty-five or thirty dollars. I still had my car, which wasn't paid off. I worked the next three years to get it paid off and finally did. During these days I would go to town but didn't drink. I would go to the cafés and clothing stores but stayed away from Hogi's and the bars. I might take off a week to rest, but I would just stay on the ranch. Work became my life. We built a barn, a machine shed, and again I took care of the cattle. During harvest we cut and made silage out of corn, beet tops, and all kinds of other things that we mixed together. We had made a big trench and would unload the silage there. My life moved back and forth between these jobs. I didn't go anywhere except to town, and I had to remember what the judge, probation officer, Henry, and my dad told me about staying away from the reservation.

Well, the three years were finally over, but there were still two years that they told me to do good in. They were in front of me even if I was off of probation. Well, I wanted to trade my car, so I went to town and bought a different one. I came home and told Henry I would like to go visit my dad. He hesitated and then told me to make sure that I don't get into trouble. It was 1960, and he told me a lot of things before I left. He said that the big jail is not a place for you. He would hate to see me go there, he said. I told him that I won't do that so he should take my word for it. He gave me some beans, twenty-five pounds of beans. He told me to go to the potato cellar and gave me two hundred pounds of potatoes. Then he wanted to go to the grocery store, so I went over there and he bought me coffee, sugar, and all kinds of things like cans of pork and beans and corn. Then he pulled twenty dollars out of his pocket and gave it to me and told me to give it to my dad. So I left and went back to Parmalee and saw my dad and Eugene. It was New Year's and there was a celebration in Parmalee with lots of drinking, but I didn't drink. I stayed away from it. I stayed with my dad for the second, third, fourth, and fifth. Then on the fifth I told him that I wanted to go home and that I would come back again. I took off and headed back.

Well, Romeo Kills Enemy was looking for a ride, so I picked him up because he was going to find a job back there in Gordon, Nebraska, him and Marcella Omaha Boy. Then we stopped over at Gordon to visit Jesse Iron Star. He was living up north of Gordon where he worked on a ranch. So we stayed overnight, and the next day they asked me if I could take them to Gordon and then back up there. "We are going to buy some groceries and then come back," they said. I told them okay, and we went to Gordon. They bought some groceries and bought some wine, so I started it again. I couldn't stay away, so I helped them drink. We took the groceries back. I tried not to drink too much because I didn't want to get into trouble. I had enough money to get home, which I decided to hang on to. We went up there and then went back south about four miles, and then we turned around and went back to the liquor store and bought some beer. We left and headed north to take them back to Jesse's, and they said, "Well, why don't you stop at this liquor store. If you do, I will buy some beer."

It was getting dark, a little bit dark, and we stopped, but I told them I wanted to go home. "Okay," he said, "I'll just get a couple of six-packs of beer and you can take us home, and I will give you a couple of six-packs of beer so you can go home." He wasn't too drunk. So we stopped there, and here were two girls coming along the road. I was thinking, "Maybe I will call them over," so I called them over. One of them was a young girl named Victoria. So I called her over and asked if she wanted to drink beer. She said she didn't drink beer. The other one told me that she just lost her mother a few days ago and they had a funeral not long ago. They had just come here yesterday, she said. She was the niece of Victoria's. "Oh," I said, "why don't you get in and we will just drive around." My friend went into the liquor store and then we went back to Jesse's. They got off and Romeo and Marcella got in and then we headed back to Gordon. Victoria and her niece asked if I could drop them off at her house. So I said, "Yeah, sure I can," and I took them to their house. Victoria almost went in, but she was young then so she just drove around with us. I wasn't drunk, so we drove into town. I finally told her I was going back to Scottsbluff to work. I said, "Do you want to come or do you want to stay?" She said go ahead, and we took off. I didn't know her. So we went back and we did pretty good together at Henry's. I was really pleased she came. I worked and she stayed home all the time. But then sometimes she was crying. She missed her mom a lot.

One time she was crying and I was not around and that time my boss came over. He saw her crying and asked her if I hit her or something. She said no, but that she was sad. From that time on his wife would come and get her and take her back to her house and have her work with her. But Victoria was still sad. Finally her brother came over and told her that her dad missed her and didn't know where she was, so he wanted her to come back for a visit. He said, "All of a sudden you were gone and everybody was looking for you." Victoria and I talked. I told her if she wanted to go she should go, if she wanted to stay she should stay, but that if she wanted to go that I would give her money so she could go. I would take her there and bring her back if she wanted. I told her that I was working so I couldn't go for long. Her brother was there, but his transmission was broken so he couldn't take her. I told him I didn't like to go over there because I always got into trouble, so I sure hated to go over there.

But she said she wanted to go, so I talked to Henry and he gave me fifty dollars and we went to Gordon and saw her dad. He told her that her auntie wanted to see her near Mission, South Dakota. Her aunt was Ted Thin Elk's mother. So we went up north of Mission to the Thin Elk place to see her. It was February. All of a sudden there was a really big blizzard with deep, deep snow. We were snowed in there for three days. Her auntie talked to her every day and told her that she was too young to get married. But then she said, "You don't have any place to go, and I don't think your dad can take care of you. So if you are going to make a good marriage, it is up to you. I am not going to say anything; it is your decision."

At last the blizzard let up and some relatives came from Mission. They took a bus and were going to go back. I told Victoria that I was going to walk back to the bus and go to Mission and then to Parmalee. She said she would come because she didn't want to stay over at her auntie's any longer. The snow was kind of deep, so we had to walk one way and then another. When we got to the bus stop, it was an old converted pickup truck, but they brought us to Mission. We caught a ride to Parmalee and stayed there for two or three days at my dad's when the police came over. They asked her name. She told them, and they said, "Well, we have to take you back to the Rosebud jail and I guess you have to come along," so I went too. They took us to Mission, where they said someone wants to talk to Victoria. They put her in jail but let me out. I stood on the corner across from the old jail in Abourezk's grocery store. I saw a police car come over, and the police went inside, brought her out, and put her in the car. They then came over and told me to come and get in. They took us over to Rosebud and put us in jail. Two days later we went to court. The judge said, "There is a complaint that you are living with a minor. She is under sixteen, so you can't be married." "It all depends on her father," the judge said, "so we have to wait. You will wait in jail." We waited thirty days before we had to go to court again. She was waiting there to see what her dad was going to say. Well, finally he came over and signed a paper that said we could get married. The judge told us that you now have consent to get married, so you better get married and not just live together. They let us out, and we went to my dad's. Two days later we went to Martin and were married by a justice of the peace.

After the marriage we returned to my dad's and stayed with him for a few weeks. I wanted to go back to work but didn't have any money, so I called my boss and asked him to send me some money. He did, and I went back to work. We stayed over there for about a year and a half. About that time they were having a sun dance in Pine Ridge. We went over there and camped with my dad. I had not gone to ceremonies but just worked and traveled. Well, we stayed over there at the sun dance for four days. I liked it. After that we went back to Scottsbluff. At this time we had no kids. Then Victoria became pregnant and was going to have our first child. We went over to visit her family in Kyle about January, the last part of January. Then after that we went over to Parmalee to visit my dad, and over there, it began to look like Victoria was going to have our first child. So we went back to Kyle and she was ready. It seemed like something was wrong, so we hurried to Pine Ridge, and on February 2 my oldest boy, Jesse, we call him Chop, was born. Victoria was in the hospital for ten days, and I stayed right there. I did not know anybody there, so I stayed in the hospital lobby. They gave me blankets and stuff as well as food. So if they brought Victoria food, I was there and they gave me food. I had my car outside, so after ten days we went home, but we stopped first at Victoria's sister's place in Gordon. I didn't have any money, so I called my boss and he wired some money to me. We went back to Kyle because Vickie left some stuff over there, and then again we went back to my dad's in Parmalee for about a week before I went back to work again.

Auntie Rose's brother, Herman, Herman Arapahoe, stayed with us. He wanted to go after my dad and bring him over to our place. He wanted to hire me to take him, so I did and we brought him back. So Herman wanted to put up a lowaŋp̄i and he did. My dad did two nights of ceremonies. Jesse, Chop, was about five months old at the time, and I worked every day. Then Herman told me his oldest son was doing a vision quest, so we went over there to attend it and helped out with the praying and singing. I still couldn't sing, but I could help a little. I tried. When it was all over, we left for home and arrived there, so I started to work again every day. Then Herman came back and said he wanted to talk with me. He said, "Joe, there are a lot of lowaŋp̄i and sweats, so you should come over and participate." Jesse was about a year old then. We went over and went into sweats and ceremonies with Herman and others, but mostly with my dad.

We went home many times during these months. I attended ceremonies with Frank Arrowside, my dad, and others. Frank was a real powerful medicine man. He stayed down on the river with Abel and Kenny's mom. I could sweat a lot in those days, and nothing bothered me. I liked them and never got tired of sweating. We also went to Pine Ridge to the sun dance again, and Romeo danced for four days. We stayed and supported him, but after the dance we went back to Scottsbluff. Then one day we heard that Victoria's cousin died, so we returned to Kyle for the wake and funeral. After the funeral we went home and back to work. Jesse was about two and half then, and we had a baby girl. We went back to Rosebud to have her, so she was born at my home reservation. We went home again to Scottsbluff and worked for quite a while without leaving. Then in March my girl got sick, really sick. We took her to the hospital and she died. So we took her back to the reservation and had a funeral and buried her. It was tough, really tough on us. We went back then to the ranch where I worked. I worked again every day but started to feel real bad. I got sick, very sick. I had pneumonia. I did not work for two months and almost died. I just stayed in the house and gradually got better and was able again to work, but Henry went for a one-month vacation to California. Before he went he had sold all of his cattle. He said he would buy new cattle when he returned, so there was nothing much to do at the ranch while he was gone. He told me to take a vacation and build up my strength for the new herd. When he returned he would call my Uncle Ernest and tell him to have me come back. So we went home.

Johnny Strike was doing his vision quest, so I helped out. He did it over at Paul Stone's place, so we were there, and when he finished I went home to Parmalee. There was another person doing a vision quest with Arthur White Feather. I don't remember who it was, but it was someone. I thought it was a priest, but that was later. After that vision quest I went over to Wagner, South Dakota, with my dad, who was putting someone up on the hill for a vision quest. There were ceremonies all of the time which I helped in. We finished these vision quests and headed to Pine Ridge to attend a sun dance led by John Fire and Peter Catches. John was an old man at the time, and Pete was younger. We went there and spent the time at the dance helping in whatever way we could. It just seemed like my life was these ceremonies.

Then Henry returned home and called. He said that I should come home, which I did. We then had Diane. She was sick right away, going in and out of the hospital. We didn't have much money, so it looked like half of our paychecks went for doctor bills. Griswold really helped me when I had nothing. He would say, "Joe, I will pay for this." This was not just a little bit but a lot. She stayed for thirty days in the hospital. This was a terrible time for us, but especially for her. She finally left the hospital after the thirty days, and we had no way to pay. I went to Henry to talk to him about it. He simply said: "Well, Joe, don't you worry about that. It is already paid for. You stay here and work for me and that is enough." I said all right. Diane got sick again and was back in the hospital. It seemed like it was for thirty-five days. But this time I could pay for some of it, not a lot but some of it. Then a big break came. Victoria got word that her dad had sold some land for twenty-three thousand dollars and she should come back and get the money. So she went back and they gave her a lot of money, and we came home and went to the hospital to pay off the bill. We paid the whole bill. It was really a lot and really difficult to see all of that money go. But it was done and it was good to have it paid. The problem was that everything around me seemed to be going from bad to worse. Everything I was part of seemed unhealthy.

One day my boss went to Mitchell, Nebraska, in a truck. I worked all day and about five in the evening I tried to start my truck to come home, but it wouldn't start. I was working on it when this white man came by and asked me what I was doing. I told him and he said, "Forget it now and come with me. Your boss has had a car accident and is in the hospital, so I will take you home." I told Victoria that he was in the hospital and the doctors were working on him. The next morning Charlie, Henry's son, came over and said, "Well, Joe, you better stay around here and work and keep things going because it looks like my dad had a car accident and is in bad shape. I don't think he's going to make it."

I felt real bad, so I decided I wanted to see him and we went over to the hospital. They were not going to let me in to see Henry when his wife peeked out of the room and saw us. She said, "Let them come in and see Henry." So I went in, and he was in pretty bad shape, broken, very broken in the chest and lung area. He still recognized me and said: "Well, Joe, you go back and stay and take good care of the cattle. If I make it, we will work together again." So I walked out, and that was the last time I saw him. I went up to the pasture and checked the cattle and fence. The next day I did the same thing and fed the cattle. Here his boy, Charlie, came and said that early this morning we almost lost our dad, but he made it and now he is sitting up and eating some ice cream, but you never know. I said I will just keep hoping. Early the next morning I went to do the same chores and Amelia, Henry's daughter, came. She said, "Well, Joe, about an hour and a half ago Dad died, but you stay and don't leave." I said okay. The next day they had him in the funeral home and the wake. We went over and stayed all day and also the next night. Then at two o'clock the next day they had the funeral. We did not go to the funeral but went to the cemetery and waited for them to bring him. They arrived and we were standing off to the side a ways with this Mexican guy who also worked for Henry. Soon one of his daughters came over and told us to come over and see him one last time. So we did and that was the last time I saw him.

He was a great man. He spoiled me, because whatever I asked him to do, he let me do it. Whenever I needed something, he helped me. When he died, it seemed to me like everything went down. It was really bad. They asked me to stay on, and we did. Charlie and his brother-in-law, John Waggoner, took over in a partnership. For the first year I liked it. But then the two of them began to argue about everything. They continued to treat me good and never did scold me. But one guy would say to do one thing and then the other guy would say the opposite. So I was right in between. I told Victoria about this, and she and I agreed we should move on. We decided to go home, so I went over and told Henry's wife we wanted to go home and visit and I don't know if I will come back, because he is not around. He died and I don't think I can stay around. We miss him anyhow. She said they wanted me to stay around and told me to stay, but I told her what was happening and she said that it would keep going that way because Henry was not there. So the next day we moved out and went to Parmalee.

It was 1965 and we decided to look for work around Alliance, Nebraska. I went to the unemployment office and right off they found me a job at a dairy farm owned by a man named Sokol, Ed Sokol. We moved in, and I started to work. But then things started to change quickly. I was sleeping one night and had this dream of thunder. It was sudden and really clear. I dreamt that a thunderstorm was coming before it came, and sure enough it came. Then the next night the same thing happened. I suddenly woke up at two in the morning and peeked out at the sky, but it was clear. All you could see were stars. But then all of a sudden I heard something and looked out and it was lightning. I saw it coming real steadily, persistently. I thought it had finished and was all through, but it wasn't. I went inside and told Victoria that we had to go to the basement. I said that I thought that a storm was coming really bad, so I went over to the bed and we got Chop and Diane and took them to the basement. There was a bed and couch down there, so Victoria laid on the bed and we put the two kids on the bed with her. I laid down on the couch. Oh boy, the thunder was really coming and it seemed like it stopped for a minute, but then the lightning was coming into the basement. We went and covered this small window where it looked like it was going to come in, then it looks like the lightning hit something and bounced off the wall and was in the basement. I went over and covered up the window again and made it real secure. Then again it struck in another place and came in. It was a blue light, a blue ball. What was happening to us was steady like this for about a half an hour and then it calmed down. But we were terrified, really scared and nervous. Victoria got very nervous, but then the next day everything was okay. So we worked there for about two or three weeks and nothing happened. But I kept thinking about the dreams and that this storm was coming and I knew it. We had other storms. You know how the plains are in the summer, but they didn't bother me.

Then one day I was out fixing fence when a storm came up really fast. It was about one in the afternoon and I was setting up an electric fence. The storm was coming really quick, so I cut those wires, made a gate, and headed for home fast. The lightning was going in that direction. I arrived at home, and Victoria was scared. It was really bad because there was this ball again. It was like it was looking for me, seeking me. I decided this was too much for us to take, so I told my boss that I had to go home for a couple of days to do something. He said that would be all right. It was a Friday. He told me to take off for the weekend and make sure I was back for Sunday evening. He was a pretty nice guy, so I went back to Uncle Ernest's and told him what was happening. I told him the whole story, what it was all about. He told me that they would help me if I came back, so I told him I would come back in August. This was July, and I told him that if I make it, I will come back then. I stayed for a couple of days, and before I left, Uncle Ernest said that in August they are going to have a sun dance in Pine Ridge. He said he talked to Henry Crow Dog, who told him that if I sun danced maybe it might help me. When we were back, we almost went to a lowaŋp̄i but didn't; we were really close.

It was July, so I went back and worked, and in early August I went to do the sun dance. I danced four days, but it didn't help me. I pierced and fasted, but when I went back that dream came, the thunder beings came, and it was tough. The last part of August I went back to Uncle Ernest's and told him it was too tough. I couldn't take it anymore. He told me to come home and straighten things out. So I went back and talked to my boss. I told him I had to quit. He asked why. I told him that I had something I had to do at home, but when I was done I would come back and work for him. He said it was all right. I didn't tell him what I was going to do. He wouldn't understand, so it was better to just say this. He said okay but asked how long it will take. I told him, "I will let you know when I am done."

We then went home. It looked like everything was going to be right; I would settle up everything, but then Diane got sick. We had to take her to Alliance to the doctor. While we were there Victoria said that maybe we could stay over here for a while, so I made a phone call to my old boss. I told him I was done with all that I had gone home to do and that I would like to work again. He said, "Okay, you can come back, but I have a man working here who is going to quit soon, so you can return if he quits." He said he needed to talk to the man first, so we stayed in Alliance for two days and he came over and said that sure enough the man quit, moved out, and I could come and work again. So we moved back and stayed there for September, October, and November. Then we went after my dad to come and visit. He stayed with us for a couple of weeks and then wanted to go home. While he was there nothing happened. It was real quiet and nice, but Diane was still real sick. We left that day, a snowy winter day with pretty deep snow on the prairie.

We were about three miles from the farm, and on the side of the road there was a highline pole. Sitting right on top of the pole was an eagle. My dad said, "Can you shoot it?" So I said yeah. I asked Victoria to hold the wheel and took out a 25-20 from under the seat. I used to be a really good shot when I was young. While we were slowing down but still moving, the eagle began to fly away, but I just had him and shot him so he fell onto the snow. It was about this deep, about the depth of the alfalfa, maybe ten inches deep. I got out of the car and walked down there and he was laying in the snow, so I walked up to him and was going to pick him up. But he was ready for me and stood up and made his call. I jumped backwards really surprised! I called up to the car and asked them to bring the rifle. When I got it I put a shell in the chamber and sighted in on the eagle and here he was standing up, and he looked like someone who was raising his hand like a stop signal. He opened his mouth and was screaming, but I had him right in my sights, right on his head, and I just dropped him right there. I then picked him up and put him in the trunk and we drove off. We made it to Hay Springs, Nebraska, and then turned to go to Gordon. We went about three miles and went south on a gravel road. My dad said he just wanted to cut the tail off. He wanted the wings, so we cut off the wings and put him in a big sack and later we put it under the cupboard. We left the rest of the eagle there and we came back and brought Dad back home, and the next day we went back to where we were working.

About a week later, yes a week later, here I was dreaming one night and somehow something happened. I dreamed that I met a man and we argued or something, so I took that gun, the same one which I shot the eagle with, and flipped in a cartridge and had him right on the forehead. Here he stood just a little ways from me, so I pointed it and sighted in right on his forehead. Then he raised his arm like this, like a stop signal, just like the eagle. He told me, he said, "Don't do that, don't do that, *eċun śni yo, eċun śni yo!*" Then I put it down. Two times I did this, but I don't remember what we talked about. I remember we talked about something. So I had this dream real clear and remember him saying "don't do it, *eċun śni yo,*" twice. About that time I woke up and was really sweating. I got up and made coffee and stayed up until it was time to go to work. I thought about this all of the time, because it didn't happen but was a dream.

I told Victoria, but she didn't say anything. Well, the next night I went to bed and was kind of thinking why am I dreaming like that. I went to sleep, and then while sleeping somebody came in from the door real fast, really fast, into the room. When he came into the room, my bedroom, he said: "You! You had a dream a long time ago. You have done nothing about it. So if you don't come through and do something with this dream, then you will do what you saw in that dream last night. You are going to do what you dreamed last night and you are not going to be with your family. So if you go through with the dream and do it, act on it, then this won't happen and you will be with your family."

About that time I woke up and sat around for a while. I was afraid to go back to bed, but finally I went back to sleep, and here in a couple of hours the dream happened again. The same man came in real fast and said: "If you don't do it, if you don't do that dream that you had a long time ago, the dream you had and you did nothing with, then this is going to happen to you. You will do this. You will no longer be with your family. You did this a while ago just like in the dream—the eagle! The same thing is going to happen to you. First you must take care of that body of the eagle and you must do it right. You have to look for the body and take care of it!"

So the next morning I told Victoria that we had to go home because this was too tough over here. But we didn't go over right away. We stayed around and one day we were driving back from Alliance and had a flat tire. I got out to jack up the car and started to do this when a pickup drove up and this old white guy got out. He said: "Well, it looks like you have a flat. Let me help you with it." He started to help us change the tire. He grabbed the tire wrench and stooped over and began to take off the lug bolts. I looked at him, and all I could see was his back pocket. There was his billfold. It was big. It bulged and must have been full of money. I wanted that money. Things were bad for us and we needed it, so I decided to take it from him. While he was working on the lug bolts, I took the tire iron and raised it up to hit him over the head. I wanted to do him in right there. All of a sudden as I was ready to hit, I was thrown into the ditch right behind me. Just like that I went flying back. The white man turned around and looked at me laying there and said: "Gee, you slipped and fell. Here, let me help you up." He helped me up and went back to changing the tire. I didn't know how I got in the ditch, but it looked like someone took me and threw me back there. So I was given another chance. I decided to take care of the eagle and dispose of it correctly. We knew where it was and went and got my dad, went back to where the eagle was, and put it to rest the right way. It was no longer alone and disrespected.

We returned to the farm, where I had milking chores to do. I wanted to do something about this dream because it still came to me, yet I just stayed there. It was winter, cold, and every day I had to milk twice a day. To do the milking I had to put the milkers on the cows. You know those old type with the tank that fit on the metal ring underneath the cow and the cups that you put on the udder. When I was doing this, the cows got a little nervous like. I would go to the other side and put them on another cow. Well, I happened to glance over toward the door and there by the door were two men. When I looked toward them, they ducked away and hid from me. They were small, two little men. So I worked and looked again and there they were. Again they quickly moved and left. So I thought I would go to another cow and did, but they were again over there in a little different place, a little bit further away. This happened for four days, but I just ignored it and toughed it out. They would come and watch me and then go away, but come back again and watch me for a while. I thought, maybe I am just seeing things.

So I finished up the milking that second evening and went to the house for supper. We sat down to eat and were eating and I looked over by the bedroom and there they were again. They followed me to the house and were standing there at the door of the north bedroom. So the next day in the morning I went to milk. I was doing the same thing and there at the doorway were the two of them standing right in the doorway. It was a little bit to my right, just a little bit that way, but I could see clearly. So I looked over there toward a little stairway with two steps. And the cow I was milking spooked. She just began to shake; she really shook. It was like a shudder. You know animals can sense the spirits better than we can. When this happened, I knew it was not just my imagination. I realized that it was real because I didn't know, but this cow knew. She just really jumped. I quieted her down.

Now that I knew it was real I went to Victoria at noon and told her. She said she didn't know anything about this but that we should find out from somebody who did know. She said maybe my Uncle Ernest or my dad could help, so we should go back and take care of this. I went to my boss and told him that I had not completed what I needed to do at home, so I had to go back to my dad's. He said okay. I told him I would come back when I had finished what I was supposed to do.

This was February, I think. We went back to do a lowaŋp̄i at Arthur White Feather's. I told him about the dream, this last one. I also told him about what I saw in the milk house. He said: "Well, Joe, you better do something about this because there are two men standing right outside of this ceremony. They are waiting for you, because this is the reason they are following you down here, so you better take care of it. If you don't, then the dream will happen to you, so if you want to stay with your family, then you better do it." Me, I don't want to kill anybody. I said okay, so the next night we had a ceremony. I took my pipe. I had made it myself. It was the one I had made earlier but had put away when Diane got sick right after I had the thunder dreams. I had made other things which were part of my earliest dream and brought them to the ceremony. So Arthur prayed and talked strongly to the spirits for me. Things quieted down a little, but not completely.

That spring we went to another medicine man, Frank Arrowside. I decided to ask him to put me on the hill, so he agreed. He told me, "Joe, you do this vision quest and I will open everything up for you. But you must pray and stay there for the whole time. You can't run away. If you leave the hill and run, then they will keep following you. When you are up there, some things are going to happen to you. They will make you want to run away, but don't run or it will be worse."

So I prepared everything. I had to have everything that was in my early vision. I was ready. This was the first time I did something like this. We sweated first, and then they took me to the hill. It was about sundown, and as the sun set I said to myself that I couldn't pray. And, I could not pray. It was going to be dark very soon. I was out there all alone, and I wanted to see what was going to happen. I wanted help, so I began to pray and kept praying, but I didn't want to be out there alone. The sun went down and it got really dark; everything was completely quiet, silent. I could hear voices, but I did not see anything. It looked like these voices could not come in to the circle where I was. The voices were so quiet that I could not figure out what they were saying. All night and the next day it was the same. The next night the same way. Finally, the fourth day came and it was the same way. About noon on that day they came to get me, and we went back to their place and had a sweat. That evening we had a ceremony and I told them everything. They laughed and joked a bit and told me that I was too scared. They said I was really scared and that was why the spirits could not come to me. So they instructed me that I should prepare again and next summer I must do it.

But I refused. I told them I couldn't wait. I told them I would fix it all again and prepare to do the hanbleċiye again in August. I wanted to go through it and have it over one way or the other. Finish it up. So I told Uncle Ernest what I thought, and he said that I just as well do it and finish it off. At least I would be better off, he told me.

So we prepared. We had a lot to do again. It was tough for those two months because the thunder would not stay away from me. But I got everything ready like in my early dream. I had to have two gourds and a bow and arrow there, so I prepared them. My grandma was in my dream but now she was dead and could not be there, so I went to her grave and took some of the earth from the grave to be with me. We made a sweat lodge and covered it all up. It was new. I had to go in there and then they would take me up to the hill. Right over to the west was this thunder cloud which looked like it was coming fast. I took off my shirt and shoes and stood up to take off my belt. About that time the lightning was coming and it really hit hard. It missed me, but right across the river it hit this cottonwood tree right on the bottom of it. It was so close that it raised all of the hair on my neck. The wind was powerful, so powerful that it made us lean like the trees. Everybody was leaning as if they would fall over. None of them wanted to come near to me. So I took my pants off and went to the other side of the sweat lodge when another flash came which looked like it just missed the top of the lodge. There was an old stump over there, and it hit that stump. Everybody came inside the sweat right away and the thunder disappeared. Everything was ready and was there, so when we finished the sweat, we left for the hill.

We got to the hill and prepared everything like in my dream. I made my altar with the earth from my grandma's grave, the gourds were leaning there with the bow and arrow. I sat behind the altar and said to myself that I must go through this and when I finish I will be better off. But then, oh boy, everybody left. Here I was sitting all alone. I sat and right away it looked like somebody came and squeezed my neck. It was tight. I could hardly talk. So I sat down, but I couldn't even pray. I just wanted to see what it is going to be, what was going to happen to me. Am I going to go through it? Will I make it?

Then suddenly a man came and stood near me. I couldn't see if he was a man or what, but a man came and stood there. He said, "A man is coming to you. He is coming to speak to you, rather than me speaking with you. I will be right here with you, so there will not be anything bad that will happen to you. I will be right here." At this point from over there somewhere, somebody came right up behind me and took hold of me. It looked like at that moment that I just about died! This man started to talk directly to me. The other man stood to the side and supported me. The man talking said, "This is the way we show you. This is how to use this dream. This is how you are going to use everything in front of you to help the people. But you can't just push your dream out of the way. You can't go on your own, by yourself, because we are going to follow you. Whether you run or stay, we will be there anyway. If you push this out of the way and think you are finished with us, you are not going to be finished. So just hang on to the dream. That is the gift you have received. This is the only way you are going to be. If you push it out of the way, your life is not going to last."

So this man kept speaking, telling me if I pushed it away that death was going to be there. He said to carry the dream and what they have shown me with me, and they will come to be with me so that everything will be all right and I will help the people. Then he started to sing and said when you sing this song, we will both be there. He then told me that others would come, but I had to wait until they got used to me and I got used to them. Once we became friends and worked together, then those others will come and work with us. So I was to work with those two for now. They told me their names: *heyoḱa čik'ala* and *heyoḱa iŝnala,* or little thunder being and the single thunder being. They were those thunder powers that came to me on the farm. They were those two men that I saw at the milking barn. They were to be my friends.[1] They told me that the eagle I had shot would come to me as a friend to help in my work, but that for now I had to work only with them. They said, "You can only doctor in this manner for now and don't try to push it further until we are all familiar to you." So these are the four things they told me: how to set up my altar, the song for the ceremony, who to call, and not to push for more until we were all ready for each other.

So at the end of the four days, Frank and the others came to get me and took me back for the sweat lodge. I did that and that same evening I set up my altar. Abel Stone was there as well as Frank and Arthur, my family, and others. We had the ceremony at Frank Arrowside's place. He knew a song, and he and Abel sang it for me. During the ceremony those two men who were on the hill with me came and were talking to me, but I couldn't quite understand them. I could hear them a little, but it was like they were still a bit of a distance from me. For a while they just couldn't come near to me. We were still getting used to each other, I guess. I don't really know, but it was that way for a while. It was okay. So I set up my altar and did my ceremony that night, and Frank told me that I had gone through it. I had to follow the directions, and everything would work as they said. So from that day forward I started to do as my friends said.

8 Origins and Gifts before the Pipe

As you know, my vision did not have the sacred pipe in it. I use the pipe in my ceremonies in respect for it and for what the people know, but it is not in my vision. There is another way that is very ancient which I want you to know. I had told Albert White Hat the story of the original way that the people prayed. This is what I told Albert.[1]

I have been thinking about many ceremonies we have, and the traditions and the ways of my people. I thought about and prayed about the many things I want to say or pass on. I thought about the different ceremonies and traditions. I believe that as we pass these on to the younger generation, we also must record them and share them with other people. I believe we are doing this more today, and if we are not, it will happen soon.

There is one story that is more important than all the stories and ceremonies. As you know, yesterday and few days before that, the weather was bad. I'm keeping an old man here at my place. This old man put out his thoughts and said, "You know, we really need the sun to shine, but the weather prevents us from working outside. It really sets us back on many things. So if you spread the word among yourselves and help me, when the next big blizzard comes, I'm going to do the sun dance!" he said. "You know, I am sitting here now just waiting for the blizzard to come." Well, as you might expect, it started to snow a little and the old man started getting pretty nervous. He started pacing the floor and he kept looking out the window. But as they say, if you say you're going to do something, you have to do it! Of course, I am joking about my friend here. This didn't really happen. We use humor like this to entertain ourselves. No matter what kind of a day we get, we give thanks and praise for the day. And so, let me tell you a story I have witnessed being told about a long time ago, when the Lakota people lived in the old ways, before the sacred pipe was brought to them.

One evening a woman was frying some dried meat over the fire.

When she was finished with the meat, she took a piece of dried fat and fried this over the fire also. As she took the fried fat and laid it on the top of the fried meat, a woman came in saying, "Your cooking smells so good. I just had to come over."

"Thank you," said the first woman. "Please sit down."

The visitor said, "Back there my grandfather and my son are hungry. That is why I came over. So if you could give me part of your meal, I will take it back for them."

"Yes," said the woman. "I will give you part of my meal so you can take it back for them." Saying this, she cut part of the meat and laid it on a big leaf. I don't know what kind of leaf she used, but it was a big one. She used it because she had nothing to put the meat on or wrap it in.

After she put the meat in the leaf, she took a piece of the fried fat and laid it on top of the meat. She took the whole thing and handed it to the visitor, saying, "Here, take this to them."

The visitor took the gifts and stood up and said, "Behind your camp there is a big hill. On the other side of this hill there is a valley. Tomorrow at the point of this valley there will be a large herd of buffalo. Tell your people to be there then so that they may get plenty of meat by killing the buffalo. When they get enough meat and when everybody is full, they must think of us." Saying this, the visitor disappeared.

Immediately the woman went to the leader of the camp and delivered the message.

At dawn the next day, the leader gathered his people and followed the directions the visitor had given. They went over the hill and down into the big valley and headed to the point. As expected, when they reached the point, there was a large herd of buffalo. The hunters charged the herd and made a big kill. Everybody went to work and butchered the buffalo and cut off the meat and had everything done in due time.

When everything was finished and cleaned up, the leader picked a virtuous man to do the ceremony. They fried some meat and fat, took part of each and laid it on a big leaf, and the leader took the gift and handed it to the virtuous man. The man took the gift and made the offering. They said he said these words: "Hear me! Recognize this gift! Your son and grandfather shall be full! In return, I want the same for my son and my grandfather. They shall never go hungry. Give me help in this manner. Hear me! Recognize this gift and live a happy life in the future!" After the offering, the leader picked another man of good virtue, and this man took the offering and delivered the gifts to an isolated place.

To this day we still practice this particular ceremony. Since that time we carry out and practice this ceremony each day and night. You will notice now that on occasions when men and women will sit down to eat, and before they take the food into their mouths, they will take a small portion and offer it, saying, "Recognize this gift, I shall have it again!" Lakota people believe in this short prayer because they have received whatever they prayed for.

This is how it was told to me by my grandmother, who was the older sister of my dad's mother. I remember the day she told me this story exactly as I have related it here.

It was later on that the sacred pipe came to the people. When the news of the pipe came to the people, they gathered all the wise men and asked them to make a decision on what to do with the sacred pipe.

At the conclusion of the meeting, they picked the wisest man to deliver the message to the leader of the camp. The wise man came to the leader and said: "A very sacred pipe has been brought to the people. But along with the pipe there are some strict laws that the people must observe. Also, they must be very careful of what they say when they hold the pipe. Since we are humans, I am afraid that down the road people will divide and fight each other. The people must be very careful and work hard together, and good will come to them."

One of these people answered him, saying, "If that is so, I will not take a step toward that life. Ever since we existed we have had a ceremony that we practice daily, and I was told we must always do our prayers in this manner. For this reason, I myself will continue to keep the spirits and continue to live with them."

9 The Fish and the Man

Nothing is more present than an unspeakable absence.

—Françoise Davoine, Lacanian psychoanalyst

I had not met the young man. Rather, a friend, Frank, who visited me had spoken of him and asked me for advice. He told me that this young man had been on life support with a bad cancer and was just now taken off the machines which kept him alive. Frank mentioned that he expected a call any time that the young man had died. We talked and I was thinking about this situation, so I told Frank that I would try to help and that "death is not your business." Although I did not usually ask my helpers for such advice without the person in front of us, this case kind of struck me. As he talked, it made me feel that something special was there. It is one case which I have not understood well and one that made me question why did things go the way they went. Usually I know that maybe things will go one way and maybe they will go another, perhaps the person will get well and perhaps they won't. I just accepted that as a fact, but this case became a puzzle for me.

The friend who spoke to me of the young man and his sickness was a psychologist in Wyoming. Frank's wife often came to our sun dances and had some special powers, so Frank and I had become acquainted and became friends. I liked him a lot, and he is one person who I think you should know. He spoke to me about this person, who also was his patient. He had many problems which Frank treated, like depression and sadness, but he had one big problem that was beyond Frank's work; the young man had cancer. He had been given four months to live, and now they said he would soon die. Frank felt that perhaps some new hope and a cure could come from the spirits and our ceremonies, so he asked for help.

So I asked my helpers, spirit helpers, for their advice, and to my surprise they spoke right up. They explained to me that cancer was like a flower. It grows, buds, and blooms. It can continue to grow and become larger and occupy much of the body or it can stop growing and become smaller and then die. Cancer is a living being. One has a relationship with the cancer, but too often the only way it speaks is through the body's pain. The person speaks to the cancer only about how much pain it is causing. My spirits said that they would stop the cancer from growing and budding. But the cancer would only stay as it currently was and would not grow or spread. If the young man did something else, it might make it go away. What the spirits wanted this young man to do was to go fishing. It would be best if he went fishing alone, but it was also okay if he went with another person. They knew he was sick and weak, so if he needed help that was fine. He would go fishing, and once he caught the fish he was to take it in his hands and look it in the eye and say to it that he wished it a long life. He should talk to the fish. The fish would speak to the young man and he was to speak back to the fish. He was to say something to the fish and the fish was to say something to him. Only this young man could maybe understand the fish and only this young man could speak what was to be said. Maybe he would say something, but what I don't know. He would know at the time. What the spirits said is that he should speak to him about his sickness and then return the fish to the water. They thought that the fish would take something with him. We don't know what. Well, I told Frank what to tell his patient and what to do. After he left, I said to myself that this case was very different. I was very curious about what would happen.

Frank returned or reported to me every so often what was happening. The doctors were amazed that he had not died. He began to steadily improve and was discharged from the hospital but had to return for chemotherapy. In June the young man began to react again to this medicine and got really sick. The young man would try to go fishing with Frank. They would make plans and then the plans would fall through. One time something came up for the young man and another time something came up for Frank. So they would get really close to going fishing and then not get there, just right there and, then, it didn't happen. They came to the sun dance one time, and this was the first time I met the young man. He was a little scared, but we had a nice talk and I told him that he should just go fishing, because all he was doing was going fishing, and when he went he would have his chance to speak to the fish. This man had now lived well beyond the four months and had now lived well over a year. The reports from the doctors showed that the cancer was still there but was not growing.

Frank told me that he often had bad days and would become sick. I told the young man that if he was sick, he would just postpone the trip and he would have another chance. Both Frank and the young man kept trying to find a time to go fishing, but they still just seemed to get real close and then they had to cancel. I sure wondered why this was happening. As you know, I first talked to you and the others up in Manitoulin Island,[1] because I wanted to have some advice from you all about why this might be happening. He came to see me in July. We had a nice talk, but he was sort of shy.

Well, finally, they found the time to go fishing.[2] From what Frank said, they had quite a go of it. They went from place to place and were skunked. Finally, they went to a place where you pay to go fishing and were skunked at all of the ponds. The man who owned the place had told them if they went to one of the tanks that they could find a fish for sure. Finally, they did this and after a little casting the young man had a fish on his line. The trout came quickly to the hook he had baited with cheese and took it. The young man reeled in the line and then pulled in the fish hand over hand. Frank said that as soon as the young man took the fish into his hands, it quieted right down.[3] He looked right into the fish's eyes, and the fish looked right at the young man. The young man began his speaking, his prayer, Frank thought. He could see his lips moving as he spoke to the fish for up to two or three minutes. As he finished and was preparing to let the fish go, it happened. The fish spoke to the young man. Frank described the sound as a "meow," almost like a cat's cry, and it happened twice. They were shocked but listened closely. The young man was really surprised, excited, and very happy. Frank said that he grinned and smiled. Then he put the fish back into the tank and they left.

The young man and Frank could not understand what the fish said, but they knew it had spoken to him. He had spoken to the young man. He had not understood what the fish said to him. Unfortunately, he was not able to throw away the cancer with the fish by finding the words that would talk to the fish. Well, what really puzzled me was why the two of them couldn't meet. They just couldn't find a time to meet. This was the big problem, maybe. But I didn't quite understand it when I talked to you all on Manitoulin Island. I felt a real pity for this young man. He died from the cancer fourteen months after that January that he had left life support, and I wished there was another way, but there wasn't. The young man and his friend were in between and sort of stalled in between my ways and their ways. And this in between made it really hard for them to meet. They did not really understand the Lakota way or my way of doctoring. He and Frank both had a desire to believe in the Lakota medicine but couldn't lend their whole mind to our ways. If he would have come to me immediately after the fish spoke to him and put up a ceremony, the spirits could have told him what the fish said, but he didn't. Even if he didn't really believe, he could have asked and they could have told him. Whether things would have turned out different if he had done this I don't know, but he would have known what the fish said to him. I really felt pity for them. But this is the way it happened. Frank came to see me two months before the death, and I told him that the young man had more suffering to do. But this young man was doing okay. He said that the young man lived with the words of the fish and felt much better and was more confident that he was going to a better place.

4 Wisdom

The only true wisdom lives far from mankind, out in the great loneliness, and it can be reached only through suffering. Privation and suffering alone can open the mind of a man to all that is hidden from others!

—Igjgarjuk, Eskimo shaman

10 Life and Struggles of a Medicine Man

Hečetu! Takuni siče śni! [It was all truly all right and there was nothing bad!]

—Eagle Elk's comment on his life

The two men became my main two friends. They stayed with me for the next two years, a pretty long time. At first when I had the ceremonies with them, they seemed to stay a little ways from me. They were really hard to understand at first—it was almost like a whisper. I had to listen real close to hear them. Gradually, we got more and more used to each other, and finally I could understand them real well. People started to come to me, and I was pretty nervous about it. I was bashful and shy. But everything was good, once I finished it all. I said to myself, "You just as well do it." So I gave myself to them. We left the ranch and never returned to that life. Now my life was with their directions. I would sing the songs they gave to me, set up my altar as they instructed me, and they would come to me and tell me what to do to help the person or whether we could help her.

I remember one of the first people I doctored was from Pine Ridge. I don't remember when it was or how early, but I remember her. Her family came one day. They had to bring her, because she could not move. She had a really bad case of arthritis. She was thin and her hands were already crooked.[1] She was on a board in the back of a car. She had been to the hospital over the years, but just kept getting worse and worse. She told me that they were going to give her gold treatments, maybe they had started. But she didn't feel any better. Well, when I saw her, I didn't know what could be done for her. It really made me nervous, because I wondered if they could help her. But I accepted her request to doctor her. We had four nights of ceremonies. The first night they told me they could help her and what medicine to use and how she should take it. I doubted them, just really wondered about this. But I did what they told me. I went and found the medicine, prepared it, and gave it to her. I saw her for a long time, because this was a very tough case. Each day after the ceremonies she got better and better. She had some movement in her hands and feet right away. In a few days, I don't remember how many, she could begin to sit and move around. The pain was still there, but gradually she got better and better. Pretty soon she was off the medicine and was walking real good. Today I know this person and she is fine, but I really didn't think she would get better. I was surprised.

So I worked with these spirits for about two years. Then they told me I had to go back up on the hill. I had to do the yuwípi, where they tie you up and you wait for the spirits to come.[2] Well, they tied me up, and sure enough that man came from over there. It seemed like he was a long way off, and sure enough he came over and they untied me. They sang me some songs which I was to use when I did this ceremony so I could call them in. I was up on the hill for two days. I came down and we sweated, and then that night I did the ceremony for the people. Again my friends stood far off, just a little distance away. It stayed that way for a while. Then they came closer until we got used to each other, maybe after a few months. I worked with them for the next two years, them and my wakiŋyaŋ friends.

Then one day they told me I had to go on the hill again. Two years from the last one. So I went. This time the same thing happened to me. They came, but held back a little and then came up close. The one who came was the eagle who I had shot that time with my dad. I was really surprised, but it was him. He told me that things were going to become very difficult and that I would have very hard times, but he said: "Joe, I will help you. I will come to you and stay with you and this will be our home, so later I will come!" Sure enough, the second night after the sweat, he came to me when I put up my altar like he had shown me in the vision. He helped me a lot when I would have difficult cases. So again for the next two years I performed these ceremonies. Sometimes one type and other times another one. I sang the songs they gave me. Abel or another singer would sing them, and they would come into the ceremony. I had more friends now, and they seemed to have become really comfortable with me. But still I doubted that they would come or they could doctor this person and still I was bashful. I don't know why, but that is just the way it was. Then after about a year of working with both the waŋbli (eagle) and with the yuwípi, the yuwípi spirits asked me to do some new things in a new way.

So I did it for them. This man, a spirit friend, came to me and told me that there were two spirit women that were ready to work with me and that I had to go south of Kilgore, Nebraska, and that I would find a big cottonwood tree there and that right below that cottonwood tree I should hanbleċiye for two days. So I went there and found the place. I prepared everything and went up on that hill. That first time I heard their voices but couldn't see them. I heard them but couldn't understand them. For two days I stayed there and never could understand them. So I finished the hanbleċiye, and my spirit friend, the yuwípi friend, told me I would have to do another hanbleċiye in the same place. So the next year I did another one. This time they came close to me and spoke to me. They gave me a song to call them into my ceremony. They told me that I should call them to help with very serious problems, those of great difficulty. These *wiŋyaŋ nup̄ap̄i* (two women) ceremonies were really different than the other ones.

Finally, two years later, again I went on a hill for a vision quest, and this time the *wanaġi* (spirits of former medicine men) tried to come close to me and again they couldn't. They did come close enough to tell me that they would work with me at first from a distance. They gave me my wanaġi song, and when I put down their altar and sang their songs, they would come and help me doctor.

So these are my ceremonies, my friends, the powers and songs that help me to doctor. Each came in a vision quest. First, two nights for the heyoǩa and wak̄iŋyaŋ, then two nights for the yuwípi, then two nights for the waŋbli, and then two nights also for the wanaġi, and finally the two nights for the wiŋyaŋ nup̄ap̄i. *Ho hehaŋl mit̄a welo!* (So these are mine!). After the first vision quest, life was a straight line. There were hard times, but nothing really bad. But there were some very hard times. I would always call my one main spirit friend with this song:

K̇ola le miye ċa wau welo, wau welo
(Friend, it is me, so I am coming)
K̇ola le miye ċa wau welo, wau welo
K̇ola le miye ċa wau welo, wau welo
Wiyoȟpeya t̄ak̄iya lena waŋji na ahit̄uŋwaŋ nawajiŋ yelo
(Toward the west I am standing, look on me)
K̇ola le miye ċa wau welo, wau welo, he ho!

I would have them repeat this for each of the sacred directions, and during this song he would come.

So my life had changed from the way it was before. I seemed like I went from ceremony to ceremony. I continued to work but did not go back to the ranches. I worked mainly in Rosebud. Sometimes I worked as a janitor, and then Stanley had me work at the college. It is hard to work jobs and then have ceremonies every night. They didn't mix too well, but I did them. Victoria and I had three more children: Chris, Cheyenne, and Cork. Victoria always worked. One day she went to Rosebud to look for a job. We drove here and there for her to look for a job, but no one would hire her. She was from Pine Ridge, so they seemed like they gave the jobs only to someone who was from Rosebud. We didn't stop, but every day we would drive around until finally she found a job. She became a cook at the hospital. She worked there quite a while and made money for our family.

One day my friends told me Victoria should do a hanblečiye, so she did it. She had to do this because she held the sacred pipe in the ceremony and prayed for the people who needed doctoring. During my ceremonies she prayed all the time while we were singing or doctoring the people. They also told me they would someday give her a vision. Someday she could interpret, understand what they said, and have power. But they still have not come to her. She can't understand them, but someday in the future she will. It is she and I together with the singers and the people who complete these ceremonies.

So we went from our work to our ceremonies. The children were alone a lot with other relatives. I didn't have the time that they needed, because we were always busy. I wanted to quit the work at times. I said to myself, "Joe, you should quit. It is too hard. Your kids need you. It is time to quit this right now." I was still bashful about the ceremonies. I still felt nervous each time a person would come for healing. But each time I thought this, my friends would come to me and tell me, "Don't do that. There are some people coming to see you." And sure enough, someone would come and I would help them. I went on and on with my work, and I was fine and my family was fine. I was really happy, even if I was shy and unsure of myself. I stayed home and followed my friends' directions. My children grew, and we were very proud of them. We started to travel more. People in different cities would ask us for help and send for us. We would take some of the kids with us sometimes. The kids were healthy except for Diane, who was better but was never strong in her body.

One day while I was at home this one guy who had hemorrhoids really bad came to me. They were bleeding, and he could hardly sit

Joseph Eagle Elk offering a prayer at the Bell Rocks, Whitefish Bay First Nations, Ontario, in honor of the ending of the Elders Conference.

Joseph Eagle Elk, 1985.

Victoria Eagle Elk and son, 1985.

Joseph Eagle Elk and son, 1985.

Joseph Eagle Elk and Stanley Red Bird, 1985.

down. He came with the pipe and asked me to do a ceremony, so I agreed. We had a sweat to see what we could do for him and what ceremony to hold. He told us his story. He had this problem for many years and had gone to doctors but they gave him medicine which he didn't take. He had tried medicine from the drugstore. He was told that he would have to change his eating habits, but he refused because he said he didn't like these doctors' orders. So now they said they wanted to cut on him—operate. He wanted us to help him so they would stop bleeding and he would get better.

Well, I said, "Why don't you come into the sweat and we will see what they say."

So he came in and we started. I called my spirit friends into the ceremony, and they took one look at him and told me to tell him they couldn't help.

"He needs to go to the doctor and have surgery right away or he might get an even worse problem," they said.

They told him that they would send one of their friends to be with the doctors and help them in the operation in order to make it all come out as he wanted. But they could not help him because he had let it go too long. I found it hard to tell him what they said, but I did as I was instructed and we did not hold any further ceremonies to doctor him. If he wanted a ceremony to pray for the doctors and the surgery and for his own strength, we could do it, but not to doctor his hemorrhoids. Many people come too late and do not take care of themselves, so the problem has to go to the white doctors. Sometimes they had been to many doctors and came to me for one last chance.

There are other problems which are not like this but are the kinds that are not in the body. Sometime during my first years of being a medicine man I was brought these two young people who were adolescents. They were brother and sister. They had always been very close, really good friends. But they could not get their minds off of each other. They wanted to get married but couldn't because they were brother and sister. So the parents were very afraid and brought them to me. My spirits looked them over and told me that there once were two young men who were very, very close and also really good friends. Well, these two young guys died. About the same time, this family is having these two children, and the two young men's spirits were put in this boy and girl. So they were just really close like them, but they got mixed up at adolescence because they wanted to get married. So my spirits had to stop this. They helped them to know themselves and to understand what had happened to them. They told them they would have to leave each other. They could not stay close to each other or they would have this problem. So the woman got up and left. The boy too, so they were separated and had to stay that way. So sometimes they doctor with the truth and that is enough. But they have to come early and have to follow the directions given them.

So our lives moved between everyday work and our evenings in ceremonies. We would come home from work, do some cooking, and all of a sudden somebody would show up and ask for a ceremony. Maybe there already had been a ceremony scheduled and we would have to schedule another one for the new person. But most of the time the person came because they needed help right away. So we might have to have more than one person being doctored at the same time. This is not so good. It is better if the ceremony is only for one reason, one person. But the people are suffering and we could not say no.

There was a lot of work raising the children and having these ceremonies. To have a sweat lodge, we needed wood and rocks. We had to keep the lodge clean and ready for an *inik̄aġa*. I had some real good helpers. Vincent Brings the Pipe stayed with us a lot during these times. Sometimes he liked to leave, but when he was around he helped us a lot. He cooked for the kids, watched them, and helped with the ceremonies. He was also a great joker—full of jokes—practical jokes. He could always see the funny side of what happened.

One of my other main helpers was Abel Stone. Abel sang for me and knew all of the songs for my ceremonies. Abel was my close relative and friend. We were neighbors down in Grass Mountain. He sang at my first ceremony after the vision quest. We also had a lot of fun. Back in the old days they used to have dances, white dances. One night Abel and I decided we were going to go to this white dance. Our wives told us to stop acting so foolish and behave like men of our age. But we were hell-bent on going to that dance. We made our plans and went to our homes to get ready. Our wives told us we didn't fit into those dances, but we didn't care. We took baths, shined our shoes really bright, and really got spiffed up. One of us had some cologne, so we splashed that all over ourselves so we smelled really good. I greased down my hair so I looked great. The time had come for us to go to the dance when there was a knock on the door. Victoria went to the door and answered it. Someone was there to see me and they brought me a pipe to put up a ceremony. I couldn't say no, so I had to do it. Well, when we sat down for that ceremony, Abel and I smelled the best. We looked the cleanest, the most well groomed, and everybody teased us about how we smelled. My spirit friends, they even commented on how good we looked. People used to love to tell this story, and Abel and I would act mad when they would tell it.

Ken Stands Fast was also one of my helpers, as well as Duane and Celeste. Herman Arapahoe, Auntie Rose's brother, helped me many times in my ceremonies. John Around Him sang for me, and we worked together on the sun dance. When John had his first sun dance in honor of his father, I asked Ken to come and help me. He helped me, so I asked him again when I had to do one in Cherry Creek, on the Cheyenne River Reservation. I told him he would have to go out into the arbor with me and help with each of the rounds by bringing the people around to pray in each of the directions. Lots of things he would have to do. I told him everything, and he helped for the four days. It was really hot. I bet it was 114 or more. I felt mercy for the dancers and the people and decided to stop the dance early, about three or four in the afternoon. So we did this for the four days, and I kept looking at Ken and smiling, because he was getting redder and redder. He would smile back at me, but I didn't say anything to him, but just smiled. I felt good about how everything was turning out for the dancers and the people. Everyone was together! So we left and went home. I was still looking at him and laughing to myself at how he looked. Ken went to his house, went in, and his mom was sitting there in her chair, the single chair in the living room. She looked up at him and said, "Who are you?"

Ken said, "It's me!"

His mom just started to laugh, and he wondered why but decided to put his stuff away. Finally, he went into the bathroom and looked in the mirror and was shocked. His face was almost black. He came out laughing and understood why I was grinning at him and why his mom laughed so much. They took his picture, and he still has it. Boy, was he dark! We always enjoyed teasing him about how nobody knew who he was.

So I depended a lot on these guys to help me. One day, my friends told me I had to do another hanblečiye. They told me it would be a yuwípi one and so I would have to be tied. So I started to think about who could put me up on the hill. I got in my car and drove to Spring Creek, St. Francis, Parmalee, Soldier Creek, Mission, and Rosebud and thought of all the people I knew—trying to find one to help me. So I thought about this for about two weeks after they told me to do the yuwípi hanbleċiye. Well, I would drive around and think and visit people. We would sit and drink coffee, but then I would leave and go home. I always ended up back in Grass Mountain. I kept thinking of Kenny Stands Fast. He was a good helper. So I went to him and told him, "I am here to ask you to put me on the hill for a yuwípi hanbleċiye." I said we would do it the right way. He agreed, so we made the preparations. It was necessary for us to do four days of sweats before I went on to the hill. I had picked the hill west and south of our house with the pine trees around it. It is a powerful place—a place where others have prayed and others have been buried. I was very happy with Ken. He was going as far as I wanted, further than many others. He helped with all of the preparations. We were ready. The day came. We did the final sweat. We headed that evening right about sundown to the hill. Victoria and relatives and friends came with us to support me.

Ken put the blanket on me and began to tie me as I had told him. I had a really beautiful leather rope which my Uncle Silas had made for me for these yuwípi ceremonies. He tied my fingers, interweaving them behind my back. I looked like a mummy, all tied up. He had helped me fix the place up, and I told him to put me on the sage near my altar. The others who came stood to the side and prayed for me. As he and his helpers laid me down, I knew I was beginning to change. I could feel my friends come to speak with me. Once I was down, I began to make the *hi haŋ* sounds, the sounds of the owl who was coming to me. I told Ken to sing a particular song and then another. He started to cry, because he felt I might not come back, maybe I would die, maybe they would take me and I would never come back. I often wondered about that myself, but I just let them come really close and told him to keep singing these songs to the four directions. They left me there alone. The spirits came fast and they took me away and showed me many places among my ancestors, where they are now. At times I was happy with what they showed me, and other things made me very sad. But I was happy in the place they took me to because I had no worries or troubles. I don't know how long I was with them, but when I came back, my spirit friends untied me. Victoria stopped by on the third day, and I told her I could return. She went and got Kenny, and he came and took me home.

We sweated right away and then had a yuwípi ceremony that evening. Ken tied me again and put me down near my altar. As soon as this happened, my friends came in, really fast. The gourds flew around the room. It happened in seconds. They startled me because it was so fast. I kind of jumped myself. They told me to voice myself to the people and tell them about my journey. So I did. I told the people how sad I was to see how difficult it was for them, all of what they were going through and all of the suffering they experienced. But I told them that there was a place I had seen where there was no more of this suffering. I knew that this ceremony would help the people have courage. I knew that I should continue to work with them.

So I worked with all of these friends. At times I worked with the wak̄iŋyaŋ, thunder beings, who had first come to me. I drew a picture on my earth altar of what they told me was their sign so that when the songs were sung, they would come to their altar. I used the wak̄iŋyaŋ for Ken's sister's daughter, who was twelve years old and lived in Minneapolis. She was diagnosed with cancer, so they asked for help. Even though she was not much involved with ceremonies, she really wanted help for her child. They told me the doctors had tried to stop the cancer but couldn't get it done, so she had only a few months to live. We had a ceremony, and my friends looked really close at the spot and where it had gone and how far it had gone. They told me that we would need to doctor her for four nights, which we did. My wak̄iŋyaŋ spirits came in real strong and worked on her. They are lightning and electricity. They have the power to burn out the sickness. They can stop it. As the ceremony went on, I felt a little dizzy. It was hard on me. I felt the full burden of the cancer. I was drained at the end of each of the nights and felt weak, so I asked Ken to come to the center and get the medicine which the spirits had advised me to give her. Ken came in and took it and gave it to the girl.[3] This was a medicine which they picked for this particular cancer of this here girl. It was not a medicine for anybody else. They told me they had killed the cancer; they had stopped it with the medicine, the power of the wak̄iŋyaŋ medicine.

Sometimes people got better, like this person, and I felt really happy. Other times they didn't and I was sad. But I learned that sometimes they weren't ready to get better. Other times they got better and never returned and never seemed to want to have the *wopila,* thanksgiving, ceremony which would complete the cycle. In our way, the people give you a gift after the ceremony. It is a *woȟyak̄a* (an exchange for the help). Sometimes they would give money, but other times food or animals or a quilt or something. Sometimes they would give a handshake or a cup of water. Whatever they had, whatever they could afford, they would give. I was always happy when they gave me whatever they could. It is our way never to ask for money for our work. It is wrong to do so. Medicine men have rules, lots of rules, for how to do their ceremonies and how to live their lives. They are hard rules, but they are necessary. The rules are not just for us, but also for the people, so they can live and become strong. Today many of the people have forgotten the rules. One is wopila. We should thank the spirits for what we received by holding a ceremony after our doctoring and remembering what we got from them. So we depend entirely on the people who come to us, so the cycle of healing is completed.

I worked, but it was too hard to keep a daily job and spend every evening in ceremonies. Once people started to ask for help in their homes and their homes were in Minneapolis or Denver, I had to go there. So we went. Victoria stayed home and worked so we could live and have enough money. One of our rules is that we can't keep what we are given, so we never did have any savings. We had to depend on others for the money for gas, a car, furniture, and everything. It is a hard life for children and a wife. They helped me much, but I know it was tough on them.

So life became hard—really hard! The kids grew and they got into trouble. This really bothered me. I was very unhappy and at times did not even want to be with them when they acted this way. They would become angry or start fighting and get drunk—nothing good. But it was their life and I seemed helpless to stop it. But sometimes the police were wrong when they came to pick up one of the kids. I could not stand for it. One time when they came to pick up Jesse, they were really rough, so I slapped the policeman and told him to treat my son with respect.

I kept doing my work as a medicine man and then the kids started to straighten themselves out and there was nothing bad going on. I was really happy. So what do you think happened, but my health got bad. My heart was really bad. So I started to get sick and got weaker and weaker. I had noticed I was dizzy at times at sweats and ceremonies.

I could only walk a little ways. I went to the doctor, and he told me I had valve damage, a little hole in my valves. They gave me medicine but wanted to doctor me by surgery. They told me I could maybe get better if I changed my diet and stopped smoking. I didn't smoke a lot, but it was too much. Well, I didn't really follow their directions, but I ate what I liked. I really liked doughnuts and sweets, so I ate them. Sometimes I slowed down just a little. I talked to my friends, spirit friends, about it and they said it was my decision, but that I had part of my vision left to complete. I doubted about surgery: do it or not? I decided not to do it.

We stayed around but traveled too. Vincent stayed with the kids a lot. He and I had to work to make sure that there was enough wood for the winter. One time we went to get wood down on the river. So we hooked up the cart up to the wagon and off we went. We headed out to the road and started down that long hill to the Grass Mountain road. I drove and Vincent sat in the wagon. You know how steep it gets and really gets curvy at places. Well, I was driving, sort of daydreaming, and not moving very fast and all of a sudden I look up and here is the cart moving past me lickety split—moving right along. Vincent had this look on his face, his mouth sort of dropped open, and he was waving his arms. Well, lucky for Vincent the wagon ran off the road and into a bank and not over the cliff. It tipped over, and Vincent was a little shook up. We laughed and laughed at how that cart just took off and passed me by. That night we had a ceremony and before it everyone is sitting and visiting, joking and teasing each other. Vincent claimed I was trying to get rid of him but that I now knew how lucky I was to have him around.

So I kept at my doctoring. One day we were sitting around visiting and the phone rang. It was a call from Salt Lake City. There was a man named Fred Hardy. He had been in a car accident and his leg was crushed. They said it would never be better at the hospital, that his bone was like little shattered pieces of glass which you couldn't put back together. I asked Stanley to go with me. This was one of my first times doctoring a person in a big hospital. I did it other times, but this was one of the first. We went there, and they had the ceremony right there with doctors and nurses around. It was okay. They brought him into the ceremony in a wheelchair. So we started the ceremony and there was no problem for my spirits to come and examine this man. They said the same thing about the condition of his leg, but they said they could help. They would go in and redo the leg with the help of this one medicine. Sure enough, they did it, and he was able to walk.

I really had to wonder if this one would work. After what the doctors said and my spirits said about how badly crushed the leg was, I really wondered. The doctors x-rayed his leg and found it was all put back together. I was really happy that the ceremonies worked for this man. He had a drinking problem, and after this he worked really hard to help others with their problems. I helped with this by coming there and holding ceremonies. He has died, but they have named a center with his name where they doctor people with drinking problems.

So we went home and I rested up and stayed close to home for a while. One day I was sitting outside. It was a warm spring day, and the kids were all playing around the house. I saw one of the kids carrying a 30-30 rifle and wondered what he was doing with it. He was very young. All of a sudden he pulled it up and shot it at close range right in the stomach of my nephew. I almost fainted. It made me sick, very sick. This was Abel's grandson. They rushed him to the hospital, and he was almost dead. The doctors were able to keep him alive but couldn't give him what he needed, so they sent him by plane right away to Fitzsimmons Hospital in Denver, the V.A. hospital. We knew they would be operating on him, so we had a ceremony right away that evening. We let everyone know. I was sick and worried. Many people came, and our little home in Grass Mountain was full. You and Stanley were there. I asked to be tied up, and they tied me up for a yuwípi ceremony. My singers sang the song, and my friends all came into the ceremony. They were there and looked at all of the people. The people were there for only one reason, to help this young boy survive. Sometimes my spirits will play around or stay away or not cooperate. Everything is not quite right. Not too often does the power really come into a ceremony. But that night, it was right; we were of one mind. So I was brave. I told my spirits right out what had happened. That the boy was close to death. That he was not expected to live. I told them that they had to save him. I told them I had done everything they had told me to do. I had suffered and followed their directions. I threatened them. Either they saved this boy or I would quit my life as a medicine man. There was no other choice, no other way. They owed me. They listened. They listened to the prayers of the people. I told them to go immediately to Denver and help these doctors with the surgery. They agreed. They went and they helped the doctors and the boy. The boy survived in spite of what everyone expected. He is alive today. I learned that day why the spirits stayed away or did not often come into the ceremonies really strong. What we had that night, and you felt, was *ṫawaċiŋ waŋjila*—we were of one mind, one desire. No one was there to get their cold fixed or get a relative out of jail. We did not have two or three patients all sitting there looking for help. No, we had one people. We had one desire. I learned how great power comes when we are one. In my many years of practice, I have not seen the power really come that often. But when it has come, we were all of one desire, one thought locked on the person to be doctored. I also learned about how my spirit friends could respect me. I shamed them out; they had to do as I told them.

So there are many different kinds of doctoring. They are not all the same. For a medicine man, we may take the ceremony even if it is something that we or the spirits might not agree with, but we can still help. When this happens and the spirits don't want to deal with the problem, I have to use my human judgment. One evening I was at home and a woman came to me because her child was caught with drugs and put into jail. She told me how sad she was and how she didn't want her son to stay in jail. Well, this is not what my spirits want to doctor. They are there to help people with serious sickness, with big problems. But I felt pity for this woman and held a ceremony, but the spirits stayed away. So I told her in my own way during the ceremony that it would work out, but that there would be a delay. I said to her that the boy was going to get some time and go to the big house. He would come out later and become a better person. I did this myself and did not get my spirits involved with this.

You know there are other limits. Lots of times it is your limit. You have a doubt. You doubt the spirits and what they can do. You doubt the medicine and what it can do. But if the person has a doubt, then maybe that's their limit and the medicine can't work even if everybody there wants the person to get better.

I was at home one time and, Jerry, you called and asked me if I could go across the ocean. We like to travel there and had friends in some of the places over there. So we went, and when we were there people would ask us for help. This one woman had been injured and her injury would not heal, so she asked me for help. We had the ceremony at her home. It was hard to doctor her because she knew nothing about our ways and we were a long way from my medicines and my place. They also had a dog in the house that stayed there during the ceremony but was not in the room. That made it difficult also, but not too hard. But we tried anyway. It was a really good ceremony, because everybody was of one mind to help this woman with her problem. Her family was there. You and our friends were there and her doctor was there. Everybody really prayed hard for her. They had prepared really good food, and my spirits were very happy at the respectful way that we were treated. So they came in strong and examined her very closely. I described to her and her doctor after the ceremony what they saw under the bandages on her leg. It looked to me like that doctor was pretty surprised when I told him what they saw and how it could heal gradually over time. My spirits had a medicine just for her leg, but I had to get it when I returned home, prepare it, and send it to her. I told them, her doctor and her, how to gently use this medicine, how often, and what they would see happen. Well, when she got my jar of medicine, she found earth in it. She told our friends that she could not use it because it was not, how do you say, sterile. She had a limit. That was hers, and we could only work up to that point. But from what I was told, she did change after the ceremony. She went back to work and was happy, I was told. So a ceremony that is a strong and respectful one, like that one, works to the point of the patient's limit. It is best she didn't use the medicine. She wasn't ready. But she received what she needed at that time from the ceremony.

Other people have different limits. This one doctor came to the Hollow Horn Bear sun dance. She had a sickness which made it hard for her to bear heat. So when it came time for the sweat lodge, I told her to just stay outside and maybe put her legs into the sweat lodge and they would doctor her. She said no and told me that if she was going to die, she was going to die. So she went right into the sweat and went through it. Afterwards she started to get better and wanted to fast and dance in thanksgiving. It must have been 90 or 100 and some days it was way over 100. We danced and she was smiling and made everyone stronger. I was very impressed. She never did get rid of her sickness entirely; but whenever she felt bad, she would think of those four days and pray harder and start to feel better.

This is the way it is. I kept up my practice. I still had my doubts, but I knew that this was my way. My health kept getting worse. I had the bad heart and would get pretty dizzy. It worried everybody, but I still traveled a lot. I couldn't walk as much or as long, but every so often I got a lot more energy and it seemed like I was back to normal. I remember what my friends told me about my vision. Someday I must fulfill it in front of the people.[4] My vision was the wak̄iŋyaŋ or heyok̇a vision, so I had to perform the *heyok̇a woze* in front of the people. My friend had pressured me. He asked me why I had not done this ceremony.

He said, "All these years you do ceremonies and you need help and you call on me and I come in and now I want you to do this and you didn't do it."

He was right. I put it off and then I got sick and almost died. I couldn't figure out what was wrong. I knew what the doctors said, but I felt there was something else that could help. I felt like I needed to do something. So I finally decided I must perform what my spirit friend wanted me to complete. So I decided I would do it the summer of 1979 or 1980, sometime around then. I prepared everything like it was in my vision.

We held it over by Arthur Running Horse's place near the canyons out that way in August. I put four people in the center: one with a cane, one with crutches, one blind, and one in a wheelchair. I told them this was not going to cure them but I wanted the people to look at them and know that these are kinds of sicknesses we have today. I told them that we must pray that we do not want these sicknesses around anymore. If we pray sincerely, we will end these sicknesses. This is what I told the people. Well, I prepared myself.

I was dressed with my face black, with heavy black cloth, on my eyes were mirrors with the shiny side out. I wore gunny sacks, a breech cloth, and a big turtle on top. From the turtle there hung two bull snakeskins. This is the way they told me to dress. I came out of the canyon forwards. I would turn backwards, then forwards, then backwards to fulfill my vision as a heyok̇a (a contrary). I had placed some cottonwood branches in between the canyon and where the people were and around the area at certain spots. There were two tip̄is and two sweat lodges there. As I came out of the canyon and approached the people, I would run and jump over these branches. I was very light. They say there were four hundred or five hundred people there. I don't know.

As I came in, there was no one there. I saw no one. I thought maybe I shouldn't be there, so I went back out. That is why I went in and out. As I would start to go back to the canyons, I heard a voice say,

"*Ķawiŋġa yo!* (Turn around!)" It was not a human voice, and it really scared me. So I turned around and returned. I was light on my feet and just jumped right over these branches. I came close to the people and looked around and saw the pot with the dog boiling in it.

I looked again and again at the people and saw their prayers. They were very few! I saw just a very few. The rest of them did not have any prayers. I looked again and saw the people had many different thoughts and desires. I knew that they all could come true in this ceremony, good or bad. I saw a medicine man there, and he was pushing his power toward me. He was challenging me with it. I saw all of this. I looked at the pot in the center with the boiling dog and knew that everyone wanted me to pull the head out and show it to the people. This would complete the ceremony for them. But if I did this, then all of what the people were thinking could come true. The sicknesses, like those of the four with us, would go untreated. I could not do what the people had come to see me do. Instead I pulled an arrow onto my crooked little bow that I carried with me and zeroed in on the head of that dog which was sticking out of the water. I shot the arrow into it, and it went back into the water. Then I went over to the medicine man who was throwing his power toward me and shook his hand and went out of the center and left. Well, that was it. You know the heyoǩa has to tell the people the truth; only when they had strong prayers, one thought, and could push it forward could I complete this ceremony as they desired. Only then could they heal the types of sicknesses of the people who were there. Some thought I was afraid, but others thought about it and may have learned from it. But this was my decision, and my friends only wanted me to tell the people the truth. I have only told a few people about this. I might have to do this ceremony again someday when the people are ready. My friends will give me a sign when I should do it again. So far I have not had a sign.

A few months either after that or before that ceremony, a group of the medicine men and helpers were sitting in your office with Stanley discussing the way people talked about the medicine men and the way the medicine men acted in their human life. There are medicine men who drink alcohol. I still continued to drink beer even after I became a medicine man. I haven't got drunk, but I drink. Some of the medicine men drink too much and go on drunks. Well, we were sitting there talking about this question of whether a medicine man could be a drunk and still have power or could the medicine man have other problems and still be a medicine man. Could he be in prison and still be a medicine man? Frank Picket Pen, Bill Schweigman, Arthur Running Horse, Robert Stead, and some of the helpers and singers, like Narcisse Eagle Deer and Ben Black Bear Sr., were discussing this. We all had many different opinions. Many ideas were brought up. Maybe the power would leave this person, because they were no longer acting with respect. Maybe they would hurt the people they doctored. Maybe the people would lose their respect for the medicine man and his spirits. But the more we talked, the less important these ideas became. We didn't believe the power leaves the medicine man. I don't remember who said the final thing we agreed on, but he said that even if a medicine man set up his altar and was drunk, the minute that the lights went out and the song was sung, the spirits would come into the ceremony and sober up this man. There was no limit on what his spirit friends could do and who they could use for their healing. The healers and the people have to understand that we are just men; we are interpreters; we are used by our friends. Well, I know the spirits would humble this man and make him suffer if he did that or if he does not act in a respectful manner. But they could still use him. Some of the medicine men I know who are the humblest and have strong friends drink the most. They feel very weak. They are sorry about it, but that is the way it is. It is not for us to put a limit on the spirits.

Well, you know I have had hard times. You and Stanley helped Victoria and me when we were having problems. She took off and didn't show up for a while. When they brought her back, you guys met us and took me to Valentine and we got back together. We drove down there together, and I was scared. It was a sad moment; me and Victoria both cried and felt sorry for what had happened, but then we got together and kept on going. We knew people supported us, so we kept on going. It is tough to be the wife of a medicine man. Victoria cooked for people who were going to have a ceremony. Sometimes she had to make the tobacco ties and prepare the offerings, because people had an emergency and did not have anything ready. Sometimes she spent every night in a ceremony and then the next day she worked as the cook at the hospital. Sometimes she could not be at the ceremonies, because she had to work. We did not resent it, but it was *otẽȟkelo,* very difficult.

The people have a really hard time too, especially the young people. Today is not like it was. I see the young people on drugs, some of them sniffing glue, young people who drink Lysol to get high. I don't scold them. That is not right. I know they are lost. They are trying to find a vision but in this wild and crazy way. They are all alone. They are not supported by the people, by ceremonies; no one is there to speak to them and to speak about the ancient knowledge, to speak about how you find your vision. They don't need preaching. In the old days, the children would go down to the creek, by the river, to play. The people would go with them, and they would spend the time watching the children. When they left to return to the village, one person was responsible for staying behind and calling the children's names, each child's name; in this way they called the children's spirits to return with us to the village. As they did this, the person would wipe away the tracks in the sand. Today no one calls the names of the children, no one calls their spirits home or wipes away the tracks, so they remain and go in all directions and the people are lost.

I remember a young man who came to me because he was homosexual. He was ashamed. His family was worried. He wanted help. He had a friend who he could not keep his mind off of. He was always after this other young man, and the young man was not happy about it. They had been really good friends and their friendship had been okay before they became young men and then it started to go bad. I had a ceremony. In the ceremony the spirits told me this young man had within him the spirit of a young woman who had loved the other young man and now he was within this young man. Well, they told me I must tell him that he was a man. He was the man that he was right now. He had this spirit of a woman in him, but he was this very man. He was not a woman and he was a man. He could not have this other man who was the man in the former life, because this man was not homosexual. But he was a homosexual. I did not explain more to him about him as a homosexual. I simply was to tell him he was a man and why he felt the way he did about this other man. Just tell him who he was. So there are these problems which we must help with. It is very interesting for me.

Well, these days my biggest problem is that my health is not too good. I have learned that I should have followed those doctors' directions. But I didn't, and my body is in bad shape. So here I am today. We travel a little bit to where they want us. There are some places I really like. We go to see Mary Lou and her people in Ontario.[5] They really treat us good. They put us up, and the people come and ask for help. I know they need much help and are finding their own ways, but sometimes they just can't go far enough because they don't know our way really well. I have lots of rules to follow for my ceremonies, and it helps if the people know them and can do them. Many of the people come and can't understand about the tobacco ties, and flags, so it is hard. Like the ceremony at Mary Lou's which was so short, maybe twenty minutes. I could not do what they wanted. They must learn more and come ready to speak and ready for the ceremony. This is not their limit, maybe now it is, but they can change. It is hard for me too, if I am not at home where my medicines are. I learned about my medicines in my vision, and I use them when my spirits tell me to. So sometimes we have to go home and send the medicine back. If they came to my home, I could help them better. But they have really good hearts and have many needs, so my spirits take mercy on them and help them up to their limit and our limit. But I like this place. It is a very powerful place over by the bell rocks and the dreamer's rocks. The people there must find their own way and they will become very strong.

After you moved up to Alaska, you had me and Stanley come up one summer and we went to that one village, Huslia, way out in the woods. Boy, I was a little afraid of all of those trees, but we found paradise there. At least that is what Stanley called it. We found a place where people lived with nature. They ate real food from animals who were free. They ate berries they picked and fish they caught right from their river. They had many medicines there that they could use. I really liked that place. In Huslia we held no ceremonies but talked with the people so they could get to know us and we get to know them. They were a little afraid of me, I think. But they didn't know our ways, so they didn't ask for healing. But I learned that there was a place where Indians still lived like we did before these reservations. We talked when I got back, and I really think you and Stanley are right that the people there could become very powerful if they found their own rituals. They could join the natural life and the ceremonies and they could heal many sicknesses. Our people have lost their natural life. We tried to get it back with the Tiośp̄aye Project, but it was not enough.[6] If we could join our ceremonies with a natural way of living, eating those foods and living in that way, we could heal many sicknesses.

On another trip with Cecil White Hat, we traveled also to Nome and spent time with Eskimo people there. We held a ceremony and tried to help the people. Everybody treated us real good. We learned a lot on these trips. Many people came to us, and they asked about their dreams. Young people told me that the dreams bothered them. They talked kind of quietly. They almost seemed afraid to talk about them. But then they really talked strongly. I was sure they have the same kind of dreams sometimes that I had and they don't know what to do with them, because the people have put away their old ways of knowing and interpreting. It is like those old ways are starting to peek around the corner but then duck back behind because the people are afraid. You can help them by taking them into a sweat and letting them pray. They can then begin to find their own way.

Every place I went I took some earth with me back to my home. I mixed the earth from these places into the earth I use in ceremonies as my altar.[7] So now I have the strength and spirit of that place and I remember the place and people in all of my ceremonies.

We traveled overseas to Austria, Germany, and France. We had many of these people come to me for help. I have had many white people come to me for help. Well, it was really interesting in Germany. The people there know a lot about our ways and tried to practice them very closely. They are looking for their way, and we can help them to find their own power in their own land. Like Stanley said: "They come to experience our ways but must return to find their ways." I really like how sincere they were. Like I told you, I just have not met a bad person, not when I was young and not after I became a medicine man.

Victoria and I lived in our home above Grass Mountain. We have many animals, and the kids come and go. They still have lots of problems. Sometimes it goes good and then sometimes it goes bad. Vickie has not had her vision, but maybe it will happen, maybe today or maybe tomorrow. I don't know, but she will someday be able to understand the spirits. We have met many people and doctored many different diseases. Our people have great problems, sicknesses which are real deep and real hard to doctor. So our life is good. I am happy, but not too happy about my health. I wish I had taken care of myself, but I didn't. You know how they say you should take your own advice. I sure didn't do that. Well, people wonder if the reason I am sick is because the people have not returned to the spirits what they should. Maybe or maybe not, I don't know. I do know the people need to think real hard and speak to the spirits, their body, and the medicine as their relatives. I know they should do a thanksgiving, but some of them don't.[8]

One last thing I want to tell you about is these people I have seen who have big troubles, maybe not in their body. Well, you know we have to find the *ok̄o,* the crack, through which they can go. When somebody is having a real hard time and could not get over it, the medicine man can help them find the crack through which they can go. We have to be real clever, tricky, to find that crack so the person can sneak through it. The spirits help us to find that crack, but then you have to work with the person so they can squeak through it. For people who suffer from *ṫawaċiŋ gnuni* (soul or spirit loss), they might have had a sudden and startling event and something bad happened and they can't remember it. Well, it is really important to get to them soon after this or the spirit leaves, because the longer they are in this condition, the harder it is to heal. And if it goes on a long time, we might not be able to do it or it will take a long, long time. We use a medicine the person inhales to doctor this, but the person needs help fast.

So I guess that is it. Once I had my first set of friends, everything went fine. There were tough and hard times, but it was all right, just fine. One song they gave me I often sang in my ceremonies. It was important.

Ṫuŋk̄aṡila, Wak̇aŋ Ṫaŋk̄a, heya hoyewa yelo! (Grandfather, Great Mystery, I pray to you. I throw my voice to you!)
Ṫuŋk̄aṡila, Wak̇aŋ Ṫaŋk̄a, heya hoyewa yelo!
Ṫuŋk̄aṡila, omakiye yo! mak̄ak̄ije lo . . . he ho (Grandfather, help me! I am suffering.)
Ṫuŋk̄aṡila, Wak̇aŋ Ṫaŋk̄a, heya hoyewa yelo!
Ṫuŋk̄aṡila, Wak̇aŋ Ṫaŋk̄a, heya hoyewa yelo!
Ṫuŋk̄aṡila, omakiye yo! mak̄ak̄ije lo . . . he ho

When I am gone, I don't know what will happen. Maybe one of the boys will have the power and a vision. Maybe they will follow it. But then maybe it will skip them and pass to the next generation. I don't know, but it will continue.

11 Further Teachings

Yes; a power that we call Sila, which is not to be explained in simple words. A great spirit, supporting the world and the weather and all life on earth, a spirit so mighty that his utterance to mankind is not through common words, but by storm and snow and rain and the fury of the sea; all the forces of nature that men fear. But he has also another way of utterance, by sunlight, and calm of the sea, and little children innocently at play, themselves understanding nothing. . . . When all is well, Sila sends no message to mankind, but withdraws into his own endless nothingness, apart. So he remains as long as men do not abuse life, but act with reverence towards their daily food. No one has seen Sila; his place of being is a mystery, in that he is at once among us and unspeakably far away.

—Najagneq, Eskimo shaman

THE BODY AND MEDICINE

People seem today to misunderstand how to be cured. They go in to see a doctor or a medicine man, and they never think of that doctor or medicine man much. They just take the medicine and don't think much about the medicine or their body. When a person takes a medicine, white medicine, herbs, Indian medicine, whatever, they need to understand that medicines are people. They are persons. You need to treat them like people who you invite into your body. You need to welcome them into your body by talking to them, telling them you are happy that they have come to help you. You also need to talk to your body. We are made up of both body, spirit, and our destiny, but our body is intelligent and has a spirit that understands. We should talk to our body and ask him to welcome the medicine. We need to explain to her [our body] that the medicine is there to help with the pain or the sickness. We should say, "I know you get real tired. I know that I have not treated you too good and I ask you to forgive me for this, but we have a friend who is coming to help us. Here is a medicine that I am going to take, so I ask you to give him a hand, help him, and you will feel better." Sometimes we try to keep our hurt and pain. Sometimes it doesn't want to leave us, but this medicine is our friend and she can help us, so help the medicine. Then tell the medicine you have talked to your body and asked her to help with her work.

Tell him you will follow the doctor's orders so that the body and medicine can get to know each other and work together to heal. We have to do this because they don't know us very well and they don't know each other very well. If they are not welcome in our bodies, then they are not free to do their work. Ask them to talk to each other. So the most important thing for the medicine to work is to build up that relationship so the medicine can talk to the body and the body can talk to the medicine. They need to become friends. Maybe even more, they need to know that they are relatives. You need to help with this if you take the medicine. Some of the plants and foods that are the medicines are the ones that are relatives to other plants and foods, so if you eat them together then they know each other and can build up your body. It is no good to have a fight going on inside of you by eating things or taking medicine where no relationship is possible.

Well, medicine and the doctors are the same way. People today don't put anything into their relationship with the doctor. The Western doctors are just like Indian doctors. They are doctors because they have a gift. They cannot do their work without the help of the people. The patients have to think real deeply about the doctor and think real deeply about the medicine and talk to the medicine so it will be filled with its power to do the work that it can do. They need to put all of their thoughts into this doctor so he can become strong. The physician or medicine man has the same responsibility to think deeply about his medicine and about the patient and to use his gift fully. But today it looks to me like the reason a lot of physicians are having a hard time and are troubled is because the relationships between them and the patients are not good. I see that people want more and more, they want to get and to get, and too often they do not want to return anything for the doctoring and to the medicine. There has to be equal responsibility and equal giving.

I see a lot of people, just like the white doctors. I remember a case of one woman who came to me with the pipe and asked for help. She was very sick with a heavy and difficult sickness. I told her I would doctor her, but about that time another person came with a very light and not so serious a sickness as compared to the first woman. But this second person kept following me around and would not let me go. She did not need my help. She could help herself, but she just kept demanding more and more. To me, this made it hard for me to concentrate on the woman with the serious sickness. We know that in order for our ceremonies to work and people to get really better that we must have a single focus. We must have everyone of a single mind in the ceremony for the power to come. But this is hard if you have to doctor many people, all demanding equal treatment when they are not equal. Some need to take care of themselves. They don't need us. So people need to take time to think deeply about the medicine, their body, and the doctor and put all their energy into creating the relationship. More and more, people will find that there will be less medicine men for a while because maybe the people need to learn to do things on their own.

Doctors, white doctors, have come to me and asked for advice, but it seems they mostly want to know about my medicines and how they are prepared. I try to tell them that each medicine man is different. He has different powers, his own vision and gift. I want them to know that they have a gift and they have to find their own source of healing. I can't help them with medicines. I can tell them how to think deeply about the medicines, the body, the person, and the healing.

POWER AND ITS USE

As told by an anonymous person

Joe spoke about the power that seldom came to heal. He and many of the elders spoke of power they had witnessed but no one could reach in today's world. I often wondered if this was only the musing of those growing older.

Joe connected power to the human community. One could not understand the power to heal unless one understood the power to destroy. Each resided with human beings.

Joe talked a lot about energy, about the thunder spirits. We drove for nine hours, and he talked nonstop about them. He said that fire originated from the thunder and was how people discovered fire. He said that they were given the gift of fire by the thunder spirits, who allow them to understand how to use it. But what was critical was that the people were full of gratitude for the fire. They only used it when they really needed it, because it was precious for them. They learned to work with the fire, how to treat it, and they were very careful. They knew that this power was sacred. It was both a life-giving and a life-taking force, and what you brought to it would determine whether it would function as good or evil. As he explained it to me, the force of fire was neutral, so you could bring evil or ignorance or harm to it and hurt others or yourself. However, the people were very careful to use it to give life. They were so grateful for its warmth, its power, that they used it right and did not abuse it.

Then there came a time when there was a people. They were *tok̄a,* different, not Lakota, who forgot about it as a gift. They stopped being thankful. They stopped thinking deeply about the fire and its origins with the thunder beings. They stopped doing their wopila—thanksgivings. So the hearts got hard. Joe said this is what happens when all the people start treating their gifts in this way. He said it became widespread. In fact, he used the term "all the world around" to tell me that the people started doing bizarre things with fire. They began to use it for destruction. So when gratitude left them, their hearts became hard and crazy things began to happen. Then the people took sort of a huge jump and created electricity. Joe compared the creation and use of electricity with his own power that he received from the thunder beings.

Every spring Joe would open all of the windows of his house before the first big thunderstorm and invite the thunder spirits to come into his home. He waited for that first thunderstorm to come at night in order to do this. Lightning would illuminate the sky in the west. The thunder would shake the foundations of the house, yet he would speak to them and ask them to come into his home. They would come and enter. Prior to opening the windows Joe would have packed his sacred pipe and would have it lying there. The lightning would come right into the room and into his pipe and light it, so when he used it they were there. They had entered his house and he was grateful for their presence, and he could remember them each time he loaded his pipe.

He told me that the white people had a similar experience with the creation of electricity: there once was this man who sat in his house with the windows open and a jar on a table. He too was waiting and had the jar there for the thunders to come into. So he harnessed them by putting a blanket over the jar and a lid on it so that when he needed light he could take out this jar, take off the blanket, and there would be light. Joe talked in his own way about the creation of the electric light bulb. He said electricity was a gift from the thunders. It would bring health and life. So, from the beginning, people used their creativity to receive this gift of electricity from the thunders and were in awe of it. In its earliest times electricity was good. Certainly no one would want to go back to the pre-electrical times. But then some crazy minds overpowered this awe and sense of gratitude and started to apply electricity in ways that were inappropriate and hurtful. They produced pain and death. The people again forgot about it as a gift, so their hearts became hard. The harder the hearts became, then the easier it was to do crazy things with electricity. It is like a progressive thing. Well, then the people took a real quantum leap. They created nuclear power.

Nuclear power is not really nuclear power in Joe's way of thinking. He said the thunder beings said it was an imitation. It was an imitation of the real power, of them. In fact, that is the thunder spirits' name for nuclear power—imitation of the real power. They say they are worse than imitations and are really monsters. They will turn around and eat us if we do not destroy them. He said that the thunder spirits don't trust the people anymore to know what the real power is, because they have become so crazy and bizarre that they either would not recognize it or, if they did, they would abuse it. He said the same thing is true of the Lakota people and the wak̄iŋyaŋ, the thunder spirits. They no longer are thankful. They no longer treat the gifts of healing from the wak̄iŋyaŋ with gratitude, so their hearts too are hardening.

Whenever we lose touch with our relationships to the spirits, whenever we forget we are part of life and that at the heart of life is relationship, whenever we lose touch with our place in the scheme of things, then we start to take it all for granted. We put ourselves in the front, push ourselves forward, and then we forget what we have been given. We become hard. We begin to destroy ourselves.

12 Sitting in the Center—a Search for Words

I will tell you something I have discovered. Listen well. History is an underground river that flows underneath the present. Everything that ever happened keeps happening below us. The river empties into the present now and then. That is when catastrophe occurs. Historic catastrophes are sometimes caused by someone inadvertently digging too deep into the past and reaching the river of history. . . . This river flows simultaneously backward and forward: it has no source and no exit. It is formed by the debris of time; it is made out of unfinished business. . . . Can we never escape history?

. . . Everything we abandon before we can bring it to a conclusion continues to live until it is played out, until the story is finished. All strains will be played out.

—Andrei Codrescu, *The Blood Countess*

A story told by Maalia

June, twenty-seven days above 80 degrees, sunlight all day long, and the beautiful contrast of white bark with the light, shiny green leaves of the birch trees sprinkled into the dark, almost black spruce forests of the interior, all seen from the window of my dormitory. Every evening I sat in this room looking out, only to return to staring at the beige walls of my room. I cried and cried and cried, unable to complete the psychology courses I was taking, thinking over and over what the visiting Russian-born professor, Urie Bronfrenbrenner, said: "Every child needs somebody, at least one person, who loves him or her irrationally." He told us about the Russian orphans who had been taken out of their homes and placed in mental hospitals. They were normal, alert young children when they left their homes, but within a few months they behaved like they were mentally ill, unresponsive, self-stimulating, uncommunicative . . . Studying all of this material stirred up all kinds of feelings. I kept thinking about how my siblings had died of alcohol and felt guilt.

"Why am I sitting here? Why did I make it?" were questions which rolled over and over in my mind.

A sense of sadness and emotional upheaval had begun in the past year when I began to feel more and more pain in my body and was told that I had rheumatoid arthritis. My joints and body just hurt, and the pain at times was intense. I noticed that my work began to suffer. You know how much I was and had been involved in local and statewide educational and social advocacy groups. I just didn't have the energy to speak, and when I did speak I felt like I was on edge and sharp in my comments. I lost control of my emotions easily and would hurt people's feelings, even if I didn't want to. As the year moved forward, I was becoming drained and worried.

I had managed to fool the whole world. They all thought I was this happy, competent, and assertive person. One of my college instructors told me that she pitied the person who would give me a B, because I worked so hard, and overworked to excel. I could not bear to let anyone see how I really felt about myself. They saw the facade, yet deep inside I felt that I was worthless. I was bum and ugly; I was an orphan. My father had abandoned me. My mother had taken me and my sister and brother to the mission. She said she was going to return to get us after the trapping season, but she never returned. I asked myself that if my own parents could not love me, then who could? I could not even believe that my children loved me. I could love them and my husband, but not accept that they loved me. There was this little girl inside of me who had a name, my Indian name, but I could not speak her name. I hid her. This sensation of being two people was really strong in me. There was one who the world could see and another, this little girl, who I knew. I knew where she was and I held her safe there. No way was I going to let her out into this world where she could get hurt. So here I was, a bundle of nerves when my instructor invited us to your home for a Lakota ceremony of thanksgiving that the visiting medicine man was going to do.

I decided to go and asked my husband to go with me. We arrived and sat through this strong and powerful ceremony that Joe Eagle Elk performed in the pitch black of a darkened room. I didn't feel really too scared. During this ceremony I began to think about whether I could have such a ceremony to ask for help. I decided to speak with you about this the next day.

Before we talked, I felt very uneasy about the ceremony because I thought I might make a big mistake and the medicine man would get mad at me. He would see this bum person. Really, I was thinking how I could not possibly hold such a ceremony, yet my pain was so strong that it pushed me to ask. You encouraged me and explained how I should ask Joe to do the ceremony privately and explained how ritually to present the pipe to him and that you would loan me your pipe so I could use it to request the ceremony. I don't remember exactly when, but I do remember that I went to his house to present the pipe to him. Joe came in and sat down while I packed the pipe with six lumps of natural tobacco, Bull Durham, praying to each of the four directions, to the spirit of the winged, those above us, and finally to our grandmother, Earth, while thinking deeply about what I desired. They explained to me how each of the six lumps of tobacco placed in the pipe constituted my prayer, my desire, and my gift to the spirits.

When I finished, I stood facing Joe and turned in a clockwise circle, the path of the sun, until I faced him again. I then handed him the pipe four times, and on the fourth, Joe accepted it, which was his sign that he would do the ceremony for me. I then told him why I wanted the ceremony while he smoked the pipe. He sat smoking and listening until all of the tobacco was smoked and then took apart the stem from the bowl of the pipe and returned it to me. He told me how to prepare for the ceremony. I was to make seventy-five black and white tobacco ties, bring the flags for honoring the spirits of the four directions with tobacco tied into each of the corners, and water, cornmeal, meat, and berries, as well as enough food to feed those who would attend. He would do the ceremony the next evening. He asked where I wanted to have the ceremony, and I told him that you had offered to have it at your home, since my home was quite a distance from the city. You translated what I needed to purchase or prepare for the ceremony, explaining where I could buy the cloth and that I should bring it to your home and you would help me make the ties and flags. Joe then said to me, "Maalia, when you pray in the ceremony, tell the Grandfather and my spirit friends what hurts you."

"Hurts me? You mean what is wrong with me?" I said.

"No, tell them what hurts you."

I was very surprised and consternated. What hurts me, not a list of what is wrong with me? I didn't know what I would say, yet I had gone too far to turn back. So we made all of the preparations and came to the evening ready. I picked our most delicious foods, preparing baked salmon, meats, fry bread, and desserts. As the time came closer, my hand just shook and I trembled, growing more and more nervous about whether the food was good enough and whether I could do this. But, if I was to do it, I would do it well!

I didn't think some of my family would come because of their religious tradition but knew they would support my decision. My husband would have come, but he was working out of town. So I asked some of my best friends to come with me. You had asked me if you could invite some of my fellow students or friends to come, persons who we both thought could support me in seeking healing. Having been at the thanksgiving ceremony, I wanted to make sure that those who were there would not scare me. I knew I wanted to speak and didn't want to feel inhibited by not feeling safe.

The day arrived. You explained how you had prepared your basement with the help of your two sons. You described how you had moved the furniture around and out of the way so that the room was a twenty-two-foot by eleven-foot empty space. The room had unfinished walls and ceiling, a linoleum floor and a black Ashley pot-belly wood stove on one side which unfortunately blocked out part of the space. But for our numbers there was adequate room. You had darkened all the windows with black plastic and blankets since the ceremony must take place in total darkness. Because it never gets dark in the summer in Alaska, you were able to test it well during the day to see how it would be that evening. You joked about how you would ask the boys to stand in various places and then would turn off the lights. The boys would indicate where there was a little light showing and go over and adjust the plastic or quilts so that no light came through. Then you had to have the big test and brought Stanley down for the final checking, and he said he saw light everywhere and made you start looking closer and closer at the corners of the room until you realized that he was joking. You seemed very pleased that there was a totally darkened big space. So all was ready by evening for my ceremony.

The other people arrived that evening about eight. The food was taken upstairs to the kitchen, and I returned with a bowl of water and a bowl with a little bit of each of the foods placed in it. The cornmeal and berries were placed in the same bowl, and both it and the bowl of water would rest immediately to the right of Joe's earthen altar. People sat in a circle with their backs against the walls. Your sons had placed pillows and blankets on the perimeter to provide a bit of a cushion on the hard floor.

The medicine man meanwhile prepared his space in the center of the room. He put down a red Pendleton blanket, on which he sat. He then reached into his small blue Samsonite suitcase and began slowly taking from this suitcase everything he needed for his ceremonial altar. First, he pulled out a round buckskin pouch and opened it fully. In it he kept the earth he used for his ceremonial altar. The pouch was a circular buckskin about a foot in diameter, and once he spread it open on the floor, the dirt rested in a pile on top of it. He smoothed out the light tan pile of dirt to make a rounded mound of about ten inches in diameter and two inches high, flat on the top. He then took his right index finger and slowly drew a figure of lightning into his earth altar, his symbol for the heyok̇a spirits which would come to help him during that ceremony. While he did this, he bantered in Lakota with Stanley and you. Sometimes you or Stanley spoke English to translate or to tease each other about how slow he was and that if he didn't hurry up it would get dark. Of course it never got dark in the north in June.

The medicine man unwrapped the seventy-five black and white tobacco ties I had made, putting them around the earth altar. After this he set up my blue, green, black, white, red, and yellow flags on the cherry and willow branches, which were stuck into a piece of wood and set in front of him. Stanley and you sat in front of him about four feet away at the far end of the room and were responsible for the singing. I was very impressed that you joked with each other about how this was going to sound since neither of you was a regular singer for ceremonies. Joe said the spirits might run away after the first song, but he would warn them and coax them back to the ceremony. Joe said that at least you both were in the farthest corner of the room, so he couldn't hear well.

When Joe finished setting up his sacred center, you asked someone to turn all the lights out except for a flashlight. However, first, your boys checked all the corners for full darkness. Stanley explained to the twenty or so people present that the spirits came in the darkness, that we were all born from the darkness of the womb, and that darkness could help us to clear our minds fully so we could all concentrate on helping Maalia. I was amazed to hear him say this. Stanley and you told the group how important it was for everyone to concentrate on the purpose of this ceremony. Stanley then said that everyone should put their billfolds in a safe place and watch out for Joe because in the darkness he would steal all of their money. Maybe everybody should just give him, Stanley, their billfolds and he would "really" take good care of them.

Just as the laughter began to subside, they hit the drum and began singing the song for the sacred pipe:

Ḱola, leċel eċun wo! Ḱola, leċel eċun wo! Ḱola, leċel eċun wo!
Heċaŋu k̄i, nit̄uŋk̄aṡila waniyang u kte lo.
Hoċok̄a waŋji
Yuha iyot̄ak̄e ca
Miksuya k̄i, op̄aġi yo!
Heċanu k̄i, t̄ak̄u yaċiŋ k̄i
Iyeċe t̄u kte lo
Caŋnup̄a Waŋji, yuha iyot̄ak̄e ċa
Miksuya op̄aġi yo!
Heċanu k̄i, t̄ak̄u yaċiŋ k̄i
Iyeċe t̄u kte lo.
Ḱola leċel eċun wo! Ḱola leċel eċun wo! Ḱola leċel eċun wo!
Heċanu k̄i, nit̄uŋk̄aṡila waniyang u kte lo.

(Friend, do it in this way! Friend, do it in this way! Friend do it in this way!
If you do, your Grandfather will come to see you.
This sacred ritual,
When you sit down to begin,
Remember me as you load the pipe!
If you do this, whatever you desire
Will come true.
When you begin the ritual with the pipe,
Remember me as you load it.
If you do this, whatever you desire
Will come true.
Friend, do it in this way! Friend, do it in this way! Friend do it in this way!
If you do, your Grandfather will come to see you.)

You said later that you sang the song pretty softly, but to me it sounded so beautiful and full. I sat to the right of the medicine man and his altar. As he packed his pipe, he sat down in front of the altar with the earth in the middle, the black and white tobacco ties sitting around the mound of earth. He had put the black, blue, white, yellow, red, and green flags I had made on red willow sticks and stuck them in a board that sat in front of him. The whole arrangement was so colorful. I thought to myself, "This is my altar and it is beautiful. This is no one else's altar." I realized from what you, the medicine man, and Stanley said that everyone was there for me and that this was truly my altar and ceremony.

After packing the pipe, Eagle Elk placed the pipe in the center. Next to me sat two friends, all of us immediately to the right of the medicine man. You and Stanley stayed at the far end of the room. The lights were turned out. It was pitch black. The medicine man stood and gave a short talk about the ancient ceremony with the food that preceded the coming of the White Buffalo Calf Woman with the sacred pipe. He asked someone to translate it, so Stanley and you translated. Joe told me that I had done everything that was required and that no one could pray at this altar except me. Then it really hit me. It was unbelievable that this ceremony and altar was nobody else's. Being the oldest one in the family and because we had always had to share, I had to give the biggest share to my siblings. I had to take the smallest. If there was something hard or ugly to do, I had to do it first, like take sour medicine. So here I was in front of this beautiful altar that I didn't have to share. It was only me for me. It was awesome. I had been raised on secondhand clothes and secondhand Christmas presents. We even used secondhand yarn from old socks and sweaters to make something. Tonight this was new, this was for me, and everyone there was there for the first time just for me. I could hardly grasp this.

The medicine man then told Stanley and you to sing the song to invite in the spirits. He began it with them. The singing was so strong and powerful. During the song a soft blue and yellow spark appeared where Joe stood and then moved rapidly around the room together with the sound of a rattling gourd. When they finished the song, he began another one and they finished it with him. Later they explained that it was to honor his spirits for coming to us. Eagle Elk's voice changed a bit, becoming a little higher but also softer. He appeared to be in a conversation with his spirits, because he would say in Lakota:

"*Haŋ, haŋ, hm haŋ*" (Yes, yes, okay, yes). While they sang, the gourd came over to Jerry and Stanley and touched their shoulders and head while the little yellow light quietly flickered in front of them.

They finished the songs, and Eagle Elk said to the group, "They will stay. They are afraid of these singers and told me that these two men should learn to sing, but my friends will stay to help this lady." Everyone laughed, and Stanley and you joked that our voices were just too powerful to be heard. Then Eagle Elk's voice became more serious and he said: "*Heyoka čik'ala le miye lo! Na Heyoka mišnala le miye lo!*" (I am the little Heyoka! And I am the single or solitary Heyoka!) He then addressed me: "So now you should tell us what it is you want."

Meanwhile the little yellow and blue light silently circled around the room and moved from floor to ceiling. He had told me that they might touch me and not to be afraid, but I was afraid. I could feel heat on my forehead, like they were very close, and I could see outlines of their features, but they were just a little distant and to the right of me. Then you all began to sing again, and as they sang a bolt of lightning struck right beside me. I was terrified. The singing stopped, and Joe said, "Sister, voice yourself."

I began to voice myself very quietly. I prayed very hard with my heart beating really fast. I wanted so much to voice myself that I felt like I was. Then Eagle Elk responded very softly and quickly and Stanley translated: "They say they can't hear you. Maybe they say you need to tell them what you want." I went on, a bit louder, and told my story of fear and anxiety about my life, my diabetes and arthritis and my lack of energy. I know I spoke with a cracking voice and tears, but could only talk very briefly. Eagle Elk said: "They say you are maybe a little afraid and should come to my center and stay here and they will help you. So come on out here. Maybe you should pick two of your friends to be with you. They can stay on each side of you and give you support." I picked Kathryn and Kathy, two women friends, to stay with me. We shuffled the few feet to the center and knelt there. It was too painful on my joints to kneel and so I asked if I could sit. The medicine man told me to sit comfortably.

He then asked for a song for his spirit friends to examine me, and he began it. You all sang it while Eagle Elk's friends examined me. The gourd and light circled near me. I felt the heat and that they want to touch me, and seemed to move around the perimeter of my body. At the end of the song Eagle Elk said with a chuckle: "My sister, are you asleep? They wonder if you are maybe dozing a little. They say you are afraid and it is hard for them to get close, but that you have more to say."

I was trying so hard that I thought I was talking when I wasn't. I had this sensation of something coming from the pit of me, coming up, coming up toward my mouth, but some of the times I could tell it was stuck. Then at a certain point in the ceremony I felt it loosen a little and I was able to voice myself. I told them about my life in a boarding school, of being forced to leave my family. I spoke about being an orphan, about losing my family, about the good I experienced in the school and the pain of loss and the experience of knowing no family. I prayed for strength to overcome my illness and to contribute to my family, praying for my family, asking for help for them. Meanwhile we could hear Eagle Elk say, "*Hm, haŋ, o haŋ*" (yes, yes, okay, truly).

I finished, and each person in the room prayed in turn for me. This was hard to believe. I listened to their voices. Some prayed in English, others in their own languages. The medicine man had told us that his friends would understand. I sat there very stiff between my two friends. The one had asked the Presbyterian minister who was in the ceremony if it was okay to pray and be with me and he had said yes. He prayed very strongly. The medicine man then said with just a little chuckle: "Hum, hum, they say you are just a *little* afraid, just maybe a *little* afraid, but that these two ladies with you are *really* scared. They say that there is more for you to voice." I tried again to speak, and Joe again responded quickly that there was more for me to say. At some point in this exchange I was able to voice more and more. I began to relax and just leaned against the two friends that were with me. I had been stiff, but now I just laid against them and they held me while I voiced myself more. I again had this sensation that more was trying to rise from my stomach to my mouth but couldn't get up and out. Joe said, "Okay, you can't go further." I felt relieved. I think he knew I could only go so far or if I had let it all out they would have been picking me up off the floor. I was so wounded.

He asked the singers to sing doctoring songs and told me that his friends, his spirits, would now doctor me and tell him what should be done. Again the singer was powerful, and suddenly I heard the Eskimo woman next to me singing in Lakota. I was perplexed and wondered how she had learned this language. As he sang I felt the heat here on my head. I could again see the spirits, not real clear, but the outline of four of them standing off to my right. They would come close to me as the songs for doctoring continued. Periodically he would stop singing with you and Stanley, and in the background I could hear him listening to his friends while acknowledging what they were saying by saying something in Lakota. They told me later he was saying like, "Okay, yes, okay, for sure."

The song was over, and he said that his friends still said that I and my friends were *really afraid* and that they could not doctor me fully because of the fear, but they could help me a little at this time. He said that the spirits usually left the ceremony when someone was afraid. They loved us so much that they did not want to frighten us. But this time they stayed because she needed them and they wanted to help. They loved me enough to stay and would protect me. Again I couldn't believe it. They could see my soul, so how could they love me?

The medicine man told me that his friends had said that I had much to tell them and much to let go of. I had anger and fear. I had resentments, worries, pains that just stayed inside. I needed a friend to give these to who could keep them so I did not have them, someone who was strong and able to bear the burdens with no harm. He said that when I went home I should look for a tree near my house. I should seek one that drew me, one that I liked. I was to make friends with this tree. I was to make this relative a very special relative. This tree would become my source of help and the person to whom I could go regularly and speak to. I should talk to the tree and tell it more and more of what was bothering me. Even if I could not say it now, there was a time when I could say it. When I could, this tree would receive my pain and I could leave it there, a little at a time. His friends would help me and the tree, so all I had buried inside would come out. I would have a friend to whom I could speak these hidden and fearful things.

So that was all he said. "Is there any question?" he asked. I said I understood and thanked him. Then he told me about the medicine for my arthritis and pain. He told me that he would give me water to drink at this time to doctor me. It was pure water. This water was my doctor.

He said, "When you feel the pain, take water. Pray with it to the four directions and the winged spirits above us and to Mother Earth. Ask the water to come into you and help you."

I was very deeply moved, tears began to swell, but I felt a type of excitement and joy, because water is our very special element. Some tribes have fire or earth or something else, but for us, who are ocean people, water is our special relative. I drank the water, feeling it move through me. The pain began to diminish immediately.

After this he asked if anyone had other things to say. No one said anything. They then sang songs to honor all of the tobacco ties, flags, and other gifts that were brought by me and to bless the water and the food. We were told to pray to honor this altar I had provided. Finally, they sang the songs to send home the spirits. While they were singing these songs, I could see the four spirits, my grandfathers, just to my right. They began to move away and gradually went out. I had the sensation that I didn't want them to stay or rather didn't need to hold on to them. Joe had said they would return to help me when I called on them, so I felt this childlike trust. I simply said to myself, I can let someone who loves me leave without any panic. They were gone, the songs ceased, and they turned on the lights.

After the lights were turned on, Joe had Kathy, Kathryn, and myself return to our seats and he handed the pipe to me so that I could light it and smoke it for a brief period. Each puff, each inhale and exhale, symbolized my prayers, thanks, and desires. I then passed it to my left and it went around the room, each person in turn repeating the smoking and prayer with the pipe. At the same time, Jerry followed the pipe around the room with the bowl of water, offering it to each person to drink. It had become a medicine both for me and for all of us. I drank first and Joe drank last.

When each person had either finished their prayers, smoking the pipe, or drinking the water, each would say *mītak̄uye oyas'iŋ*. This is the ritual prayer that bound us all together with our ancestors, the earth, the animals, our families and friends—all of our relatives—our relationships. Sitting in front of the altar was a beautifully formed ball of the tobacco ties, flags, and food that had been in the bowl. Joe gave it to me and asked me to take it home and burn it as an offering. I was to find a place where I could pray and burn it.

This was a quiet time in the ceremony. People were reluctant to begin to speak and appeared overwhelmed by what they had experienced. Following this, a number of the participants went upstairs and brought down the food, passed out bowls and utensils, and then served all of the food: soup, salmon, berry pudding, fried bread, cakes. Joe had told us that the spirits were very happy with the food they smelled, the natural food of Alaska's Native people. They were hungry and happy.

We bantered while we ate the ritual food. The participants told us what wonderful singing they had heard. Joe told Stanley that pretty soon the record companies would come and find us. Stanley said he thought it could have been better if Joe was not so off-key when he started up the songs. "Maybe Joe was a frog, because he sang so low," Stanley said.

Joe then asked me what I thought about the ceremony. I replied with a laugh that, yes, I had really been scared and thought my heart was going to jump out of my body. Everyone laughed with me. I said that during the ceremony I had felt real fear, but gradually more and more memories came back. More and more, I could see and feel the hurt. I said I thought that sometimes it was like an old friend I didn't want to give up. Joe said that was how his friends also saw it but that I would find that I could let it go and use my new friend, the tree, to give it away.

He then asked Kathy and Kathryn how they felt, and they too said they were pretty scared in the center but were very happy. They really appreciated that they could be next to me and support me. I sat there thinking that all of this was for me and they were all happy that I was happy. I felt happy.

He turned toward you at this point and quickly asked you if you were still awake. Everyone looked at you and had a big laugh, because you were slumped a bit with your head down.

About this time the food had been all served and people had eaten. You took a braid of sweet grass, lit it, and incensed all of the food and people and told us that as you did this we were again to say *mitak̄uye oyas'iŋ*. As you went around, we could smell more and more of this sweet smell of the burning grass mixed with the odors of the soup, other foods, and our bodies; smells and sounds began to move in harmony as the rhythmic *mitak̄uye oyas'iŋ* went from voice to voice. We repeated what we had become during the ceremony, one voice made of many.

Afterword

Speaker: Mohatt

Everyone left. Joe and Stanley and Vickie went to their apartment to sleep, and we cleaned up the house, moved back the furniture. The next day after lunch, Stanley and I sat with Joe in my office and talked about the ceremony and the woman's needs. He explained that she had many fears and much anger. The spirits just could not come close enough to her in order to doctor her strongly. However, they saw a little opening for her when she kept giving more and more information. They stayed because they saw this crack or opening. Since he could not be with her to keep seeing her, she needed someone to speak to on a regular basis. His spirits told him that a particular tree had a strong spirit. Once she picked this tree, it could give her a place to leave her anger and fear.

"Healing is for a long time," Joe explained. "Last night it began for her, but it will continue for her life." What she experienced as a child, becoming an orphan, and other things he did not know about, were too big for her.

"They are too hard for people to carry around alone, so now she is not alone with them," he said. I questioned Eagle Elk about whether she needed to understand where this anger came from.

"Maybe she needs to speak it to the tree. I don't know whether such things that caused it are ever understandable. They just happened and they don't have to be carried alone."

He again explained to me how sometimes we have a burden that is too big for us and needs to be shared. Lots of times, he said, the family and community close to us just aren't strong enough to help. In fact, sometimes they want us to carry it for all of them. So the tree was strong enough, he said, to help her. He did think as she spoke she would find out who she was really angry toward. Sometimes it was mixed up and really she didn't know who to hate or love. What was hidden lived and was very strong. Time speaking with her new friend and time giving away would heal.

Speaker: Maalia

I went home and slept like a rock. I went right back to that dormitory and slept until the next morning. I left for home the next day, and when I got home I had to find a place to give away the offerings. We had a smokehouse down by the river which some people were using, so I asked them if it was okay for me to burn something on their fire. To my surprise, they said no, because it would spoil the fish. I went back up to the house and found the outdoor grill we had for barbecue and made a very nice fire in it. As the fire grew and became stronger, I prayed to the four directions, to my spirit relatives there, and to the spirits above us and to Grandmother Earth, telling them of my gratitude.

Then I put the offerings on the fire and they began to burn, emitting this perfumed smell. Sweetness enveloped me as the smoke moved up and around me. I was so thankful. The next day I found out that the people in the smokehouse had found all their fish had spoiled and were rotting next to the river. This seemed so odd to me that the perfumed smell of the offerings had been rejected because they might make their fish smell bad. I was sad for their loss.

My arthritis was much better. I told you that I had read that sometimes the body could become fooled so the immune system didn't know the difference between disease and distress. I think this was my problem. Joe had doctored the distress and allowed me to experience the real pain deep inside of me. Each day when I felt some pain I would get some water, pray with it, and drink it. My arthritis pain lessened, and as you can see, I have no deformities or problems with my joints.

I felt sighted. I had sight, could see for the first time. I could see clearly in a new way. Suddenly my trees were my relatives in a deeply emotional way. The animals who came around our home, lynx, moose, raven, spider, all these were my relatives. When the leaves returned, I would tell my children, "Oh, look, our relatives are putting on new clothes." During the fall as the leaves dropped, I would tell them that our relatives are changing into beautiful colored clothes and preparing themselves for the winter. One day we were ice fishing and Raven was coming overhead and I remembered what the old people told us and I said to Raven, "Grandfather, come and empty your backpack!" He flew over us and tilted a little, which was the sign that he was emptying his sack and we would have good luck. Right after that the people fishing next to us caught a big pike. I told them laughing that they had caught my fish. At the end of the day they came over and gave me the fish. So the world around me took on new meaning. I don't know how to describe how I began to feel. I felt like all of those years I had been floating and now my feet were on the ground. That was a good feeling!

I had returned home and found a tree, a big spruce tree near our home. I had trees in all the locations we traveled, and they became my friends. When I felt sad or that something was bothering me, I went to the tree with my flags, tobacco ties, and offered them to my relative. I would stand there and talk and talk until relief came. Gradually, more and more left me. I remember my husband and I were sitting one day at our camp, our beautiful home on the lake. Joe had told me that I would begin to remember some of the things I couldn't voice at the time. When this would happen, I was to voice it. So we were sitting there at Christmas. We had decorated the house and were getting ready to go back to our other home and decorate it so that they would be ready for Christmas. Our daughters would return from college the next day. We were doing this all for our children. My husband knew that as a child I had never received a present from my father.

He knew what I was thinking without me saying it, so I said to him, "We are here cleaning and decorating two houses for our children. I wonder if somebody used to think about me on Christmas?" I couldn't say my father's name, but I was thinking about him.

My husband said yes with real understanding.

So I went on and said, "I wonder what he ate on Christmas. I wonder if he gave people presents." I told my husband how I remembered that I found a quarter and kept it to buy candy. I knew I was stealing. After I had stolen it, I couldn't repay it because I couldn't get a quarter from anywhere. So this was a funny thing I just remembered and voiced. It was still there forty or fifty years after the fact. Why did I have to steal? Couldn't he give me a quarter or could he ever give me a Christmas or birthday present? This was how things got voiced and recalled. I could gradually recall things and let them be. Before the ceremony maybe I couldn't tell anybody anything, or if I did, it was in secret and there was no relief. For the first time in that ceremony, I remembered things and found relief. I could forget them. So now I am not holding everything inside ready to explode like a bomb. My arthritis doesn't bother me unless I get upset, and then I have my water to help and I can find out what hurts and let it out. It really is finding the distress rather than making it into a disease. I think much of my woundedness came from the abandonment, and others of it came from my understanding of my Catholic upbringing while I was a child. I felt that some of not being lovable was because we are not supposed to be of this world. We are supposed to suffer. My teachers had come all this way to help this poor little creature. It reinforced my sense of being somebody not lovable.

But I don't think about those things so much now. They have paled. I know I am lovable. I am a woman and becoming an elder woman. My sense is that I am entering what I call the glory of being an older woman, the power of it. I know I am a woman. Even the animals respect me as a woman. My daughter and I were out berry picking. We had just returned to the car when she screamed that there was a wolf near us. I looked up and there she sat and looked at us. As it began to run away, it would stop and sit and look back at us. I was not afraid at all. To us, the wolf is our relative and family member. She is a good mother and feeds her children by chewing food and giving it to her babies. She is a good family model, a good mother. Even the male wolves are good providers. This wolf came to me at a time I was very sad and comforted me. I had only recently lost my husband.

The worst thing happened that could happen. Right in the midst of everything going so well, my husband was diagnosed with cancer and eighteen days later he died. I sat with him in the hospital as he was moved from room to room, unit to unit. The pain was so much for me, I didn't know if I could bear it. My friends said I was too brave, trying to comfort everyone else. I sat there in the hospital with him, and each day we looked out of the window and an eagle came. When we saw Eagle, we felt happy and my husband would make a little recovery. One day my brother-in-law and I were sitting there and we saw Eagle being chased by a little bird, maybe a dove, who was trying to attack the eagle. The eagle flew higher and higher and circled until he was out of reach of the dove. I asked my brother-in-law what was going on and he said, "It must have been taking something that the little bird loves."

Eagle left and didn't return until the morning my husband died. The death was very dignified and beautiful. We were all there, and he was not expected to last too long. I had been dozing and they woke me and told me his blood pressure was very weak. But he was very strong and lasted a couple of hours longer. When it was almost to the end, I took his mask off of his face and leaned over and breathed his last breath with him.

We looked out and there Eagle was. He stayed with us everywhere we went, including our trip down the river to home. And when I went to my husband's grave before I came home, Eagle was there. I have to think that the little bird was me. I was trying to keep my husband, but, you know, Eagle could have killed the little bird, but he didn't. So somehow I have been able to bear this loss.

I ranted at God. During the wake, we had to say the litany after the rosary. As people responded with "pray for us" to the priest, saying the saints' names, I thought who is this St. Steven, probably he thought the world was flat. Who the hell gives a damn who this saint or that one is. I even began to substitute names of my relatives and said out loud St. Edith, St. Claude . . . and the people answered and said, "Pray for us." I surprised myself at how I voiced this. I don't know what they thought; maybe that I had gone off the deep end, but they responded and we went on.

Sometime later after the funeral, I went home and my friend came to visit me this one time and we went to visit my husband's grave. She told me that I had kept too much in and I should just lay on mother earth and scream. I remembered reading Maxine Hong Kingston's *China Men* and how the Chinese men had screamed into the ground. So she left me beside my husband's grave and I laid there and screamed and screamed. Afterwards I made some flags and put them on a big birch tree next to my husband's grave.

I still have lots of problems, like my son's illness and other things, but I have more strength to bear these problems. After my husband died, I was in my car next to the river. I looked at the river and thought that my husband had given me a life on the river. We spent so much time going up and down that river visiting village after village. I couldn't have known it without him. So I thought that maybe the way to get back to him was through the river. I was going to drive into it and find my husband. At that moment I knew I needed help and went immediately to the clinic. A psychiatrist told me I was symbolizing something or other and that I had to let go.

After seeing him, I went to the elders and told them what happened. They said to me, "You have walked this path with your husband for over forty years and if you take a different path, you might not reach him. So you want to die to reach him?"

"Yes!" I said.

"Well, you might be taking the wrong path."

I decided to live. So a lot of tough, really tough, things have come to me, but I have been able to avoid disaster by being more spiritual and more aware. I hurt. I feel pain. So I decided to buy this new place and live here. One day we were driving along and saw the place. It was two acres with good trees and very clean. So now I am here in my home, which we moved by barge all the way from the village. My memories are here. Once we have spring, I will clean it up and then find my tree. I will put the flags on the tree and begin again this process of honoring my relative and letting go of my pain. It will go on, but now I am at peace. I can say things without anger or without alienating the people. I can see. I want others to learn how to see and voice themselves. My world has gotten so much bigger and nicer. The animals are here. The trees and plants and lots of mosquitoes. We are all at home here. Lots of us live here. This comforts me.

Conclusion

Joe stayed with us in Alaska for about a week in June 1990 during the summer solstice. We lived on the university campus because our home had burned in January and was being rebuilt. Joe and I sat in this small apartment for many hours during a five-day period talking of his life. We taped for about six hours. Vickie did not want to listen to Joe's stories, particularly of his life before she and he met, so she and my wife, Robby, shopped. Vickie loved to shop and was able to buy some of the things that her children needed. Joe and I drove into the hills surrounding Fairbanks and visited about life and our shared memories of the past. Joe spoke each day in my cross-cultural healing class at the university.

During our more formal interviews, Joe and I broke into laughter as he told the stories of his escapades that landed him in jail, his encounters with his spirits, and his foibles during the time he roamed. A young Russian university student, Andris Ozols, who was among the first Russian students from the Far East to come to our college, was living with us. He was very impressed with Joe. Joe liked Andris and was very happy to meet a Russian. He never thought this would happen in his lifetime. He asked Andris to send some earth from Russia to me so I could give it to him for his altar. One day Andris returned home in midday with four young Russian women, students who were part of his group. They all wanted to meet the medicine man and ask him questions. Andris asked Joe if this was okay. Joe was very pleased and said to tell them to ask anything they wanted to know. They sat immobile and silent, afraid to ask anything. After a little while, they got up and shook Joe's hand and left. Joe and I laughed and laughed about how he scared these young women. He must have been too handsome for them.

We held our annual wopila (thanksgiving) ceremony in our little apartment with our children, Andris, and a few friends. I was struck by how weak Joe was. He had me fill the pipe for him and sit in the center during the special prayers for our future. He said the ceremony would be *wowaȟwala* (quiet and peaceful) and rather short, because he could not handle long ceremonies.

Before and after the ceremony, Vickie asked us to get Joe to a doctor, but when I asked Joe, he did not really want to go. He said he was okay and that nothing more could be done. We could not walk far, and he needed rest during the day. But he loved to sit and talk and drink coffee. They stayed in one of the dormitory apartments, and we had them over for breakfast each day. But because of jet lag, they woke up each morning earlier than we did and were hungry. I asked Vickie what to bring, and she said a coffeepot and sweet rolls. They really missed their morning sweets.

The last day of the visit Joe talked to me about our new home and returning to it. During the ceremony, he had sung a song that we were to sing when we moved back in, before we moved any furniture into the house. He told me this would be our song for our home and we should sing it and remember the spirits for what they gave us. The song is:

K̇ola, wamayaŋk̄e yo!
Ṫuŋk̄aŝila, Wak̇aŋ Ṫaŋk̄a, heya hoyewa yelo!
K̇ola, wahi najiŋ lo
K̇ola, wamayaŋk̄e yo!
He ċaŋnupa k̄i yuha wahi najiŋ lo na hoyeċ̄iċ̄i yelo!
K̇ola, wamayaŋk̄e yo!
K̇ola, wamayaŋk̄e yo!

(Friend, look on me!
Grandfather, Great Mystery, I pray to you. I throw my voice to you.
Friend, I arrive standing here!
Friend, look on me!
I stand here praying and throwing out my voice, holding my sacred pipe!
Friend, look on me!
Friend, look on me!)

We said good-bye the last week of June. Joe never recovered his strength. He was not able to do sweats or ceremonies as in the past. He was in and out of the hospital, and the doctors said that he suffered multiple complications with his heart condition. They said he could not have surgery, because he was too weak and would not survive an operation. I called in January to talk to Joe and was told he was in the hospital in Sioux Falls. I called him there, and his voice sounded strong. We joked, but he said he was very seriously ill.

I asked, "What do the spirits say about this, Joe?"

He answered, "They said it's pretty tough and there isn't much to do about it, but we will try."

I told him I would pray in our sweat. That evening my family and I went into our sweat and prayed for him. We repeated this often and tried to cajole his spirits into taking mercy on him. I talked to them as he had about all Joe had done for them and how they needed to take care of him now.

I called him again in late February or early March, and we talked for quite a while on the phone.

I asked, "How are you doing, Joe? And what do the spirits say?"

"No good, pretty weak. I went to Norbert and we had a ceremony. They said I have until the grass turns green and then they don't know. Maybe I could get two more weeks or a little longer, but I don't know," Joe replied.

"So won't they give you more time?" I asked.

"Maybe and maybe not. We won't know until then, but once it turns green, I have to go back to Norbert, and we will ask them for more time or what they want," he said.

"So it looks like this is the end, then?" I asked.

"Yes," he said.

"This is going to be really hard on everyone. We love you and will miss you a great deal, Joe," I said.

"Yeah, I really hate to leave these kids and Victoria. I know how much they depend on me, how much they need me. I guess I just didn't do what I needed to do. I didn't do what the doctors said, and now I have to leave my children. This makes me really sad."

"Yeah, I know it!" I said. "I just can't understand why, Joe. You have done so much for your friends. Why can't they help now? Why can't they return to you all you have given to them?" I was angry and both of us were very close to tears. "We love you, Joe. Justin and Nate admire you, and your affection and love for them really have helped them. I will keep asking your spirits to help you and not give up. Why can't they help?"

"I guess I'm guilty!" he replied.

The family and friends had ceremonies for Joe, but he went into the hospital the second week of March. He was very weak. Albert White Hat remembers going to visit him and seeing in his eyes what he called "that twinkle," which told Albert that Joe was leaving this world. On March 19, Norbert Running was working in the place where he held his sun dance and looked at the ground. Right in front of him was the first blade of grass. He told the family what he saw, and they held a ceremony that evening. During the ceremony, dogs began to bark and a car pulled up to the house and there was a knock on the door. They sang a song and finished the ceremony quickly, and Vickie went to the door. The people could hear someone speak to her, and she broke into tears. Joe had died.

Four days later he was buried on the hill with the pine trees that he loved so much. His medicine bundle was buried with him. His lineage of healing would come through vision when one of his children or grandchildren had a vision.

Four years later, in the summer of 1995, friends and family gathered to place a stone on the grave, to pray for the family and friends, and to remember Joe. Such a memorial involves the accumulation of many handmade star quilts, Pendleton blankets, woven goods, pots and pans, chests, utensils, and money. The family gives these items away to those who attend in honor of the deceased after everyone present has been fed. Such a giveaway is done after the funeral and again a year from the death of the person. Pallbearers and others who helped are given to first. A respected member of the community serves as the announcer for the event, telling people to come forward to receive a gift or to ask people to come forward to speak. At a certain point during the giveaway, photographs of the deceased are brought around for people to view. After the photographs, cakes made especially for the memorial are also brought around to be viewed by the participants. In this way, we remember the person we lost so we can continue with our lives and he or she can have rest and honor.

The memorial was held in Ghost Hawk Park on the Little White River. Charlie and Elizabeth Garriott and Elizabeth's mother, Edna Little Elk, organized this giveaway and feed with the help of Manfred Kazenmaier, Joe's adopted German son, and our family as well as many others. We fed the people and gave away in Joe's honor. John Around Him, Albert White Hat, and Duane Hollow Horn Bear spoke of what Joe had done for them, and John announced. Joe had helped each of them begin his sun dance and had been each one's mentor and supporter in many other ways. Edna Little Elk and other elders spoke of Joe and of the memorial. Manfred and I spoke of our memories of Joe and his meaning to us. We thanked all the people who came. Vickie was there, along with their children Diane and Chris and some of the grandchildren. We remembered Joe. We thanked him and his spirits, and we reminded the people of who he was and what he stood for. It was completed.

Epilogue *A Difference Made*

Herr Doktor, I said, it all depends what you mean by living. A real life, a life that leaves a deposit in the shape of something alive, not merely a photograph album yellow with age—God knows, it need not be magnificent, it need not be historic and unforgettable—you know what I mean, Herr Doktor, a real life may be the life of a very simple mother, or the life of a great thinker, someone whose life leaves a deposit that is preserved for world history—but it doesn't have to be, I mean it doesn't depend on our importance. It's difficult to say what makes a life a real life. I call it reality, but what does that mean? You could say it depends on a person being identical with himself. . . .

Are words a deposit? Perhaps life, real life, is simply mute—and it doesn't leave photographs behind, Herr Doktor, it doesn't leave anything dead.

—Max Frisch, *I'm Not Stiller*

A woman arrives in a therapist's or psychoanalyst's office. She speaks with trepidation, jerking forward to stare intently at her therapist, about the bugs crawling up her legs. She retreats immediately into angry (apparently) silence. Another patient fears the world of people so much that he lives in solitary loneliness in a small room with black wallpaper and heavy curtains, and sleeps in a monk's bed to help redeem the world. The mother of a young Lakota woman calls a therapist and tells her of the rape of her daughter. They mobilize other women, who take the young women into the purification rite of their tradition. On an intensely hot day in July a man who survived Vietnam as a warrior and is wounded in his spirit dances with his relatives in the sacred circle of the sun dance.

Each person brings a story to his or her therapist or ritual leader. Each of the clinicians or ritual leaders is focused on the patient, humble in their work because of a profound sense of the skill, knowledge, and courage needed to heal. A realization exists among each of these helpers that they have much to learn and much to give. They can use no esoteric magic, no "new age" crystals; they cannot simply pray for the patient. They don't call themselves healers. Arrogance will only stand in the way of a cure. Yet they know they must possess knowledge and skill. They know that they must "get out of the way" yet enter at the right time. They realize that much of their work is to empty themselves so they can have an indifference that allows them to listen and to hear the other. They know they must continue to learn.

The following conversation represents reflections on these questions by a distinguished group of practitioners, some psychoanalysts, some psychologists and psychotherapists, and others members of the Rosebud Tribe who are recognized leaders engaged in traditional rituals. All come from traditions grounded in their cultural frameworks. All have met and worked with Joe Eagle Elk and other indigenous healers. They speak to what they have learned about the healing process from their association with Joe. They do not try to interpret or explain Joe or his views. They say only what meaning it has for them, what it tells them about the universal questions of healing and cure. All have asked themselves and continue to ask themselves what constitutes the cure, how is it effected.

Their conversation speaks to this question. It is the most important one for each of them. What will cure the person? What will cure the society? Even when only one person sits with the helper, the cure must address the social link—that which represents the place of the patient in the society and the gaps both in the society and in the family which constitute a silence that drives the patient to madness. What truth can't be told? What must be left "alone"?

The following men and women have shared their reflections:

Matilda "Tillie" Black Bear is a leader in the area of domestic violence and in forging ways to use contemporary Lakota ritual to address healing from trauma. She has completed all her course work for her doctoral degree in counseling psychology from the University of South Dakota. She is past president of the National Coalition on Domestic Violence. Members of her family have been leaders in the sun dance, supporters of the medicine men, and deeply involved in Lakota spirituality and ritual. She knew Joe Eagle Elk well and was his niece through marriage.

Françoise Davoine is a Lacanian psychoanalyst who treats individuals experiencing psychotic states. She is a member of the faculty at L'Ecole des hautes études en Sciences Sociales in Paris. She has written many articles and a well-known book on psychosis, *La folie du Wittgenstein,* in which she refers to Eagle Elk and his work. Davoine knew Eagle Elk for ten years, attended his ceremonies, consulted on cases with him, and has integrated his perspectives into her scholarship and practice.

Duane Hollow Horn Bear is a member of the Lakota studies faculty at Sinte Gleska University on the Rosebud Reservation in south-central South Dakota. He contributed one of the cases in this book and worked closely with Eagle Elk. With Albert White Hat, he is one of the founders and leaders of the Hollow Horn Bear sun dance. When not teaching at the university in Rosebud, he lectures throughout the world on Lakota spirituality and works with youth on the reservation to promote their identification with and understanding of Lakota spirituality.

Ute Gentner is from Stuttgart, where she works as a psychotherapist. She has been deeply involved in discovering the tribal roots of spirituality among Germans and how Lakota spirituality can serve as a stimulus for its development. She has participated in a number of sun dances at the Hollow Horn Bear sun dance and brought Eagle Elk to Germany to speak with people interested in Lakota spirituality.

Jean-Max Gaudillière is a Lacanian psychoanalyst who treats individuals experiencing psychosis. He is a member of the faculty of L'Ecole des hautes études en Science Sociales in Paris. He teaches and writes on the treatment of psychosis, does private analytic work, and lectures throughout the world. Gaudillière met Eagle Elk in 1979. He attended his ceremonies, consulted with him on cases, and organized a conference in 1985 to bring French psychoanalysts to meet with indigenous healers from the United States, one of whom was Eagle Elk.

Richard Katz is a psychologist who has worked for many years cross-culturally with indigenous people in Fiji, Alaska, the Kalahari, and currently northern Saskatchewan. He has been on the faculty of

Brandeis University, Harvard University, and the University of Alaska Fairbanks and at present holds a position at the Indian Federated College of Saskatchewan. He has published three books and numerous articles on cross-cultural healing, education as transformation, and ways in which indigenous knowledge can inform contemporary education and the practice of psychology. He spent much time with Eagle Elk, who was a mentor, a friend, and a relative to Katz.

Manfred Kazenmaier lives in Stuttgart and has worked with various Lakota healers over decades. He is considered a leader in assisting Germans serious about spiritual practice to learn from Lakota medicine men. Manfred has participated for years in the sun dance. He and Eagle Elk were very close, and Eagle Elk called him his son. Kazenmaier worked closely with family and friends of Eagle Elk to organize and complete a memorial ceremony several years after Eagle Elk's death. He currently works in Germany as a personnel consultant to corporations and other agencies in need of human relations training.

John Muller is the director of education and psychotherapy at the Austen Riggs Center in Stockbridge, Massachusetts, where he also treats severely disturbed individuals in an open hospital setting. He lived on the Rosebud Reservation and for three years worked at Sinte Gleska University, where he brought medicine men into the university's faculty to teach human service students. Muller worked closely with Eagle Elk during this period. While at the Riggs Center, he brought staff to the reservation to consult with Eagle Elk and initiated forums for cross-cultural dialogue. He has written books and numerous articles on Lacanian psychoanalytic theory and practice and on semiotics and the philosopher Charles S. Pierce.

Albert White Hat is a member of the faculty of Lakota studies at Sinte Gleska University. He is a sun dance leader and the cofounder of the Hollow Horn Bear sun dance. He teaches Lakota language and spirituality and lectures widely around the United States, Canada, and the world. He is the author of *Lak̇ot̄a Iyap̄iun wowap̄i nahaŋ yawap̄i (Reading and Writing the Lakota Language)* (1999), which integrates a cultural perspective and philosophy into the teaching of language. White Hat worked with Eagle Elk to found the Hollow

Horn Bear sun dance; he sang for Eagle Elk at his ceremonies and gave Eagle Elk and his family much support.

Mohatt: Joe considered the healing of the person, the individual, as only beginning in a ceremony and then continuing after the session. His patients were healed if they faithfully followed his directions and began to make changes in their lives. Some of the directions are pretty clear and simple, perhaps to take a certain medicine in a certain way, or maybe to stop eating certain foods or to return to see him daily, or to ask themselves the questions that the spirits left for them. The last case in the book with Maalia is a good example of this. She had more to come out and needed to find the words for what was inside. She struggled, confronting a decision about life and suicide, and coped by returning to the processes she had learned from Joe and through her own subsequent work. Others had a task that seemed more difficult, even obscure, like the young man with cancer. Joe was always very conscious of this dimension of the patient's responsibility for his or her own healing, and a bit disappointed, or maybe perplexed, about how many patients failed to work on their healing between ceremonies.

I was reminded of a similar issue in our work which came up at a lunch I had with psychoanalysts Bill Richardson and Alphonse DeWaehlens in Paris in 1981. I asked them, "Why these short analytic sessions by Lacan?"[1] He was notorious, as were his followers, for having sessions some of which might be minutes in length. People were outraged or fascinated. DeWaehlens said that, for Lacan, the session had to end at a point where a question or comma punctuated it so the client went on to the real process of healing between sessions. He thought Lacan knew how difficult the therapeutic process would become if the client and therapist depended entirely on a routine fifty-minute hour. In fact, Lacan believed that the regularity of the fifty-minute hour would lead to a dependency on the session and prevent the out-of-session work. The conversation made me think that we must redefine what we mean by therapy to include the whole rather than the single or separate parts of the therapeutic hour. Of course, this has become a major factor in some of the newer therapies in the form of homework. But homework is prescriptive and does not capture the self-determined and reflexive quality of what Joe expected from patients after they left the ceremony.

In my own practice I have found that the sheer experience of the relationship, of a human contact, can have a rather dramatic effect on the client and his or her symptoms, but the work really begins only if the patient is willing to work outside of sessions. The symptom relief that often comes from the earliest contact and support is only the first step, important but only a beginning.

Gaudillière: We have instances when we see someone with a particular delusion, certain types of persons with their own particular delusion. They can have a very big delusion, consider themselves the prime minister or the reincarnation of a king. But through the power of the transference, you can help the delusions come apart and disappear, perhaps in three months. What I mean by transference is a type of relationship established between the patient and me, created in space and time, in which we could at a certain moment repeat her past or create a new moment. This of course is the fundamental task, to create a new moment from the past in the therapeutic relationship. Each of the cases in this book illustrates this in one way or the other.

But there is a danger at that very moment when the delusion disappears, not when the delusion is crashing in on the person. If it disappears or appears to be destroyed, you don't know how or with whom it will reappear. Will it suddenly return in full force, be acted out in the society, or do you, the therapist, become the cause of the delusion? This is the very moment when catastrophe can hit, and suicide of the patient or killing of the therapist is possible. For us, we must realize that we have to be alert and open to the symptoms returning in the transference, in the here-and-now relationship between the two of us. Obviously, a potentially powerful event can happen, so we must establish a frame in our sessions, a safe place, one in which clients feel protected from the destructive forces of the delusions. We cannot just let the person go from our sessions thinking that all is wonderful. Rather, they learn that their work begins with us and continues; the cure continues, it grows. At these moments we must find bold words or we are all in danger. At times we have to use orders, very direct and very strong proscriptions. From these words, the patient learns how to take the frame into everyday life.

Mohatt: I think Joe added a certain boldness to clinical practice that was not present in my experiences in clinical training or in supervision. I remember talking to him about what he told Ed Podvoll at his ceremony. Ed was a psychiatrist and psychoanalyst at the Austen Riggs Center.[2] Joe had told him that his words were "too light." He felt because of this fact, the treatment of psychotherapy took a very, very long time and that therapists needed to become bolder, crisper, and clearer with their speaking in therapy and how they connected the therapy with the person's current life.

Muller: When Joe's spirits told us in the ceremony that the words of the therapist were too light, it meant to me that we needed to learn to speak with conviction, to be clear with our patients that aggression exists, that risks are involved, that we have a passion about these risks and will speak to them. We needed to become clear in our words and in our convictions about the limits and the boundaries of the treatment. The rituals are bounded. They exist in a sacred time and space, have a beginning and an end. The ceremony marks the boundary. The ritual frames and limits aggression, fabrication, and falsity, which are challenged by the community present through their prayers and speech and what the spirits tell the patient through the medicine man.

Mohatt: So the rituals, ceremonies demand responsibility and clarity of roles. I know what you said helped me see how my work must ensure this clarity and mark these boundaries.

Gaudillière: Joe told us that the cure does not come from the cure of the symptoms. It is a question of the duration of life. To be cured, you need your own life. It is not the question of one instance, one moment. The first ceremonies are like preliminary interviews, and they sometimes take place over a few weeks or a year or even two years. There is a ceremony, but then the practice of being cured begins. It is the work of the patient.

Mohatt: In the ceremonies the symptoms can lessen rather rapidly and the feeling tone for the client can change very quickly, but Joe always said that this could easily become part of the problem. The people would think they were healed and forget why they had come and not engage in the practice of continued healing.

My sense is that much of the fear of boldness in contemporary psychotherapy is based on a therapist's sense that she or he only analyzes and interprets. Lacan had a much greater respect for his patients' resources, their capacity for their own work coupled with their need for direct, bold interventions by the therapist.

There exists a dialectic in all this. It is never just one way, and we must work simultaneously at what might appear to be oppositional levels, for example for the therapist to intervene directly but also leave patients on their own to struggle, to address dependency and autonomy. This is what I think Joe meant by the practice of the cure. It will take time. It will go beyond the first interviews, beyond our face-to-face work, beyond the relieving of symptoms, and take place through us, by the client, and in the community. The patients make the link with the community, are able to relate in new ways. They learn to trust themselves and work on themselves. Sometimes the patient becomes freer to be with others in new ways, less suspicious perhaps, or less punitive. So they start learning new things from relationships, from others. Joe spoke often of this in terms of how the patient relates to his body and medicine. Each person has the power to relate in new ways to himself and his community.

Joe's patients did not feel they were alone with their burdens, even when he was absent. They realized that they are not the cause of their symptoms and responsible for them alone. They knew if they wanted to return to Joe, they could. He accentuated their capacity to work on their own problems. Our clients need to know they have a framework in the sessions which provides some limits and boundaries to their symptoms and allows them to depend on us. But our work with them shows how to continue beyond the moment and the place. They both become more independent but can return to the frame of therapy to work with us. Both aspects are essential.

Davoine: Joe taught me about this in the very first ceremony I had with him. I asked for a ceremony for my mother. I really did not know what I was doing, but we went through it. The evening that we drove to the ceremony, it began to storm with lightning and thunder, and I said to myself, "My goodness, what have I done wrong that this weather is so hard?" We laughed about this, but I really was awestruck by the power of the plains—its storms. Then we arrived, prepared everything, while you two and the other men went to the sweat lodge. When the ceremony began, the lights went out and the door slammed shut. It was pitch black, and I asked myself again, "My goodness, what happened?" Joe told me my mother was going to die and that she was going to suffer much. He was speaking as the heyoka, telling me the truth about the fate of my mother but only by saying the opposite. You or Stanley explained that she would get better, not suffer so much, and would not die immediately. But contained in this message was the truth that she would suffer a great deal and eventually she would die. Although she is much better now, both things he told us have happened. Both parts of the message were true, but I didn't understand it at that level. I talked to him the next day, and he was shy with us. He did his work and it was over. I was so unsure what to believe. I thought that he was just trying to mollify me and make me feel good. He raised the questions that pushed me to reflect during that year and determine how I would relate to my mother.

That was the first time we came to visit you in South Dakota. Well, we returned the next year and saw him and he was very happy to see us. At that point, he began to share much with us. We held a wopila ceremony with him, and he was very happy. After we were done and the lights were turned on and we were eating the food prepared for the ceremony, Stanley asked me, "Why don't you talk about your father during the ceremony?" I had no answer. When I returned home, I discovered that my father had fallen from a ladder and hurt himself. So I wondered about this interpretation by Stanley. It was so clear and crisp, so simple and direct, and asked me what I was to do. My work had only begun in the ceremony. As Jean-Max said, the practice of healing is for a longer time. What I had begun with confronting my mother's illness now continued for me with a focus on my father.

But we also learned that we had to return to see him before this could happen, and I had to do things in between. I had both to think and to act; the moment of healing continued, yes, but could have stopped. I could have returned to find out more but without working on these questions during the intervening year. This would have constituted a failure in my responsibility.

Gaudillière: I remember how shy I was and how shy he was with us and how our exchanges evolved slowly and inexorably toward impacting our practice.

Davoine: We did not come to learn about Indians. Certainly we did learn things about them, but Joe and Stanley taught us about how to learn about our own knowledge, about ourselves and our practice. He gave us tools to work on ourselves and understand our own practice as psychotherapists.

White Hat: It is the same for me. Joe has died. He is gone. While he was with us, I depended a lot on him. But gradually he gave me more and more to do on my own. The sun dance was ours. He led us rather quickly to assume complete responsibility for the preparation and performance of the sun dance. Since he left us, I have seldom gone to another medicine man. My work is with my tiośp̄aye, and we have more and more depended on each other. We aren't arrogant about not needing the medicine men for healing. We want them to help with the sun dance and invite them to help us with the sun dance. We help them by singing for some of them in their ceremonies. But we know that the *k̇aŋ* is accessible to all of us. We know that in ceremonies k̇aŋ is increased when the people are of one mind, so we try to make sure we have the type of community that supports healing power. Our work is to become of one mind.

Mohatt: Joe said the fullness of his power could come into the ceremony only when the participants were of one mind and desire. No multiple agendas, everyone wanting help for themselves or their relatives, but a focus on one person who needed healing. So the power of the collective can come to bear on the person. To me, this is a very interesting combination. The work of the community balanced with the equal importance of the person working independently, following the spirits' direction, and continuing to give back through ritual, prayer, and a change in their lives are all critical for healing to happen.

I am continually brought back to my own experience. Joe's life made me think about my life, my work, and my experience. I started to think back on what I experienced when I did my first vision quest with Leonard Crow Dog. I thought about how naive I was and how patient he was with me. During this experience I had a very vivid dream the first night on the hill. After I completed the fast, Leonard held a ceremony and sweat in order for me to tell him what I had experienced. Both during and after the ceremony he revealed very little about the meaning of the dream, no interpretation, just acknowledgment that it was there for me to learn from. A couple of years later his father, Henry, told me that I was brought to the hill to learn about the "university of universities."

Then one evening, maybe five years later, I was at a sweat lodge and ceremony at Johnny Strike's and began to talk to him about my dream. He said nothing, but after the sweat and ceremony he told me how this dream had foretold my work of establishing the college. He explained more to Stanley, who told me more later. Johnny said that the dream only made sense after I had done the work. Maybe I would not choose to do it or maybe I would, but the dream became a path for my own discovery. The dream pushed me in certain directions. When you have a vivid dream in such a powerful context as on a hill way out in the canyon, it calls for reflection and returns periodically. At certain points in my life I would remember the dream; for example, while I was deciding to work on the college or to leave it, I would think about what I saw in my dream and try to see how it related to what I was considering doing. Sometimes it seemed like it helped me and related to my decision, while other times it seemed pretty remote. It was not easy to relate the two, and in fact I couldn't say, this says I should do this; rather, it pushed me to reflect and consider why I was considering one choice or another in terms of the dream. No prescriptive road map existed, only reflection and personal choice and responsibility.

Then later, after I had been doing the work, I thought of my dream and said to myself, you know, this seems very much in line with the work. Subsequent vision quests, later conversations with other medicine men and friends or colleagues revealed more of the meaning, but only after I had done the work and made some of the decisions. I had to make the meaning out of it, find where it fit in the society. I had to act and open myself to follow the dream rather than analyze it. But equally important was the event itself, in which a group of Lakota people prayed for me and supported me while I was on the hill and when I returned. Without both the community and my own work, I would have never had a dream or maybe I would never have been sitting on the grass outside the Community Action Program's office in Rosebud when Stanley asked me to help start the university.

In my own practice as a psychotherapist, I now pay more and more attention to what I can say that will leave a gentle or clear question for the client to work with, maybe a story to think over, or an anecdote. Something that shows we are both incomplete and complete. Sometimes it might be a joke. But whatever it is, it is there so the person engages himself and others. It is a matter of choice.

Katz: This reminds me of a story. I had made a commitment to do a hanbleċiye with Joe. He had put me on the hill once before, and I knew I needed to do another hanbleċiye, so I gave him the tobacco and asked for his help. He said yes, that he would help me.

A couple of days later we were talking in his house. He went to the back door and motioned me to come there.

"You see that ridge over there," he said, "not the close one but the next one over. You see it."

"Yeah, I see it."

"I want to tell you a story about that ridge," he said, and then he told the story of how when he was a little boy he went to that ridge, to a special place on that ridge to put his grandfather on the hill. "It was a natural place for a hanbleċiye," he said, "a hollow in the earth." He told me that as a little boy he went to that place with his grandfather to help put him up there for his vision quest, and that his father had also sweated and done his vision quests there, and that he, Joe, had done his hanbleċiye there also.

So then he said to me, "You think that place would be okay for you?" Just like that. "You think that spot would be okay?" "Yeah," I said, "that would be a pretty good spot."

I believe Joe was telling me that he wanted to put me in a place not just where the spirits are, like the place of my first hanbleċiye, but in a place he knew well, a place where he and his family had often visited and fasted in, a family place. That notion of place was very powerful. Powerful in an ordinary way. Joe did not say this place on the far ridge is where the eagles will come, where you will see great visions. No, he simply described the earth and why this was a special place for him and his family, a place they knew.

Mohatt: Certainly this was a dramatic place, but he wanted you to decide to go there not because of the dramatics, but wanted to offer you a choice as a relative.

Katz: That's right—never did he make promises or mention signs such as "The eagles will visit you there," or "There are spirits of many generations here." No mention of great visions and signs, of dramatic things. He simply offered the place as part of our relationship.

Mohatt: Very much like how he described his first vision quest and preparation for it. He talked of the wak̄iŋyaŋ coming, of the lightning striking, and of everyone, including him, being afraid and rushing for the sweat lodge. When he was touched by the spirit in his second vision quest, he spoke of it very humorously: "I almost died!!" he said. He made the dramatic humorous; he made it human.

Gaudillière: Joe told me about his experience of doing the kettle dance. When he told me this story and went through all the dramatic description of what he saw, as you have described, he then said: "Well, I danced up to the kettle four times, and each time I took my hand and put it close to the water ready to pull the head from the boiling pot. And boy! It was hot, really hot! So I just decided not to pull it out of the pot!" So we just laughed and laughed together.

He could bring the people to a point of excitement or to a point of very intense feeling and just at that moment bring in a moment of humor so the person was not laughed at but would laugh. Even if it were not laughter, he would leave the person with a question, a question about how this makes sense in the everyday life of family or community.

Mohatt: The critical issue for me in that kettle dance was that the people were not of one mind. The community was not prepared to accept what Joe had to accomplish in his ceremony. So he left the whole audience, the people, with a question.

Like in the last case in the book. Maalia could not say it all, so Joe said, "My spirits said, maybe you are a little afraid," with just a hint of teasing with the question. Everyone laughed, including Maalia. So the person had not just relief but was free to think or reflect without any persuasion, no force, just a hint of more to know. But he did the questioning in the ceremony with two of her friends holding on to her arms, and he gave her the tree as a friend and her frame in order to let go of more of her pain, remember and forget more.

Stands Fast: I told you the story of the turkey and how Joe moved him to the wilderness. I always thought that for Joe this made sense for the turkey's destiny. On the one hand, he had to find it alone, but on the other he had to find it in a place where he belonged. Joe laughed about the situation but was also sad. It was both humorous and serious. We all have our place and our tasks to accomplish, and this turkey was no exception.

Davoine: Joe never forced one to think one way or the other. He simply spoke; he said very little. This has been freeing for us and is very much within our psychoanalytic tradition of giving the patient maximum freedom to find the truth. What was new for us and helped us understand some of our experiences more deeply was Joe's attention to how healing was related to touching our origins as tribal people and, therefore, our place, our earth, our ancestral home.

We had been in Manitoba with Art Blue and Meredith Rogers and discussed with them the deep and pervasive problems that Native people in their communities faced. We then came to your place and met with Joe. During these meetings he told us the story that you related in the book about the children's tracks in the sand and the calling of their spirits. How no one called the spirits and wiped away the tracks, so they went in all directions and the people were lost. He told us how concerned he was about children who sniffed glue and the alcoholics who drank Lysol. These problems were at their roots related to this story. Children and adults dreamed today, but no one interpreted. Few were brought to the vision quest so they could experience their dreams with the help of a medicine man. Communities had abandoned their ceremonies.

Stanley went on, and he told us, "If you come to listen to us, it's because it's in your tradition and you must find it." We could not stop by learning from their tradition but had to learn how to make meaning of our own dreams and those of our patients within our tribal tradition.

Mohatt: In Alaska, indigenous people came to Joe's talks, and the young people often spoke about recurring dreams and their fears of them. Joe told them they could find the meaning in their communities. The people could use other cultures and their ceremonies to help them, like the sweat lodge or lowaŋp̄i or sun dance, but they had to go to their own community and revive its traditions in their own way if they wanted a sense of finality or completeness. Joe and I talked one evening during this visit, and he told me how the people wanted him to use the sacred pipe in his ceremonies because it was so important to them. But he said it was not in his vision and he did not need to use it. Too many people mistake the objects, the form and symbols, for the spirituality. They think they need all the "right" symbols around their sweat lodge. But healing power comes from vision, and no one's vision is the same as anyone else's. What people need is a process to discover their own visions, which are the sources of whatever they become. What one sees may not seem very flashy or dramatic, but might be very unobtrusive and common. Maybe they are to heal by simply talking to another person, or maybe they are to give them a glass of water or just listen. Maybe their healing takes place in the daylight or in the sweat lodge or maybe around their kitchen table.

Katz: Starting in 1985, I got to know Joe in another way, at a deeper level, when I would come to Rosebud from Saskatchewan with my wife, Verna. During our visits he would have these family sweats where he and Vickie, Duane and his wife, who was Joe's niece, and their daughter, and Verna and I would come. He would say, "These are our family sweats." During these sweats we would do a lot of talking, both during the time the door to the sweat was closed and when it was open. We would just be visiting, not heavy "spiritual talk," but just like Joe asking, "How are you doing?" or "What is happening back home?"

I had experienced many other sweats in Rosebud and Saskatchewan, and there was always some joking, praying, and singing. But in this family sweat of Joe's there was this quality of ordinariness in the context of a family. What the symbol of the family sweat made me realize once again was that there was nothing about the spiritual world which is divorced from my everyday life. There was nothing necessarily unspiritual with talking about everyday life, ordinary cares and concerns. The heart of spiritual work is everyday work; and the foundation of this work is the family. I was vividly reminded of these teachings when Joe did family sweats for us even when he was ill and could not stay in it for all four rounds. He would say, "We must do this sweat before you leave, because we are all family." He valued the core experience of being together as a family and would sacrifice and endure pain in order to complete that ritual of purification for our departure.

Often during our visits to Rosebud, Joe would be gone doctoring other people. He was often sick and weak with his heart condition, but he never seemed to refuse anyone's request for healing. And often he traveled long, not returning until early in the morning—and the requests for help rarely came at what one might consider "convenient" times. I said to myself that this guy has no regard for his body or limits. Joe taught me that when you get the call to help or heal another, you put yourself into a secondary role. His vision was his work, and he was faithful to this vision.

Mohatt: The roots of his vision were in Rosebud. He spoke with his life, which was in some way a sacrifice, a set of multiple sacrifices, with his death the inevitable final one. The work had an inexorable quality to it, a demand, and he followed with fidelity, but only after years of reluctance, years of suffering and struggle, doubt and fear. His family knew the road he was choosing and tried to protect him, but finally he accepted and then he was "a one-track guy."

Katz: Joe taught us that you don't say, "I want to be a medicine man." You become a healer because you have to become one. You become a healer against your better judgment, against all odds, because you know that once you begin that healing work, your life is no longer your own. He taught me this with his life. People sometimes come to me and say they have the gift of healing and they want to become a healer. I say to them, you don't desire this path, you are chosen for it, and often chosen against your will. You will wonder whether it is the right path for you, and you will at times wish that you had not taken on this healing work because it can feel like a burden. The responsibility to serve others is so great that it pushes your own life and its ordinary and legitimate pleasure—like the joys of family life—into the background.

Mohatt: Healing or one's life's work is a question of destiny. Joe doubted. He was human, and human beings vacillate between seeking certainty and accepting uncertainty, wondering if we are on the right track and wishing we could get away from what we know we must do. He told me that often he wished he could be ordinary. He could just "retire" and live like everyone else. Days upon days, nights upon nights led to fatigue and exhaustion, but he was true to his vision and to the source of his power. I would hone a bit what you said about will and substitute the English word *desire.* The healer is often chosen against his desire. Joe was chosen, and he chose. His work was predicated on his full consent.

Gaudillière: We began to think about this question of sources and discovered that what we do as psychoanalysts is just the modern version of very, very ancient practices. We did not realize this at first, but through our lives with much influence from Joe. Remember, Jerry, when we met with our friend the French archaeologist of Greece who attended the conference in Reims where Joe and Peter Catches and Rose Ella Stone presented?[3] Later he gave us a paper of his thoughts about how what he heard from the medicine people was connected to the oracles of Greece. Our ancestors listened for the spirits to speak.

Davoine: But the Roman Catholic church came and wiped out the tradition. We were like the Indians when we were tribal people, and our languages, our medicine men and women, and our beliefs were destroyed. But like all these beliefs, they did not cease to exist. They have gone underground and return in our dreams. Rituals have been replaced by Christian rituals that take place in the same time frame and celebrate those transitions. Churches were built on temples, which were built on tribal ritual sites. Early saints replaced our spirits; guardian angels, our personal helpers. So in order for us to find our destiny, as you call it, we had to find our vision, which is tied to place.

Mohatt: This resonates with Joe's sense of the importance of place. To find one's power demands in some way to know one's place and those people who can teach us about our own traditions. He said that it was very difficult for him to travel here and there and heal. It would have been much better for the people to come to his home, where he knew his medicines. His home was where his spirits were comfortable. It was the place from which they spoke. His geographic area has its own sacred places at which one can contact the transcendent.

So to find this tribal core, we have to find our home and know our place. Louie Leader Charge is an elder on the Rosebud Reservation. When I was a young guy there and just beginning my work, I was visiting with him and out of the blue he said, "You know, you have to be buried over there where you came from."

I said, "What do you mean?"

He replied, "You can't find peace without finding your home, so maybe you better go back over there and find it." He meant the place of my ancestors in Europe.

Davoine: This question of place has affected my practice. For example, I now allow my dreams to enter into the sessions. If I have a dream that I believe relates to our work, I tell my patient the dream. This often serves to move our work forward. I don't share them as a form of self-disclosure in order to try to say to the person, "Oh, I also experienced that," but rather as an interpretation or to mark an important message.

Obviously, in order to make use of dreams, I have to be very attuned to my own dreams. More and more, I find that I have dreams that tell me what must be said in the session to help complete part of the patient's narrative.

Although I have always been oriented in this way, my work was very affected by the time in Manitoulin when Joe told us the story of the fish and the man. After that meeting we went to your cabin, and on the last day right before we left, you did a little ceremony by the lake. You prayed with the cedar for our safe return and thanked the spirits of the lake for their help. You spoke to the spirits of the lake and asked them to help us in our work so that we could hear and understand them. You connected your prayer to the fish story and our work. When I returned to France, I had a vivid dream of the spring in our woods in France.[4] In this dream there is a dog who is buried near the spring. At the grave of my dog, there was the spirit of the creek and spring. There was this white face speaking to me with bubbles coming out of its mouth. It was talking to me about the book I was writing, what to do in connection to the book, about the fish, and talking to me about this place in our country from which we can hear the stories of the spirits. So after this dream I decided that the forest and spring had to be in my book. In the book I speak of the forest and the spring and the importance of connection to our spiritual sources in nature, but not generically nature. The nature of our home, of the sacred places from which we can hear the ancient spirits.

Mohatt: Really, this question of place is one of our relation to those forces who come through nature to us. As Ken says, we have to belong to a place. Wendell Berry, the nature writer, said that once he decided to return to Kentucky to make it his permanent home after years away from it, he became immersed in the place. He learned everything about its flora and fauna, about the dips and hills of the land on which he lived. He was not a visitor but a resident who grew into a real relationship with the place. I think on the spiritual level it is exactly the same. Visions are not abstractions. The practice of healing takes place in a place that is part of the problem and solution—this particular social setting with its traditions, gaps, and power.

John Berger has written beautifully about that in his fictional works about French peasants. His hero in *The Value of Money* talks about his place in ways that remind me of the continuity you have achieved in relation to your place. Marcel is describing his thoughts while unharnessing his horse, Gui-Gui:

> The horse's stall, the large table in the kitchen, the ceiling-high cupboard where the gnole bottle was kept, the cellar door—because the bottle was empty and he had to go and fill it from the demijohn—the wardrobe in the bedroom from which he took his shotgun, the bed on which he sat to change his boots, these wooden things, so solid to the touch, worn and polished, protected from the snow, placed in the house before he was born, built with wood that came from the forest which, through the window, was now no more than a darkness behind the falling snow, reminded him with a force, such as he had never experienced before, of all the dead who were his family and who had lived and worked in the same farm. He poured out a glass of gnole for himself. The feeling came back into his feet. His ancestors were in the house with him.

Gaudillière: That is why Joe had to rush the ceremony in Canada. The people were still grappling with their responsibility as a society to recover their own traditions. They were not sure, unable to connect with the ways, the spirits of their ancestors. To recover is not an idea; recovery of healing traditions demands engagement in a process that happens in a particular place to which we belong.

Kazenmaier: Joe taught us about this in a new way. He came to Germany after we had two other medicine men who had given us great help in finding our own spirituality. We use Lakota ways to open us, and we have learned from them. But, unlike the other medicine men, Joe did not lecture or say much. He listened and answered questions and taught through examples. Sometimes it was just a short sentence, and you had to listen very closely or you didn't catch it.

Gentner: Like the old man who came to the camp.

Kazenmaier: It happened at a meeting we had outside in this field. We had a big circle of all the camp members who all came together to have this lecture. We had an additional chair there.

Gentner: It was just standing there.

Kazenmaier: We just wanted to put it away, and Joe said to me, "No, just leave it there. Somebody is coming." A short time after he said this an old man came by.

Gentner: A really old man . . .

Kazenmaier: A really old man who was out of this region. We didn't know him. He came by, and Joe asked us to invite him and ask him to join the circle. So we did. Then they started to talk, and then Joe asked us later to see if the old man would share something with us. So we asked him, and he began to share with us some things about war and what impact war had on him. He was not very wealthy and in fact may have been a poor old man. But he began to talk about how people needed to live in peace and what an ugly impact war can have. And then Joe thanked him for this. Later Joe told us that whenever you have a bigger meeting you should invite an elder.

Gentner: We are lacking of elders. We have none.

Kazenmaier: This has been a problem for us that we don't have any who had gone before us, so there is no one to ask advice from or tell us don't do this or that. So Joe gave us this advice. And what was really nice was that the elder came back and brought shoes with him and said that he had noticed that there were people there who could really use some shoes, so he gave them to our people.

Gentner: Because we have some really poor people there. So he gave these as gifts. So we had this wonderful experience that we never had before of having our own elder there.

Mohatt: An elder from your own people who could teach you.

Gentner: Yes, it was very new and very wonderful because many of our young people stay away from their homes because of alienation from their parents or the older people. So it was good to experience that which would bring that back to us that we can learn from our own elders.

Kazenmaier: This was quite unusual for him to show up, since we were in a pretty remote area, so it was a rather dramatic teaching.

Katz: For me, there has been this big unanswered question about home, because I have been so mobile, living here and there. Verna, my wife, knows where she is from — Saskatchewan. Her ancestors lived and died there, and that is where she plans to live and die. Saskatchewan is the home of her people, but I have always been moving from place to place. So I asked Joe a question after we made a visit to the physical site on Rosebud of his ancestors down by Spring Creek, his "home place." "Verna has this deep sense of home in Saskatchewan, but I have moved here and there. I wonder where is my home?"

Joe thought, then said to me, "Well, for me, home is in the heart." That was said right after we had visited his ancestral home place, and the place where he grew up. He didn't say that place was his home or that Rosebud was his home. He told me you get to know where home is as you get in touch with where your heart is, and as you listen to your heart.

Mohatt: Once you make this choice of home or establish such a quality to your relationship with both the place and the tradition-bearers of your home, it means responsibility to a people and community. The old man vividly demonstrated this when he brought those shoes. A realization grows that from this community and in this place we will learn the meaning of our dreams and visions for our community.

Of course, this was Joe's big struggle for nearly thirty years of his life and was so eloquently stated by the hobo: "You won't find your home over here." His home and his source of power and responsibility was right there in Rosebud where his heart was.

Once the choice is made, then you become a relative to each other. This carries the responsibility of reciprocity. When Joe came to visit us after our home burned down in 1990, we would go out to the place and see how the building was going. The mornings we spent taping his life or going to class, and afternoons we would do other things. During one of the ceremonies we had while he was there, he told us: "I am going to sing a song now and this song is for you. You sing it right before you set foot in the new house, before you move in any furnishings." The next day we made a tape of it, and I practiced that song, because I have a tough time remembering lyrics and tunes except in a group, sort of a good ear in context but a bad memory. Joe was telling me that we had to honor this home and this gift of the fire. It focused us on a choice of where to put our heart, and he told us that if we were to stay, we had to honor this place.

Katz: When Verna and I asked Joe to marry us, he told us what we would need for the ceremony, including a pipe and star quilt. Verna and I discussed with each other how we would get a pipe and a star quilt, because we didn't want to have to buy them. Well, the next day, just before we were leaving to go back to Saskatchewan, Joe and Vickie asked us to sit down and have another cup of coffee. So we sat at the kitchen table, and Vickie went into the bedroom and returned with a quilt and a pipe. Joe said that they wanted to help us get started on our marriage ceremony, so they simply gave us these two key elements for the ceremony. I was so struck by how simply they gave these things to us. We were really sitting with our relatives and receiving a gift from them. As Joe had said to Verna and me several days before, "Vickie and I want you to call us Mom and Dad."

Mohatt: I am very struck by how much this idea of relationship heightens one's sense of responsibility and the importance of giving back and giving thanks. This was basic to healing for Joe and became for him a source of both his hope and his pain.

He was disappointed at times at how much further communities needed to grow, but he was fundamentally optimistic. He said that in time the power would come, maybe right away or maybe in the next generation. He knew this very personally because his own children might or might not carry on his work. He was careful to accept where he and others were and knew how he and the community were intertwined. Maybe one generation will not become healers, not because the people are reluctant but because the community is not ready for them. They would not have this oneness of mind, ṫawaċiŋ waŋjila.

When Jean-Max spoke of the kettle dance, I remembered how people on Rosebud were perplexed by why Joe did not complete the ceremony as they expected. Some thought he could have done it and was reluctant and too shy to do it. Others thought he "chickened out." Few seemed ready to accept that he completed the most important aspect of his vision because he told the truth about the community. He knew if he did not, the ceremony would perpetuate the falsity. If he had done what they desired, to pull the head out of the kettle, the incompleteness and divisiveness of the community would become stonelike and immutable. So he did the unexpected to teach a lesson. He was true to his vision as a contrary, a heyoḱa; he refused to be true to the desire of the community.

Hollow Horn Bear: I felt the ṫawaċiŋ waŋjila and demand for the truth when our pipe came home, both the oneness and the ability to tell the truth and take responsibility. We re-membered, re-linked. We became and are becoming a tioṡp̄aye, a large family with a future, a past, and a present. We all have places in it. At the center of our tioṡp̄aye is our great-grandfather's pipe. It links us all to our place. The healing began in great earnest when we could link ourselves through this pipe which was so much part of our place, our community. We must speak truth. The truth may not please us or be what our image or desire was, but when it is spoken we can live in new ways.

Mohatt: You were, and are, not bound by a lie or a secret. You are free to speak the truth. You are challenged to become responsible.

Hollow Horn Bear: Exactly. My father told me he could not speak for the pipe. He told the truth to the community. We could now start becoming a community and family-based on who we really are. Joe to me was a healer and a teacher. Maybe they are both the same, I don't know, but I do know that he was my teacher.

Maalia (chapter 12): The truth is what so many of those who are "off" tell the community. They fill a role that no one else can do. Like one time in a community I lived in there was a brutal murder and rape. At the wake for this young woman, the father of the murderer came to the wake. In the same room there was an alcoholic who was drunk. When the man sat down, she went over to him and began to speak in a very loud voice about what this man had done by protecting his son when he had done other terrible things, how he got him out of the trouble and never made him responsible. So it took a drunk to tell the truth. Unfortunately, no one else could tell this truth.

Mohatt: So without the heyoǩa or those who can speak the truth and are expected to we have forms of insanity that give people the space and voice to tell us what is true about our society.

Davoine: That is why we study the clowns and the harlequins of our society, because they became the people who may have been shamans or speakers of the truth in our society. Now we have the psychotics who speak the unspeakable and are labeled crazy. We find that what we must uncover to heal them is something about the social system, the family, the community which is a secret. It needs to be spoken by the person, and we give them the space in the analysis to do so.

Gaudillière: Therapist comes from *theraps* in Greek and is the ritual substitute. In the *Iliad* Patroklos puts on Achilles' armor and battles Hector and is killed. He becomes his alter ego and stands by his side. The critical similarity in the drama is one of epic proportions: Patroklos is one who acts out and speaks for Achilles and allows death to come so that Achilles lives to fight again. He is only the *therapon* if he does not go beyond Achilles; in a way, as you say, he doesn't get in the way. Gregory Nagy in his book on the Achaeans makes the case that the poets are the *therapon* of the Muses, so the *therapon* becomes the person who can stand in the place of the other. So therapists or analysts become the ritual doubles.

Mohatt: Risky business! The therapist is in the midst of the epic of the family and community, searching with the patient for the words that will kill something that has ruptured the family through the community. The patient will no longer have to take the responsibility for the silence of the family and community. I have a patient who is desperately searching for the meaning of so much loss and death in her family because of a deep fear of the inevitable nature of this. Her family is one that was shamed and left alone by the community after one parent killed the other and himself. To recount that history of the family is not enough. One has to enter the story with the person to discover how to kill the transmission of shame and inevitability and to find a new way of living.

White Hat: Nothing is free! I tell my students in Lakota spirituality classes that in our Lakota world there is nothing free. One must return. If one does not do so by choice, then one will have to return in other ways, in other times. Joe and the other medicine men lived this way, and they taught us these very serious things with humor.

Mohatt: One evening I was at Robert Stead's and we were sitting by the sweat lodge discussing this idea, and Gene Crow Good Voice Sr. started to tease me about whether I would be ready to leave my wife if, when I went up on the hill, they told me to do so, that they wanted this from me and they were ready to make me a healer. He then told me a story about someone who had this happen to him. After he finished, all the guys joked about who would then get Robby, but the point was made. What was I ready to exchange for what I might want? The teaching was through humor, example, and story but always gave me room for choice. So for the patients, maybe the issue is not so much again only what happens in the sessions, but to be a spiritual double, one has to open up a way to live a life in a new way. One thing that humor does is highlight the incongruity of now and the dual nature of life—"Things are seldom as they seem" is a line that I never forgot from a Gilbert and Sullivan musical.

Gaudillière: My first experience on Rosebud was with Gilbert Yellow

Hawk in his sweat lodge. I did not speak a word of Lakota, and everyone was talking and Jerry translated only a few words, but they were just laughing and joking. How do you say? Teasing. And I didn't know why, but I understood it. They were laughing, and it made sense to me without my understanding a word they spoke. I began to understand better the importance of laughter for my own practice. They taught me that very clearly.

I remember years later we were in Ontario at your place, Jerry, and one day Joey and I and our friend Henry, who is a social worker for small children and for those with various handicaps, were sitting on the shore. We sat for two hours, and Joey talked. We never once made eye contact. He had the capacity to be without being present. He had really smooth gestures, a smooth voice, no accent, no eye contact, but with his classical sense of humor, he would make a very unexpected statement, like about the pot of soup being too hot to put his hand into. He could just sit and think and free associate and speak. We could take from this what we needed without feeling any persuasion.

Davoine: He was really an intellectual. He had this great capacity to think about very complex ideas without any hint of trying to convince or cajole, just to think through in this smooth way of which Jean-Max speaks. He was a teacher.

Muller: The first time I met the medicine men, you brought me out to do a workshop with the community action program workers who were youth and dropout-prevention counselors. Some were counselors, and others medicine men. Robert Stead and Collins Horse Looking were two of them. I think Johnny Strike was another. We used a Thematic Apperception Test (TAT) and some TAT stories from white folks that I had and some from Indian kids you had.[5] The clinical level of discussion impressed me. I learned much about reading the story, the life of another human being. There was this natural ability to understand and interpret narrative, the story. My sense is that the medicine men and their helpers openly lived within the narrative form and so the stories they heard in the TATs were very easy to interpret.

Mohatt: I remember this very well, and it was the reason or part of it that you then enlisted these guys to help you teach in the Sinte Gleska University human services training program.

Muller: On a very practical level these were and are the clinicians of the reservation and should have been the teachers of the future clinicians.

Gaudillière: In fact, I think I told you, Jerry, that Joe and the other medicine men were your analysts. Just as in our training we have to go through both a training analysis and supervision, you had the benefit of their wisdom, of so many ceremonies and so many chats before and after these. We came to learn and share, to establish a relationship. What we have learned has helped us as clinicians.

Mohatt: I had never thought about that until you mentioned it, but it is true. I have been very fortunate to learn directly from these men how they thought about things. One day I was sitting with Stanley after seeing a client and decided I needed to speak to him about what was happening between the psychotherapy and the client's use of Lakota ritual. He told me that I should talk to the medicine man who was working with the same client. The same afternoon the medicine man, Bill Schweigman, came to my office, and I broached the subject. He did not say anything at the time but said he would come back the next day and talk to me. I waited the next day, and he showed up in mid-afternoon and began to talk: "Psychic power and spiritual power are two worlds, and you work with the psychic power and me with the spiritual. Sometimes they cross over, and we each use both and stand in both spaces, but we have our main works. Neither one is against the other. There is no conflict. I think you can help this young man while he sees me, but maybe he will have to choose one or the other road. This is up to him. We should continue to talk." The medicine man did not mix up our work, did not want to force either of us to equivocate. He acknowledged there might be a time at which the client would need to devote his time to one or the other of the traditions and other times when he could engage in both simultaneously.

Hollow Horn Bear: Joe taught by putting me in situations from which I could learn, and he watched me very closely but never directed me. He told me stories and taught me songs. He gave us advice through stories about how things were supposed to be in the world. Like he taught us a lot about childrearing. He told us that when we prepare a meal we should do so without anger, because this is nourishment that you are giving to your children and that they receive not only nourishment but it is like medicine. If it is done correctly, the food becomes stronger and affects them more deeply—spiritually. He told us that they will not go to the doctors so much if one prepares food and eats their meals like they were a ceremony.

Mohatt: He, Stanley, Abel Stone, Narcisse Eagle Deer, and the other singers and helpers as well as all of the medicine men really were teachers who believed in stories, example, and experience as the best teachers. Otto Will, who was a friend and a well-known psychoanalyst, said healing, according to Harry Stack Sullivan, Otto's analyst, was education, an educative experience. Education and healing are expandable resources because others can then support and teach. This increases healing resources for the community. Joe looked for ways that healing resources are expandable. One of the main ways is for more people to do that which will make them healthy, and another is to support others in need of help. In our Western terms we call the first prevention and the second social support.

Katz: It is also like you said earlier about healing outside of specific healing rituals or sessions. The rituals are meant as moments to encourage the people toward becoming responsible, to healing each other in everyday life. This idea of healing resources becoming renewable and expanding and accessible to all is what I experienced as a fact of life among the Ju' hoansi [Bushmen] of the Kalahari. I've called it a process of "synergy," and when this synergy of healing resources prevails—bringing more healing to the people—the community itself becomes a healing environment.

Mohatt: What you say about healing as expandable and that indigenous healing is built on a model of synergy, not a paradigm of scarcity, helps us understand Joe's message about the body and medicine, the singleness of purpose (ṫawaċiŋ waŋjila) as the critical ingredient for healing. That is my view. Joe saw that the real healing happens within the people as they become more empowered and aware of their control and responsibility toward each other. What Albert, Ken, and Duane have all said reinforces that Joe's life influenced them in ways that they are now healing resources for the community. So his single work created multiple opportunities for others to find help beyond him.

White Hat: This is very true about Lakota healing and ritual. Look around today and compare it with fifteen years ago [around 1980] in term of sweats, vision quests, and the sun dance. There are sun dances each week in the summer. Fifteen years ago there was one or two per summer. Now many people have sweats. Young people, elders who were Christians for years now attend and do the rituals. My brother Isadore was such a person. He watched. He was a strict Catholic, but he supported me and then he began to practice and did the sun dance. Today we learned responsibility and some of us made a choice to take this responsibility. It was scary to begin with, but today I am glad we did it.

Mohatt: Isadore told me that this was a moment of great meaning because he had broken so many promises in his life, but he kept this promise and completed the sun dance. I was very moved by what he said. These medicine men, singers, and the community that held onto the rituals and took them underground have seen the multiplication of their efforts. The opportunity for young people to achieve meaning in the vision quest, cleansing and freedom in the purification rite of the sweat lodge, and the opportunity for commitment and sacrifice for the people in the sun dance are now available to everyone. This is a powerful example of how access has been increased and expanded.

I would like to change the subject for a moment and get back to the idea of a story, because in some way we all and many others became part of the story. Too often writing about healers has been either on an anthropological level or in terms of "new age" searching. There are some exceptions. The Menninger Clinic has had a long-term interest in learning from cross-cultural contacts. What I am addressing is the serious question of cultural appropriation. It comes up when nonindigenous individuals take these materials and use them for their own ends, research, new age practice, herbalism . . . To get beyond the level of appropriation, we had to become part of an exchange process and become peers in sharing, to become learners and teachers.

Davoine: Perhaps because our point of departure was to exchange, I have been able to discover many simple and practical ways. It has not been an appropriation of such-and-such so that I try to do things like a medicine man. Rather, I have learned to listen and react in new ways. We did not study Joe or Gilbert or Norbert. Rather, we spoke to them as peers and colleagues, sharing our cases and hearing about their cases. We came to Rosebud, and they came to France. We met in between at other places. These were very special moments for us because they gave us ideas and courage to follow some rather unconventional paths.

For example, we were speaking before about how Joe and the other medicine men were masterful at mixing humor and seriousness. Your description of Maalia captures this. They could bring everyone to a point of excitement and then all of a sudden the humor comes, the joke, the play on words, the heyok̄a. For me, I am now freer. I can bring humor to my patients so that a new frame is created, one maybe a little lighter or one that signals that life does go on and has its twists. We did not take a technique from Joe or one of the medicine men but learned important lessons that helped our practice.

Katz: Issues of cultural appropriation become very important in this work between people of different cultural backgrounds. I was at a sweat with Joe one time and there was a man from Germany there. He apologized to Joe before the sweat, saying he was sorry that he could not speak very well in English; therefore, when each of us prayed during the ceremony, he could pray only in German. Joe said, "No problem, no problem. I don't think the Creator will have a problem, because he understands all languages."

Joe never said to me: "You are just like an Indian." Other people have said that to me, but Joe never did. But what he did say was that our blood was the same and our spirits were the same. We are the same at the level of blood and spirit. For me, what Joe meant was that one's medicine or power was received and practiced in one's own way. The most powerful use of medicines or healing power is for someone to be able to use them in the context in which they were meant to be used. Joe never meant that he and I practice healing the same way. He could not give us his ways, but we had to find our way for ourselves. So we do not appropriate, we go on this search for ourselves.

Joe and I shared. We walked the land together and were buddies. And he never said, hey, you should treat me like a medicine man. I had a deep sense of awe with his work, but we had an ordinary relationship.

Joe had the capacity to bring traditions together respectfully, to see the whole as connected, even in planning his funeral. To me, it is the lesson of acceptance. During the days of the wake there was a peyote ceremony in the basement, a Catholic Mass in the living room, and at the same time a sweat going on outside. It was a very easy mix, nothing hidden. He planned his funeral in a way that said there is no one way to the Creator. I felt that in his house powerfully at the time of his death.

Mohatt: So we have to be true to ourselves and can find our sources with Joe's help, but fundamentally we are human beings together with each other. Our relationship was paramount. You told me about how you and he would cry when you left and how he would stand and continue to wave as you drove away. I would always try to stop and see him on my way from our ranch to Rapid City to drive back here. There was the enormous capacity for him to be with me as a brother, a father, a friend, a teacher. But he pushed me to be the same to him. He pushed me toward becoming much more of a human being who was true to himself.

Jean-Max spoke earlier about something that struck a very important chord for me as another example of how this complex relationship taught him how to work in new ways. He talked about how Joe spoke smoothly and without pushing us. You, Dick, talked about this ordinary quality of the relationship. How family and relationship was at the heart of healing. He was there as himself. Kim Chernin, a Berkeley analyst, wrote a book on her own analyses with three different analysts, but in it she talked about having Otto Will as a supervisor during her last analysis. Her experience was that Otto was really Otto. He was authentically himself with no airs, pretensions, jargon, exaggeration, but was present to her and himself. For her as an analyst, this was most critical for her growth; she learned she had to become that way with her own patients. So Joe and our work with these healers brought us closer to our real self, less the mirrored or false self, never to try to be someone else or act like someone else, never to pretend or act "as if."

Katz: What Joe has given me — along with other elders and healers like Danny Musqua in Saskatchewan, Ratu Noa in Fiji, and Oma Djo in the Kalahari — is the permission to be myself and to heal in the way that comes through me. Those healers never said do it this way or that way. They didn't even say you might try it this way or that way. What Joe gave me was a feeling that I could heal in the way I have to do it. I am profoundly affected by what I learned from Joe or the others, but it is not in the specifics of Joe's way of doing ceremonies or any other's ceremony. Joe gave me permission to do the healing. I know how to do, and part of what I know how to do is influenced by his healing work, but the influence comes through his sense of being during healing, his love and respect for the healing work, not in the specifics of his ceremony—which was his.

Gaudillière: I connect this to what we mean in French when we say "*Se croire!*" or "*Ne te crois pas!*" It means "Don't believe yourself!" It can mean that we should not believe we are somebody special. We often say it to children to mean that you are only a little boy. We mean that we cannot accumulate experiences. You have to be in the here and now. So when humor comes into the ceremony, whether it is in our sessions or the lowaŋp̄i, we push ourselves right into the immediacy of the present. We must relate and speak right now and not later. Joe was this type of person. He was always present, whether in the ceremony or in a conversation.

Mohatt: My experience with Joe, as well as healers from other cultures, and in my own practice has been that the more one tries to be anything, humble or strong, the less likely one will become how he or she wants to be. There appears to be an inverse relationship between desire and achievement of healing. Dick talks of the straight path, but it is not a single set of moral prescriptions of the collective. At its heart is humility and struggle for authenticity to one's vision and purpose.

Katz: Joe taught me about the quiet way. We all know how quiet and unassuming he was. He never presented himself to me as "a healer." In my first visit to Rosebud for the healing conference you held, Jerry, I noticed all the other Lakota and Navajo medicine men who were attending that gathering. Some of them sought me out and talked to me and invited me to their ceremonies, but not Joe. He was there, but he blended in with everyone. He was sort of invisible. He never called attention to himself. From the very beginning of my time with him until the end, that quality was a consistent and a constant theme. The lesson was in the quietness of his work.

I have learned that same teaching from other healers—that healing is quiet work. Healers are not supposed to promote themselves or call attention to themselves, but people seek them out when they need them. Joe really taught that through the way he lived. He never went looking for people. People found him, and he responded to them fully.

Gaudillière: I think of it as "the power of the powerless." We have to undress, in a sense. We have many, many dresses or clothes, maybe they are our fears or memories or experiences. If you have very little you need less time to undress, and if you have more you need a long time to undress. It is really very hard to be in a healing space and wear many dresses.

Mohatt: Joe told Stanley and later me that when he takes the pipe from a person or receives the request for a ceremony, he must feel empty. He must have an "indifference," which is a lack of his desire. He can't become cluttered with his desire or he will interfere with the possibility of healing. I find that in my doing therapy the more I think I have found the clever interpretation or reflection, the less likely it will work. I am more preoccupied with myself, rather than hearing the other. I need this indifference to open myself to the unexpected that a client brings or for an experience to educate.

Hollow Horn Bear: One day Joe came to my home and said he needed to go to Minneapolis that evening to doctor a little eight-month-old baby that was into its third coma. The doctors want to pull the life support, but the family did not want to do so. Well, Joe doctored the child and was able to bring it back and heal the child. During the ceremony I was one of the singers. There were other drums there, and we began very quickly with the ceremony, maybe, because of the emergency situation. I could hear Joe in the center calling upon his helpers, talking them into coming out there. But all of a sudden it was very silent. It appeared no other singers were helping me. I felt like I was on my own and heard this voice. It did not sound like my voice. It came from somewhere, everywhere, and the sound of my drum was not the sound of my drum. So I looked around and here I could see inside of the ceremony, but it was in a haze. I could see forever, but there was nothing to see. Suddenly, as I was singing, my song come out of my mouth like a light, like a beacon coming out of my mouth. I thought to myself, I should stop singing, so I looked around to see who this was. I stopped and looked below me, and the space extended on and on. There was a cold cement wall behind me which I reached for, wanting to touch it so I would have some anchor. But, when I leaned back, it was gone. I wasn't nervous or scared but just kept singing alone. When they got to the last song, I was back in the ceremony.

After the ceremony I asked Joe, "What happened tonight?"

He said, "You tell me about it."

"Well," I said, "if you know, then you tell me."

Joe said that whenever there is a ceremony he sets up his altar in manner that is correct for the power of those spirit friends who will help him. To do this he uses something on the altar like the blacktail deer or water or little hoop or whatever is on the altar. It is through this symbol that they can make connection. Tonight it was the drum, but he didn't have time to tell me. When this happened, the spirits came to him through my drum and took me to places to show me things and perhaps teach me new songs. He said if the singers become afraid, they may decide after the experience that they may never sing again. They may cut themselves off from the learning and power of such experiences. So Joe was telling me that part of this education is not just advice, it really is experience. For one to experience such things, you have to be open, anchored to this world, and brave. You have to suspend your judgment.

Katz: Joe had the capacity to make dramatic, powerful spiritual experiences very ordinary—and, therefore, very accessible and effective. During one of the first ceremonies I went to of Joe's, my deceased father came to me. He actually came, as real as could be. He stood by me and talked to me and we talked. Then my deceased spiritual teacher, Mr. Nyland, also came to me. Again, he was really there—in flesh and blood. He just stood there next to me and we talked. And then I was visited by my son Alex, who was at that time a young boy. I saw him grow, and as he grew he became first an adolescent and then a young man. At each stage of growth, he was there, actually there, a real person, and we talked at each stage—and he was showing me how strong and beautiful he was to become. It was very powerful. Much was said to my deceased father and Mr. Nyland, much that was not said when they were on earth. And I was filled with awe. I felt pushed to speak to Joe, telling him something like, "This is just incredible!" I felt that I had to talk to him right away.

My first words to Joe were, "What happened?" At the very same time I told him what had happened to me. He responded, "Yes, that's good. That's what happens." I was thinking, did he hear me? Then I realized that he had heard me and he was trying to calm me down and tell me that what I had experienced was not "extraordinary." These supposed different worlds of the "living" and the "deceased," or the past, present, and future, are not separate but a seamless web. Of course, the deceased and those of the future come to visit you. But for me, since it was the first time something like that had happened, I needed to be brought back to the ordinary, in order to fully experience the depth of the communications I had received.

Mohatt: He made it very human, very common and safe for you. I think he felt very secure that it happened in the ceremony. If this was happening in your everyday life, then he may not have treated it in the same way because there is a place for these experiences, which is ritual, the healing ceremonies, vision quests, sweats. They are places of interpretation or of learning, frames for such experiences. The ceremony taught you about how to face the uncanny, the spiritual, the transcendent. This capacity to confront the uncanny demands a special type of realization and understanding.

Davoine: Remember the time Joey, Stanley, Peter Catches, Tillie, and Victoria came to Paris and Joey gave a seminar that Françoise Dolto attended? She was the greatest of the child analysts in Paris. During this seminar Stanley and Joey told us a story about a ceremony in a hospital in Nebraska of a child who had a serious disease. He said that during this ceremony the child was brought into a hospital room with all his IVs and so forth in him. During the ceremony, which was in the dark, his body left the bed and was illuminated as it moved around the room above the people.

We asked Françoise Dolto what she thought of this. It does sound like an apparition or something out of our rational world, like what you just spoke about, Duane and Dick.

Gaudillière: She said to us that this was precisely her experience with the autistic and terribly disturbed children she treated. You remember she would hold the infants in her arms, and she could feel at their place the roots of the imaginary. She saw it as light and dark, as primary opposites that were in a separate space. She was able to see and heal in that space. The space where this exists for us is the collective. The child is not alone. It is not her solitary experience, but one of being enmeshed in the society where this primary opposition lives on, in the family and the community. Françoise Dolto simply told us: "Yes, I see light and dark. I see the children as such, and it is in this space of the nonverbal that I must speak." She spoke to these little children. She told them stories, and they got better.

Hollow Horn Bear: Joe knew that such experiences would help me learn how to work with the spiritual. But he told me to be careful not to become lost in the other world, to become afraid or maybe seduced by it.

Mohatt: Françoise Dolto brought this world to her patients and to her students through her stories and speech. These events were not some form of hocus-pocus. She, like Joe, used her human powers to address these oppositions. She healed the children who had experienced something without words while they were in the womb. Rather than leaving this gap that the children had experienced in the womb, she created a relationship of communication; she repeated the moments in new ways by holding these disturbed infants and finding a story to tell them.

With adults it was the same: they had to be grounded in the relationship of a human community, able to relate, before they moved to the spirit world.

Katz: Once we brought someone to Joe to be doctored. But that person was very agitated, at times delusional. Joe said he could not take him into the sweat or ceremony in this condition, because he first needed to be with other humans to be comfortable with them. So Joe said, "Let's take him over to the sun dance ground so he can be around people." You have to calm the person down first.

Mohatt: We had the same thing happen with a hospitalized schizophrenic person who was in the state hospital in South Dakota. They brought him to the sweat from the hospital, and he couldn't stay in it but crawled out under the coverings and ran away. He wasn't enough with the human community in order to be with the spirit community. As you say, they are seamless, maybe two sides of the same coin.

Black Bear: I am reminded that, as Lakota, we believe that the child is primarily spirit prior to birth and is very intelligent. The children are genderless until around the fourth birthday, but are formed by hearing the sounds, the words, and the stories that the community tells while they are in the womb. It is their introduction into their community, their ground.

Mohatt: I was told that the child picks this particular family and community. Because of this, the responsibility rests on the people around the mother to treat the child as a guest, to treat the child (*činča*) with great respect. The child is a stranger to us and us to them. So we have to tell them about us so we can open up communication, a quiet, gentle, and loving communication. We need to begin to learn about them and feel and hear them.

Black Bear: Shocks and loud noises are bad for the unborn or young child. We don't want to startle them. We have to speak very softly and carefully, encouraging the child, loving the child, and welcoming the child to our world. The people often looked really closely at the child's body to see if there were birthmarks like those of relatives. Perhaps this is a child with a reincarnated spirit of a relative and with a destiny to rework their lives or bring their wisdom to us.

Mohatt: Such care allows us to communicate that we don't want them to decide not to come here or to come here and become the symbol of our gaps. It appears to me that Dolto was talking about this. She could see these stark oppositions in the youngest infants, and she could heal them. Also, when we speak of the first stage of healing being to reestablish our link to people, family, and relationships, we acknowledge that ruptures in relationship are at the heart of madness. Joe knew that in order to make use of the spirit world, the human world of the patient was the point of departure.

Black Bear: That is why, in a way, that we go to the sweat for healing. The ceremony of purification is reentering the womb, reliving its warmth and darkness, reexperiencing the pain and joy of leaving. We speak of this ceremony as one of birth repeated, where we all have another chance to welcome and be welcomed to this world.

Katz: Joe taught us that the spirits were our relatives and our friends. I didn't know this at first. Then one day in the sweat I realized that the reason the spirits were coming into the sweat was because they were related to us. The spirits want to help us because they are our relatives. In Fiji, people trace their lineage back, generation after generation, until they reach the time of the great gods—who are then seen as relatives. And when you see this, then you realize gods and the spirits are close at hand, and you can ask for their help when you really need it. This is opposed to concentrating on, for example, the flashing lights in ceremonies and wondering where they come from. The lights are there, but what is important is that we know them as relatives.

Mohatt: This means we are ready to be with patients as relatives, as humans, at whatever place they are, in whatever condition they are. We are on call for them. We can reach them through our sense of kinship as fellow human beings and family.

Davoine: Dolto had this capacity of finding the right stories for the children. I find that since I worked with the medicine men, that I have been much more open to finding stories and myths to use in the sessions. We are moving together in a story, and every so often a story from the past fits in very nicely.

Hollow Horn Bear: Stories certainly are powerful. My experience with the pipe of my great-grandfather is a good example of that. We as a community were relinked to our story. Our story began anew and now continues. This was a very powerful experience of healing.

Black Bear: Songs are also our stories. The songs in the ceremonies, the songs we sing to our children and grandchildren, the way in which we treat each other is like those songs, especially how we treat our young ones.

Mohatt: Therapy and healing is a process of narrative. We enter together into a story and move through it together. We punctuate it. We fill in the gaps. We explore the myths and legends that articulate the deepest meanings, and we capture what Harry Stack Sullivan called the "uncanny" in one's life (1953). In January 1991 Joe knew he had to move on, even though he was reluctant to do so. He felt pain leaving his family. He worried up to the end about what would happen to his children and grandchildren. In the end, unlike Black Elk, Joe did not seem as worried about the people being lost or the hoop broken as about the future of his family. The people were responsible for themselves. But Joe was concerned for his family. He knew his work had led to stark choices. He longed to be the typical family man but chose to serve the people. He made the choice, followed faithfully his vision, and served his people, because he felt it was best for his family. He never felt he was a hero. He felt very fallible. He regretted mistakes made with his children and wished it had been different. He was convinced that loyalty to his vision, faith in his destiny, and authenticity in his life were all choices he made in order that his family would live and be strong. So what is a real life, a life that leaves a deposit, as Stiller asked? Joe knew his story was part of a longer story of a family and a place. His work was a work of his own life. It was preceded by the work of his father and grandfather. Children or grandchildren, friends and relatives, would follow him with their own visions and work. Healing is not just for the duration of one's own life but for the duration of a family.

Notes

INTRODUCTION

1. Wallace Stegner, in *The American West as Living Space* (1987), captured the uniqueness of the West as more than simply geographical.
2. To make the account vivid, I have made Stanley's story the young girl's personal narrative.
3. A Lakota children's story, or *ohuŋk̄ak̄a,* tells how Ikt̄omi, the trickster, gets some ducks to come to shore and dance with their eyes closed. While they are dancing, Ikt̄omi begins to eat them. One duck sneaks a peek and sees what's happening; it warns the others, and they escape.
4. *Ao zi* was used as a derogatory reference to half-bloods who became assimilated.
5. Subsequently, Paula Lang, director of the Indian Health Service Mental Health Clinic, initiated meetings between the medical staff and the medicine men.
6. Stanley Looking Horse spoke of this in an interview in 1978 done by Stanley Red Bird as part of the National Institute of Mental Health project "Identity through Traditional Lakota Methods." The keeper of the pipe, Orville Looking Horse, caretakes the original sacred pipe given to the Lakota by the White Buffalo Calf Woman nineteen generations ago. It has been in the Looking Horse family for all these generations.

1. JOEIELA

1. In Lakota conversation, when men meet they often greet each other in a joking manner and have sayings that tell the person to come on over and sit down and begin to spill out his story. The words they use have strong images, such as speaking like a duck spreads his feet.
2. Lakota medicine men receive their powers through vision and are given instructions about which ceremonies they can perform. The powers listed here—e.g., the sacred clown (*heyok̄a*), the tie-them-up (*yuwípi*), the deer (*tah̄c̄a*), and the ghost (*wanaġi*)—are distinct, and each carries new responsibilities and the ability to do certain types of doctoring. Each medicine man has distinctive powers depending on his vision. Although common types exist, such as *waŋbli* (eagle) visions or *heyok̄a* (sacred clown/contrary) visions, each medicine man's vision is his and no one else's, each is unique, and the instructions given by his allies are for him only. To generalize to all other visions of a particular type would go beyond the particularity of one's own vision.
3. I discussed the reaction of Joe's father and grandparents with a number of

people who knew Joe, and I include the comments of two of them here. Albert White Hat knew Joe well, and it was his father who worked with Father Buechel to give Joe instructions for his first communion. Françoise Davoine is a French psychoanalyst who knew Joe well and visited the reservation with her family a number of times.

Albert White Hat: You know, for Joe's parents and grandparents, they knew what a difficult life a medicine man lives. They knew what the dream meant and the type of life it would be for Joe. My sense is that they wanted to protect him from this life and did not want him to take on that responsibility.

Françoise Davoine: Joe told us—or maybe it was Stanley—that Joe's parents did not want him to live that life because of its difficulties. He said they knew that his life would no longer be his own, that he would have to work all of the time, that he would have to face many illnesses, that his wife would live a life in which she cooked, prayed, and prepared ceremonies, and that they would have to stay away from powwows and groups. He said that his father and grandma did not want him to take on this responsibility.

4. *Mit̄ak̄uye oyas'iŋ,* all my relatives, is either spoken at the end of a prayer or serves as a prayer at certain points in a ceremony. When one leaves the sweat lodge or completes drinking the blessed water at a ceremony, one will say, "All my relatives." This prayer is for all of creation, our relatives: the animals, the people, the rocks and earth, all the living. In the Lakota world everything natural is alive and our relative. One does not say that rocks are inanimate; in fact, they were the first in creation and carry great power. It was the life blood of the rock, *inyan,* that gave creation form.
5. *Albert White Hat:* He was the same age as one of my older brothers and lived in Spring Creek like us. My mother and his father are cousins, so we grew up as relatives. We knew him for his gentleness and his being sort of on the side. He didn't grow up violent like we did. We rodeoed, raised hell, and drank. He drank too but didn't get involved in those other things we did. We were always riding horses and breaking horses and doing pretty violent kinds of activities. Joe, he sort of stood on the sidelines and watched. He would always avoid a confrontation whereas we looked for them or jumped right in, while Joe would withdraw from them. I think that is what we always sought. It was his friendliness and relaxed style that we all liked.

2. DESTINY AND LIFE'S PURPOSE

1. Duane Hollow Horn Bear tells us about himself in the next chapter. He commented on Joe's views about instant medicine men after reading what Joe said.

   Duane Hollow Horn Bear: One of the big dangers that Joe saw was these "instant medicine men." We would have people come to the sun dance or do a vision quest and then go back east and publicize themselves as medicine men. One even said he was sanctioned by Joe. This hurts us all. It is a long and an arduous process to become a healer, and there are no shortcuts.

There are a lot of rules to working with people. Sincerity is most fundamental, but one can get in over their head if they are not careful and hurt themselves, others, and give the Lakota a bad name. He would say, "There is someone watching." We must take care not to dishonor our ceremonies. He said that we should bring those who are doing this back to the reservation, feed them, and talk to them and try to get them back onto the right road.

4. STEPS AND MISSTEPS

1. *Haṡap̄a* literally means "black" (*ṡap̄a*) and "skin" (*ha*) and is the name given African Americans by the Lakota. Other races are also represented by physical characteristics: *sk̄a wiċaṡa,* "white man," for Euro-Americans; *peċoka haŋsk̄a,* "the long braid of the Chinese," for Asians. Euro-Americans are also known as *waṡiċu,* "those who steal fat," because the first white man was found stealing fat that was hanging near a village.

5. ALL OF MY RELATIVES

1. "All of My Relatives" (Mit̄ak̄uye Oyas'iŋ), the title of this chapter, is the name of a ceremonial prayer and a phrase that signals a person has completed his prayer. It acknowledges that we — humans, animals, and nature — are all relatives imbued with life and spirit. This is one of the key concepts of Lakota spirituality. White Hat (1999) discusses it in his book, providing a good explanation of how to understand the centrality of kinship, the connection between the sacred, and the common nature we share with all that has a spirit.

7. MARRIAGE, FAMILY, AND VISION

1. A Lakota medicine man refers to his spirit helpers as his friends; in the contemporary literature they are often called spirit allies or guardian spirits.

8. ORIGINS AND GIFTS BEFORE THE PIPE

1. This translation was provided by Albert White Hat.

9. THE FISH AND THE MAN

1. In 1988 the Ojibwe Cultural Foundation sponsored a seminar on psychotherapy and healing in a cross-cultural context. It was held at the Wikemikong Reserve's new health center in the new ceremonial space and was attended by Joe and Victoria Eagle Elk, Jean-Max Gaudillière and Françoise Davoine of France, Tillie Black Bear of Rosebud, and Mary Lou Fox-Radulovich and other staff of the reserves and area health and mental health professions. During one of the sessions Joe presented this case for the first time to us.
2. The following account is based on my notes from Joe, discussions with Frank's therapist, and the therapist's notes on the case. The therapist has chosen to be anonymous.
3. This detailed description is taken from notes of the young man's therapist.

10. LIFE AND STRUGGLES OF A MEDICINE MAN

1. In 1979 I interviewed the woman who was doctored by Eagle Elk about what happened. The tapes became part of the Sinte Gleska University archives on the Tiośp̄aye Project. She had suffered from rheumatoid arthritis and was completely cured of the devastating effects of the disease. She still had some discomfort at times but now had no deformations, significant pain, or lack of mobility. Her physician was also interviewed.
2. For a detailed description of yuwípi, see Lame Deer and Erdoes 1972. Much that has been written about such ceremonies makes all the healing ceremonies of the Lakota appear to be yuwípi ceremonies. This is inaccurate. Only those in which the person is tied and in which this set of spirit friends is present are yuwípi.
3. Ken Stands Fast commented on this ceremony: "You are out there and feel that energy, and you can almost feel what he goes through when he is sitting out there. He went away and stood in the dark, and I gave her the medicine. Healing cancer is strong, hard, a strong disease. So I felt a little of what he was feeling."
4. The following is based on what Eagle Elk, Stanley Red Bird, Albert White Hat, and Duane Hollow Horn Bear told me. I have constructed it as a narrative by Eagle Elk.
5. Mary Lou Fox-Radulovich was the director of the Ojibwe Cultural Foundation. She died in 1997 after a long and distinguished career in revitalizing and strengthening Ojibwe and Ottawa traditions. I introduced her to Joe Eagle Elk, and she invited him to come to the Ojibwe-Ottawa reserves of northern Ontario to doctor people and participate in meetings of elders and medicine men. He and Victoria went there periodically to hold ceremonies. Victoria continues this work.
6. The Tiośp̄aye Project, funded by the National Institute of Mental Health, was an experimental process designed by the medicine men to help a community return to subsistence roots, increase the use of traditional ways of resolving conflict, support Lakota rules for interpersonal and kinship behavior, and increase a community's sense of control over its destiny. The project showed that intervening in one community could significantly reduce the probability that social and psychological problems would increase. A full report can be found in Mohatt and Blue (1982).
7. When Eagle Elk set up his sacred center for a ceremony, he would put a small mound of earth in front of where he would sit. On this earth he drew in the symbol of the type of ceremony he would do, for example, an eagle. Joe carried a bit of earth from each new place he visited in his medicine bundle in order to combine the power and earth memories of all these places as well as to remember each when he prayed.
8. Bill Schweigman, another medicine man, also had a heart condition. I asked him why so many medicine men had poor health. He said to me: "Wap̄ośt̄aŋ [my Indian nickname, "hat"], you know why, somebody had to return

what's necessary to the spirits. The people do not do what they should, and we carry it in our bodies. The spirits take it out on us."

EPILOGUE

1. Jacques Lacan, who taught and practiced in Paris, was one of the most influential psychoanalysts of the twentieth century. His work was informed by Ferdinand de Sauserre and Claude Lévi-Strauss, and he interpreted Freud in terms of linguistics and structuralism.
2. Riggs is the only hospital in the United States that treats psychotics with long-term psychotherapy and psychoanalysis. A group of three of the staff came to Rosebud in the late 1970s after I had given a talk at Riggs and had consulted about some of my cases with Ed Podvoll, John Muller, Bill Richardson, and Otto Will.
3. Rose Ella Stone is an Inupiat healer. Peter Catches, now deceased, was an Oglala Sioux healer.
4. Davoine and Gaudillière spend a great deal of time in a forest area near Burgundy where they have built a small cabin. They have developed a deep knowledge of the forest, have bees for honey, and harvest mushrooms.
5. The Thematic Apperception Test is a projective personality test that shows a picture to the client, who then tells a story with a beginning, middle, and ending and describes how the person or persons in it are thinking and feeling. The story is analyzed psychologically to reveal pathology, intrapsychic and interpersonal conflicts, and personality dynamics.

Glossary of Lakota Terms

aṡk̄aŋ: Breast or cords and veins of the breast (Buechel 1979).
ċaŋup̄a: The sacred pipe. The origin of the pipe is central to Lakota spirituality. The story can be found in a variety of books, including Neihardt (1979) and Brown (1953).
ċekp̄a nup̄ap̄i: Literally, the two (*nup̄ap̄i*) twins (*ċekp̄a).* This is a *wowak̄aŋ,* or power, that Eagle Elk received in one of his later vision quests. He describes it in part 4, chapter 10. The power gave him the right to perform a ceremony for healing in which the two twin women spirits would serve as his friends or allies.
c̄ik'ala: Small, little.
eċun: To do; he does or she is doing something (White Hat 1999).
ehaŋt̄an: From, a shortened form of *ehaŋt̄ahan.*
haŋ: Yes, or used to signal agreement. *Ohaŋ* means okay.
hanbleċiye: The vision quest, traditionally done by fasting for four days and four nights and used as a rite of passage for young people at the advent of adolescence. It was also done by individuals who had a strong dream, in order to discover the meaning of it. Today the hanbleċiye is still actively done by many Lakota people. It can vary in length, depending on what the person commits himself to—one night, one day, one night and one day, etc. Each medicine man has his own way of instructing the person, but the structure of fasting from food and water while praying on a sacred hill is the core process. Typically, one prepares oneself over the previous year. Then four days before the vision quest, one fasts and does a purification ceremony each day. On the final day one does a purification rite and is placed on the hill by one's mentor. If he or she is a medicine person, the mentor holds a ceremony to support the person crying for a vision while he or she is on the hill. When one returns, one goes immediately into the sweat lodge and during the ritual tells the people what one saw. That night one has a thanksgiving ceremony to thank the spirits for their help. During this ceremony one relates to the people what one experienced on the hill.
heċanu: To do something.
heȟak̄a: Elk. *Heȟak̄a wowak̄aŋ* is sacred elk power.
hehaŋl: Then, at that place.
heyok̄a: The contrary, or sacred clown. A person who has had the vision of the contrary may have *wak̄aŋ k̄aġa* power (Powers 1986) or the responsibility to perform a ritual at certain times to help the people

pay attention to what is real and true. The contrary does things backward at these times. He walks backward, washes with dirt, and speaks in opposites. When the healer has the *heyoḱa wowaḱaŋ,* he doctors with the thunder spirits. One can hear his voice change in the ceremony, taking on an exaggerated form and then saying the opposite of what one would expect: for example, you will die and all your children will die, you will never see your grandchildren . . . The heyoḱa has always provided some comic relief for the people, but he also has the responsibility to speak and act in a way that reveals what is hidden and what the community does not want to recognize. Lame Deer and Erdoes (1972) describe the role very nicely. The *heyoḱa woze* is the ceremony that is done by the person who has had a heyoḱa vision, as described by Eagle Elk in this book.

hiŋhaŋ: Owl.

ho: An exclamation, "Well" or "Okay, listen." Buechel (1979) translates it as an interjection of affirmation, such as "Yes, all right."

hoċo: A shortened form of *hoċoḱa,* or center; originally, according to Buechel (1979), it was the center in front of a circle of tents or houses. In a powwow it is the center of the arbor. In an evening sing (*lowaŋṗi*) it is the place in the center where the medicine man sets up his altar and sits.

hoyewa yelo: "I speak to you in prayer" or "I send my voice out" (White Hat 1999). This phrase often occurs during ritual songs.

huŋḱa: A person made a relative by another, although not a blood relative who is part of the *tioṡṗaye.* This status carries all the rights and responsibilities of being a relative, including being addressed with particular relational terms and using the correct terms and behavior toward one's relatives.

ikṫomi: A spider, a trickster, or a spirit power used for *wapiyapi* (depending on context). In this book the last meaning is used to designate the ikṫomi power that Eagle Elk received through a vision quest and the *ikṫomi lowaŋṗi* or ikṫomi evening songs he performed.

iniḱaġa: Purification rite that is often called sweat lodge. Literally, the word means "to make alive." *Nipi,* the root word, means "they are alive." Brown (1953) and Lame Deer and Erdoes (1972) both do a very nice job of describing the structure and meaning of the ceremony.

iṡnala: Alone.

iṡna tiṗi: The place where one is alone. This is the place women go during their menstrual periods in order to pray and to be cared for. In the Lakota philosophy a woman is especially sacred during her period and possesses great power at that time. When a young woman had her first period, she would go to the tiṗi away from the community to meditate, pray, and learn about herself as a woman from older women. The cosmic and spiritual power of the moon is tapped during these moments. Because of this increase of power, menstruating women are not allowed to attend ceremonies or be near the pipe when it is being used. The Lakota are very concerned to avoid an overconcentration of power in one ceremony. It can harm the participants and particularly the medicine man.

iyeċet̄u: To be so, become so, to be as was expected; to come to pass or take place (Buechel 1979). That's the way it is.

iyesk̄a: Interpreter. Literally, it means "to speak white" or "to speak English." The medicine man is the interpreter of the spirits. He can understand their speech in order, during his rituals, to translate or interpret for us what they want us to know.

iyok̄ogna: In the middle, not too far to the right or left.

k̄ak̄a: Everyday word for grandfather, for addressing or referring to one's grandfather.

k̇aŋ: The blood veins in a body (White Hat 1999). Also the source of energy or power. *K̇aŋ* is the root word for *wak̇aŋ,* or sacred energy or mysterious power.

kaŋak̇p̄a: To let blood with a sharp instrument in a ceremony, as described in part 2, chapter 6. It was often done each spring to let the old blood out and new blood flow more freely.

k̄awiŋġa yo: Imperative: turn or turn around.

k̇ola: Friend. Also used by medicine men to refer to the spirits who are their helpers.

la: As a verb, it is translated "to ask." As a suffix, it seems to make a word a superlative but often is used as signifying "only," as in *waŋjila,* only one (Buechel 1979). It is also used as a suffix for an endearment in the superlative, as in *bebela,* a lovable infant.

Lakota: The people; the western band of the Dakota, Lakota, Nakota Nation or Great Sioux Nation. The Lakota dialect uses *l* where other dialects use *d* or *n.*

leċel: This alone, thus, after this manner, so.

lowaŋp̄i: They sing. Also refers to the evening ceremony, done by the medicine man for a variety of reasons. There are many different types of evening songs, which are related to both the purpose of the ceremony, such as thanksgiving or healing, and the *wowak̇aŋ,* or power of the medicine man, for example, *waŋbli lowaŋp̄i,* or eagle ceremony.

mak̄ak̄ije: I suffer.

mat'e: I die.

miksuye: Remember me.

mit̄a: My, or belonging to me.

mit̄ak̄uye: My relative. *T̄ak̄uye* is "relative," and *m̄i* is a shortened form of *mit̄a,* or "my."

nac̄a: Chief, headman. Buechel (1979) indicates that in former times there were only *nac̄a,* and the white man introduced *itacan* for "headman." White Hat (1999) indicates that *nac̄a* is a shortened form of *nac̄a oḱolaḱiċiye,* which was the elite society of men who made decisions for the people and resolved conflicts. It is used to address a leader who has been selected for a position of power by the people.

niṫa: Yours. Often shortened when added to another word. For example, *waṗoṡṫan niṫawa* (your hat) can be shortened to niwaṗoṡṫan.

omakiye: Help me, from *okiye,* "to help," and *ma,* "me."

oṗaġi: To pack or fill a pipe with tobacco.

osṗaye: Group.

oṫeḣkelo: A difficult time. This term is used for times of struggle, such as a death or other tragedy.

owaŋḱa: Altar of a medicine man which he constructs each time he does a ceremony. How the altar is arranged and what constitutes it comes to him in his vision.

oyas'iŋ: All, everyone. *Miṫaḱuye oyas'iŋ,* "all my relatives," is the ritual prayer said at the end of any group prayer.

oyaṫe: People.

pejuṫa: Medicine, herbal medicine, but also any medicine given by an herbalist, medicine man, or physician.

pejuṫa wiċaṡa/wiŋyaŋ: Herbalist. Literally, "medicine man" (*wiċaṡa*) or "medicine woman" (*wiŋyaŋ*). Individuals with this gift have great knowledge of native plants and their pharmacological powers.

peyote: A natural form of the hallucinogen mescaline. The peyote religion, or Native American Church, is well described by Slotkin (1956).

Ṡahiyela: The Cheyenne Indian tribe.

Siċaŋġu: The Burnt Thigh band of the Lakota, who live on the Rosebud Reservation of south-central South Dakota.

siċe: Bad.

siċuŋ: According to White Hat (1999), "one's presence," that intimate aspect of one which is unique and which is communicated to others and can exist in a sense separate from another. In English we speak of one's presence as palpable even when the person is not physically there. Walker (1980), who translates it as "guardian," goes on to say that it is a very complex concept, "an influence that forewarns of danger, admonishes for right against wrong, and controls others of mankind" (p. 73). Powers (1986) translates it as a power given to human beings by the supernatural. Our siċuŋ is our own and immortal. Powers agrees with Walker that one may acquire the siċuŋ of another and that the concept of siċuŋ is basic to understanding the Lakota belief in reincarnation. My discussions with many of the older medicine men were inconclusive on the precise meaning of the concept. My sense is that it is the unique gift of self and character with which one is born and which provides a particular presence that distinguishes one from others and is returned to the immortals when one dies.

slusluṫa: Slippery.
ṡni: Makes a negative. *Mni kte ṡni,* I will not go.
ṫaȟċa: Deer.
ṫaḱiya: Toward.
ṫaḱoja: Grandchild. Plural is *ṫaḱojap̄i.*
ṫaḱu: Something, or the interrogative "what."
ṫawaċiŋ: One's will, mind, purpose. This is an important Lakota faculty because it lends a person his or her strength of conviction, desire, and purpose. One works to develop *ṫawaċiŋ ṫaŋḱa,* or strength of purpose and will, in order to endure suffering. One cultivates this faculty in contrast to *ṫawaċiŋ huŋkeṡni,* or a weak and vacillating mind and will. *Waċiŋ* means "will" or "desire," and *ṫa* makes it one's own. It seems to me that cognition, conscience, and will are interconnected in Lakota epistemology. Elucidating this concept and understanding how it relates to the virtue of *wowaċiŋ ṫaŋḱa* is an area for fruitful reflection and scholarship.
ṫawaċiŋ waŋjila: Singleness of desire and will. This is something to seek in a ceremony and demonstrates that everyone is there for one reason, the healing of a particular person. Eagle Elk and other medicine men indicated that great things could happen when this existed, and it was essential if the power was to be truly present and effective in a ceremony.
ti: To live, he lives. Third-person plural is *tip̄i,* "they live someplace."
tiblo: Older brother of a woman. *Ċiye* is the older brother of a man.
tioṡp̄aye: The larger extended family group into which one is born, based on blood line; literally, "the group with whom one lives." Traditionally, Lakota people lived in small units in which they were led by a *naċa* who was consensually chosen. There existed many tioṡp̄aye. An example of one is the Aṡḱe tioṡp̄aye, the Hollow Horn Bear group. Tioṡp̄aye living had carefully worked out rules governed by kinship and tradition. For a modern application of the tioṡp̄aye concept to understanding how to prevent social and psychological problems and a description of the tioṡp̄aye way of life, see Mohatt and Blue (1982).
ṫohaŋ: When.
ṫuŋḱaṡila: Grandfather. Used to address the divine in Lakota prayers as the oldest, first, the original and dearest relative.
ṫuŋḱaṡilapi: The grandfathers, that is, the United States government.
uŋċi: Grandmother.
waċiŋ: I wish or want.
wahi najiŋ: I arrived to stand here and pray. Used as a verse in sacred songs.
wakaŋ: Energy, power. A controversy exists about the original meaning of this word. Christian scholars such as Buechel (1979) have translated it as "holy," like the Christian concept of the holy, giving it a sense of

having a unique quality. White Hat (1999) translates it as the sacred energy that imbues every living creature and from which we can draw power for good or evil. *Ḱaŋ* is the blood vein, and in the Lakota creation story Inyan gave his blood to establish the rest of creation. The blood vein is the source of life and power, so wak̄aŋ goes back to the very beginning of creation. As White Hat says, it is "the power to give life or to take it away. In our philosophy every creation has that power" (1999, appendix K).

wakaŋ k̄aġa: Ceremonies which are not doctoring ceremonies and for which one does not have to have the power of the medicine man. Examples are the purification rite, the vision quest, and the sun dance. Many individuals have the authority to perform these for the people even though they are not medicine men, or *wapiya wiċaśa.*

wak̄iŋyaŋ: Thunder beings. The *wak̄iŋyaŋ wowak̄aŋ* is the power of the thunder beings that comes to a person in dreams and while he is on the hill crying for a vision. Eagle Elk discusses it in the story about his concept of nuclear power (chapter 11).

wamayaŋk̄e: Look at me.

wanaġi: Ghost or spirit. The *wanaġi wowak̄aŋ* is a vision in which one gains the power to doctor using the spirits of former medicine men.

waŋbli: Eagle. One of the powers of a medicine man if he has had an eagle vision.

waniyaŋ: To cause to live.

wapiya(pi): To repair or fix. The medicine men refer to themselves as *wapiya wiċaśa. Wapiyapi* is "they repair or heal," third-person plural.

wau: I come.

wayaġop̄a: The sucking process. Can refer to traditional doctoring in which a medicine man would suck out the foreign body causing the disease.

Wiċiyela: Yankton Sioux Indians of the Greenwood Reservation in southeastern South Dakota.

wiċok̄aŋ: Noon.

wist̄eċa: Shy, bashful, modest.

wiyok̄peya: West.

woableza: Realization, a type of understanding that is profound. Plural is *woablezapi.*

wobliheċ̄a: Courage. Buechel (1979) defines *wobliheċ̄a* as activity and industry and *woohitka* as courage. Contemporary use distinguishes between *woohitk̄a,* "bravery," and *wobliheċ̄a,* "courage."

woḣyak̄a: Gifts presented to the medicine man and others who helped him after one has been doctored or participated in a ceremony. The woḣyak̄a is sometimes money, quilts, maybe a horse or car. It can be whatever one wants to give and is in proportion to what one has as resources and the value of what one received. Many of the older medicine men would say, maybe the person who was helped has nothing, is poor, and can give me only a glass of water or shake my hand. Such a gift would be sufficient. Non-Indians who come to a medicine man for help often feel anxious and unsure of themselves when they find that there is no fee. In fact, it is not possible for medicine men to charge a fee. Some medicine men cannot keep the wohyaka, so they give it away.

woihaŋble: A vision.

wopila: A thanksgiving; a thanksgiving ceremony done after one has been doctored or done a vision quest. The thanksgiving ceremony is critical for completing the circle of asking for help, receiving help, and thanking the spirits for help, and full healing does not occur without it. Eagle Elk advises us in the book to thank the spirits when we are happy and remember their gifts to us.

wowaċiŋ taŋka: Like *tawaċiŋ taŋka, wowaċiŋ taŋka* is the strength of conscience or mind that allows a person to persist in times of difficulty. Stanley Red Bird advised that the two most important qualities to cultivate were wowaċiŋ taŋka and humor.

wowakaŋ: The power of the medicine man that comes into the ceremony.

Yanktonais: The Yankton Sioux Indians of eastern South Dakota.

yo: Imperative form used by men.

yuha: He has.

yuwípi: A power of a medicine man with a yuwípi vision is *yuwípi wowakaŋ*. The verb means "they are bound." In the vision quest a person is wrapped up in a quilt with his fingers and hands carefully tied behind his back. He is laid down in the sacred place on the hill and left there for four days and four nights. During this time the yuwípi spirits come to him and untie him and tell him how to conduct his yuwípi ceremonies. In the *yuwípi lowaŋpi,* or evening yuwípi ceremony, the medicine man is bound in the same way and laid in the center of his sacred space where he has set up his *owaŋka* (altar). During the ceremony his spirit friends untie him and doctor the person seeking help. The yuwípi ceremony is typically done only for very serious sicknesses.

Bibliography

Achebe, Chinua. 1983. *Things Fall Apart.* New York: Fawcett Crest.

Becker, Ernest. 1962. *The Birth and Death of Meaning: A Perspective in Psychiatry and Anthropology.* Glencoe IL: Free Press.

Boyer, L. Bryce. 1961. Notes on Personality Structure of a North American Indian Shaman. *Journal of the Hillside Hospital* 10:14–33.

———. 1962. Remarks on the Personality of Shamans, with Special Reference to the Apaches of the Mescalero Indian Reservation. *Psychoanalytic Study of Society* 2:233–54.

———. 1979. *Childhood and Folklore: A Psychoanalytic Study of Apache Personality.* New York: Psychohistory.

Brown, Joseph E., ed. 1953. *The Sacred Pipe: Black Elk's Account of the Seven Rites of the Oglala Sioux.* Baltimore: Penguin.

Buechel, Eugene. 1979. *A Lakota-English Dictionary.* Pine Ridge SD: Red Cloud Indian School.

Codrescu, Andrei. 1995. *The Blood Countess: A Novel.* New York: Simon & Schuster.

Coles, Robert. 1970. *Erik H. Erikson: The Growth of His Work.* Boston: Little, Brown & Co.

———. 1975. *The Mind's Fate: Ways of Seeing Psychiatry and Psychoanalysis.* Boston: Little, Brown & Co.

———. 1989. *The Call of Stories: Teaching and the Moral Imagination.* Boston: Houghton Mifflin.

———. 1990. *The Spiritual Life of Children.* Boston: Houghton Mifflin.

Deloria, Ella Cara. 1988. *Waterlily.* Lincoln: University of Nebraska Press.

Deloria, Vine Jr. 1973. *God Is Red.* New York: Grosset & Dunlap.

Devereux, George. 1961. *Mohave Ethnopsychiatry and Suicide: The Psychiatric Knowledge and the Psychic Disturbances of an Indian Tribe.* Washington DC: U.S. Government Printing Office.

Erikson, Erik H. 1963. *Childhood and Society.* 2d ed. New York: W. W. Norton.

Feraca, Stephen E. 1961. The Yuwípi Cult of the Oglala and Sičaŋǧu Teton Sioux. *Plains Anthropologist* 6(13): 155–63.

Frank, Jerome D. 1974. *Persuasion and Healing: A Comparative Study of Psychotherapy.* 2d ed. Baltimore: Johns Hopkins University Press.

Frisch, Max. 1958. *I'm Not Stiller.* New York: Abelard-Schuman.

Goethals, George W., and Dennis Klos. 1976. *Experiencing Youth: First-Person Accounts.* 2d ed. Boston: Little, Brown & Co.

Hiatt, Lester R., ed. 1975. *Australian Aboriginal Mythology: Essays in*

Honor of W. E. H. Stanner. Canberra: Australian Institute of Aboriginal Studies.

Iverson, Peter, ed. 1985. *The Plains Indians of the Twentieth Century.* Norman: University of Oklahoma Press.

Jahoda, Gustav. 1995. In Pursuit of the Emic-Etic Distinction: Can We Ever Capture It? In *The Culture and Psychology Reader.* Ed. Nancy Rule Goldberger and Jody Veroff. 128–38. New York: New York University Press.

Lame Deer, John, and Richard Erdoes. 1972. *Lame Deer: Seeker of Visions.* New York: Simon & Schuster.

Lévi-Strauss, Claude. 1962. *The Savage Mind.* Chicago: University of Chicago Press.

Lewis, Thomas H. 1990. *The Medicine Men: Oglala Sioux Ceremony and Healing.* Lincoln: University of Nebraska Press.

Looking Horse, Stanley. 1978. Interview. In *Identity through Traditional Lakota Methods.* Ed. G. V. Mohatt. Rosebud SD: Sinte Gleska University.

McClelland, David C., William N. Davis, Rudolf Kalin, Eric Wanner. 1972. *The Drinking Man.* New York: Free Press.

Mohatt, Gerald V. 1988. Psychological Method and Spiritual Power in Cross-Cultural Psychotherapy. *Journal of Contemplative Psychotherapy* 5 (summer): 85–115.

Mohatt, Gerald V., and Blue, Arthur. 1982. Identity through Traditional Lakota Methods. In *Prevention in American Indian and Alaska Native Communities.* Ed. Spero Manson. 91–119. National Center for American Indian and Alaska Native Mental Health. Denver: University of Colorado Health Sciences Center.

Momaday, N. Scott. 1968. *House Made of Dawn.* New York: Harper & Row.

Neihardt, John G. 1979. *Black Elk Speaks: Being the Life Story of a Holy Man of the Oglala Sioux.* 1932. Reprint, Lincoln: University of Nebraska Press.

Paracelsus. 1941. *Four Treatises of Theophrastus Von Hohenheim, called Paracelsus.* Ed. Henry E. Sigerist. Baltimore: Johns Hopkins University Press.

Pommersheim, Frank. 1995. *Braid of Feathers: American Indian Law and Contemporary Tribal Life.* Berkeley: University of California Press.

Powers, William K. 1977. *Oglala Religion.* Lincoln: University of Nebraska Press.

———. 1986. *Sacred Language: The Nature of Supernatural Discourse in Lakota.* Norman: University of Oklahoma Press.

Rasmussen, Knud. 1952. *The Alaskan Eskimos as Described in the Posthumous Notes of Knud Rasmussen.* Ed. H. Ostermann, with the assistance of E. Hotvad. Copenhagen: Gyldendal.

Silko, Leslie. 1991. *Almanac of the Dead.* New York: Simon & Schuster.

Slotkin, J. S. 1956. *The Peyote Religion.* Glencoe IL: Free Press.
Stegner, Wallace. 1987. *The American West as Living Space.* Ann Arbor: University of Michigan Press.
Sullivan, Harry S. 1953. *The Interpersonal Theory of Psychiatry.* Ed. Helen Swick Perry and Mary Ladd Gawel. New York: W. W. Norton.
———. 1964. *The Fusion of Psychiatry and Social Science.* New York: W. W. Norton.
Walker, James R. 1980. *Lakota Belief and Ritual.* Ed. Raymond J. DeMallie and Elaine A. Jahner. Lincoln: University of Nebraska Press.
———. 1983. *Lakota Myth.* Ed. Elaine A. Jahner. Lincoln: University of Nebraska Press.
White, Robert W. 1948. *The Abnormal Personality.* New York: Ronald Press.
———. 1975. *Lives in Progress: A Study of the Natural Growth of Personality.* 3d ed. New York: Holt, Rinehart & Winston.
White, Robert W., ed. 1963. *The Study of Lives: Essays on Personality in Honor of Henry A. Murray.* New York: Atherton Press.
White Hat, Albert Sr. 1999. *Lak̄ot̄a Iyap̄iun wowap̄i nahaŋ yawap̄i (Reading and Writing the Lakota Language).* Ed. Jael Kampfe. Salt Lake City: University of Utah Press.
Will, Otto. 1959. Human Relatedness and the Schizophrenic Reaction. *Psychiatry* 22(3): 205–41.
———. 1968. The Reluctant Patient, the Unwanted Psychotherapist—and Coercion. *Contemporary Psychoanalysis* 5(1): 1–31.
Young Bear, Severt, and R. D. Theisz. 1994. *Standing in the Light: A Lakota Way of Seeing.* Lincoln: University of Nebraska Press.

Index

Joseph Eagle Elk is referred to in this index as JEE.